# THE BIG SIT.

## DES MOLLOY

*Kahuku*
Publishing Collective

**Kahuku**
Publishing Collective

**The Big Sit**

© Des Molloy 2024

Text design by The Design Dept.
Cover design by The Design Dept.
www.thedesigndept.com.au

Editing by Kahuku Publishing

Photo Acknowledgement: Des Molloy.
Map images:1996. A3 Folio Map of Australia.
Geoscience Australia, Canberra. https://pid.
geoscience.gov.au/dataset/ga/65186

Printed by Ingram Spark

First published in 2024 by
**Kahuku Publishing**
PO Box 149 Takaka
Tasman 7142, New Zealand
www.kahukupublishing.com

**All rights reserved.**
This book or any portion thereof may not be reproduced or used in any manner whatsoever without the express written permission of the author except for the use of brief quotations in a book review. All inquiries should be made to the author.

ISBN.  PB: 978-1-7386002-8-1
       ePub: 978-1-7386002-9-8

*To my families ... without whom Penelope and I would never have crossed five streets let alone five continents. My blood family for their enduring love and support, and the worldwide Panther family for the encouragement and unconditional assistance when needed.*

*Champions all!*

# CONTENTS

A Worthy Peregrination .................................................. 2

Meandering to a Muster .................................................. 22

Cairns or bust ........................................................... 42

Cairns to Birdsville ...................................................... 66

Birdsville to Uluru ....................................................... 94

Uluru to Darwin ......................................................... 118

Darwin .................................................................. 146

Darwin to Broome ....................................................... 164

Broome to Toodyay ...................................................... 186

Toodyay to McLaren Flat ................................................. 204

The final surge .......................................................... 224

October 2022 ........................................................... 246

Tassie, Tassie, Tassie! ................................................... 262

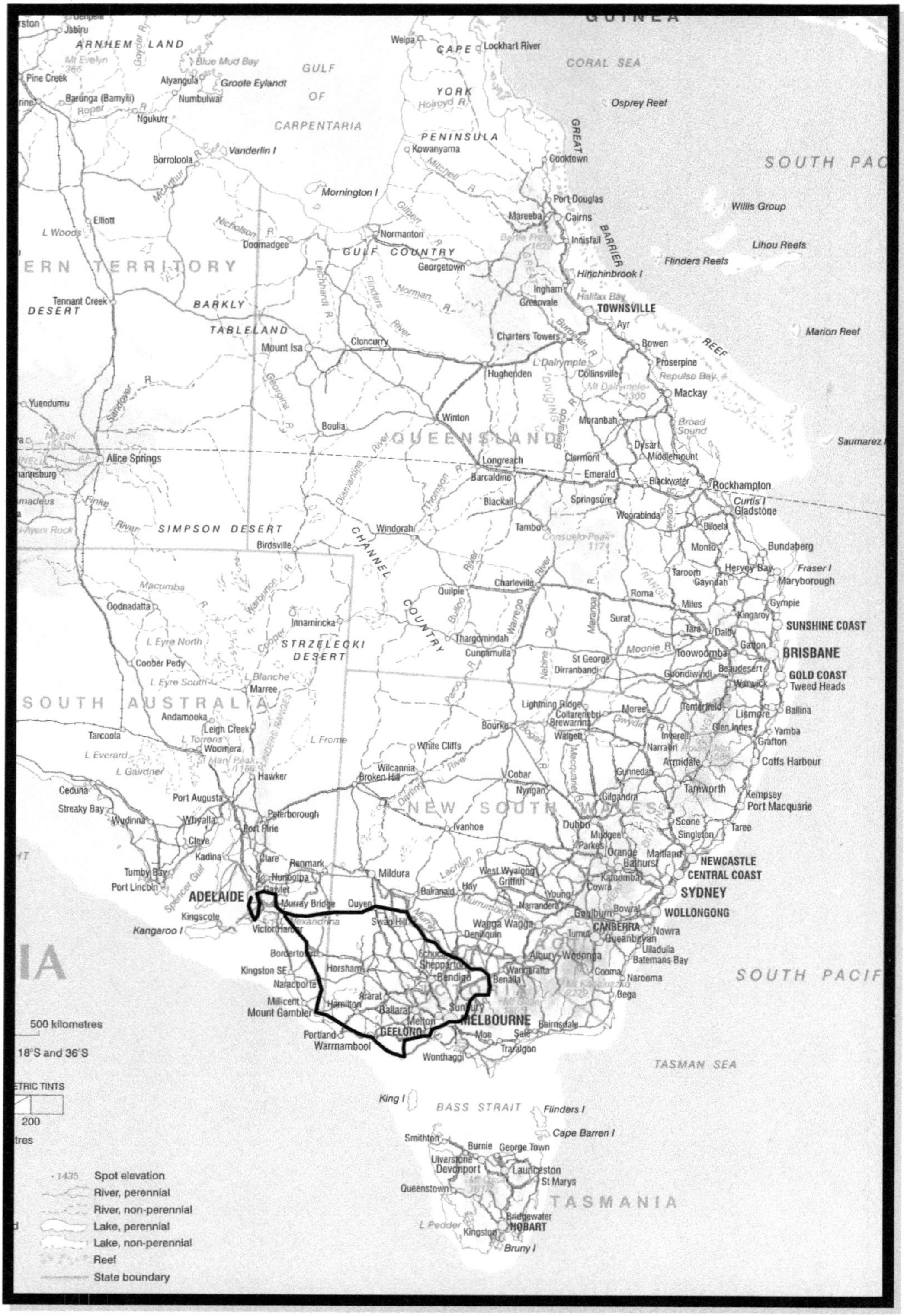
ARNHEM LAND
Jabiru
Pine Creek
Barunga (Bamyili)
Ngukurr
Alyangula
Groote Eylandt
Numbulwar
Blue Mud Bay
GULF OF CARPENTARIA
Weipa
CAPE YORK PENINSULA
Lockhart River
CORAL SEA
Osprey Reef
Kowanyama
Borroloola
Vanderlin I
Mornington I
Cooktown
SOUTH PACIFIC
Port Douglas
Willis Group
Mareeba
Cairns
Innisfail
Lihou Reefs
Flinders Reefs
GREAT BARRIER REEF
Elliott
L Woods
Normanton
Doomadgee
GULF COUNTRY
Georgetown
Hinchinbrook I
NORTHERN TERRITORY
Ingham
Greenvale
Tennant Creek
DESERT
BARKLY TABLELAND
TOWNSVILLE
Ayr
Charters Towers
Marion Reef
Mount Isa
Cloncurry
Bowen
Proserpine
Hughenden
Collinsville
Mackay
Yuendumu
Winton
Boulia
Moranbah
QUEENSLAND
Dysart
Middlemount
Alice Springs
Longreach
Clermont
Barcaldine
Emerald
Blackwater
Rockhampton
Gladstone
Blackall
Springsure
Woorabinda
Biloela
SIMPSON DESERT
Windorah
Tambo
Birdsville
CHANNEL COUNTRY
Monto
Bundaberg
Hervey Bay
Fraser I
Maryborough
Taroom
Gayndah
Charleville
Roma
Quilpie
Miles
Gympie
Oodnadatta
Surat
Kingaroy
Innamincka
Thargomindah
Dalby
SUNSHINE COAST
L Eyre North
STRZELECKI DESERT
Cunnamulla
Toowoomba
Gatton
BRISBANE
Coober Pedy
St George
Dirranbandi
Beaudesert
GOLD COAST
Tweed Heads
L Eyre South
Marree
Goondiwindi
Warwick
SOUTH AUSTRALIA
Andamooka
Lightning Ridge
Collarenebri
Brewarrina
Moree
Tenterfield
Lismore
Ballina
Leigh Creek
Bourke
Walgett
Glen Innes
Yamba
Tarcoola
L Torrens
Woomera
L Frome
White Cliffs
Inverell
Narrabri
Grafton
L Everard
L Gairdner
Armidale
Coffs Harbour
Wilcannia
Broken Hill
Cobar
Gunnedah
Hawker
Nyngan
Tamworth
Ceduna
Port Augusta
Gilgandra
Kempsey
Port Macquarie
Streaky Bay
Wudinna
Whyalla
Peterborough
NEW SOUTH WALES
Ivanhoe
Dubbo
Scone
Taree
Port Pirie
Cleve
Mudgee
Singleton
Kadina
Clare
Parkes
Orange
Maitland
NEWCASTLE
Renmark
Bathurst
CENTRAL COAST
Tumby Bay
Port Lincoln
Mildura
West Wyalong
Griffith
Katoomba
SYDNEY
ADELAIDE
Murray Bridge
Ouyen
Balranald
Hay
Young
Cowra
WOLLONGONG
Kingscote
Narrandera
Goulburn
Bowral
Kangaroo I
Victor Harbor
Swan Hill
Wagga Wagga
CANBERRA
Queanbeyan
Nowra
Ulladulla
Deniliquin
Bordertown
Echuca
Shepparton
Albury-Wodonga
Batemans Bay
Kingston SE
Horsham
Bendigo
Wangaratta
Benalla
Cooma
Narooma
Naracoorte
Ararat
Bega
Millicent
Mount Gambier
Hamilton
Ballarat
Sunbury
Melton
MELBOURNE
Bairnsdale
Portland
Warrnambool
GEELONG
Sale
Moe
Traralgon
Wonthaggi
TASMAN SEA
500 kilometres
King I
BASS STRAIT
Flinders I
Cape Barren I
Smithton
Burnie
George Town
Ulverstone
Devonport
Launceston
St Marys
Queenstown
TASMANIA
L Pedder
Bridgewater
Kingston
HOBART
Bruny I
Spot elevation
River, perennial
River, non-perennial
Lake, perennial
Lake, non-perennial
Reef
State boundary

CHAPTER ONE

# A WORTHY PEREGRINATION

*"Don't wait too long, as before you know it, you're knackered."*

This was a wisdom given out by my old riding mate Dick Huurdeman on national television a short while after we had returned from our 2005 ride across from Beijing to Arnhem (*The Last Hurrah*). He was 72 and had recently suffered a small stroke. I don't claim that his words totally inspired this ride, but they were simmering away in the background … although I was just a youthful 67 when the embryo finally started to germinate.

In 2016 I told Penelope that we were going to have another adventure. This was to be the *Circumambulation of Big Red* also known as The Big Sit. In the words of an almost forgotten advert for Pantene Shampoo … *"it wasn't going to happen overnight, but it was going to happen."* My idea was that we would chunk our way right around Australia beginning with the spring-time Australian Panther Register's Rally in South Australia. Over a period of years, we'd do the job, matching the seasons to the ride in hand. There would be no rush. I'd been telling her this same refrain since our Last Hurrah ride of 2005, but finally the time seemed right … the stars had aligned. I was nearing the end of a four-year construction project and I could be spared for a spring break. And for those who came in late … Penelope is a 1965 Panther Model 120, one of the last made by Phelon and Moore in the small Yorkshire town of Cleckheaton. Although made in the 1960s she is a crude, long-stroke single-cylinder motorcycle of a design dating from the mid-1930s. Together we have had good times and bad times across about 50 countries during a 40-year relationship. Our rides have even spawned a couple of books – *No One Said It Would Be Easy* (our youthful jaunt from New Orleans to Buenos Aires) and *The Last Hurrah* ( the Beijing to Arnhem epic). Penelope's never been the most suited moto for any journey and it has to be said is quite a flawed model, but so am I, making us a matched team. Neither of us would make the 'Firsts' and are happy to be in the 'Extra Bs' enjoying ourselves. Loyalty and history bind us together.

There were minor grumblings upon learning that she would have to become an Aussie for us to do it in such a leisurely fashion. If we'd been going to pop over, rip around and go home within a year, we could have travelled on a *Carnet de passages en douanes*. This is the international Customs' document which guarantees you will take your vehicle home. It is pretty effective because often you have deposited monies with the authorities, promising not to sell while you are passing through. Sometimes that requirement can be two and a half times the new value of the vehicle. Being that we were going to spread our adventure over several years, there was no alternative to emigration. The process of getting Penelope legal and on to Victorian 'Club Plates' was daunting ... a bit confusing and convoluted. In desperation I turned to Richard Scoular, a Kiwi ex-racer from our past. He was then residing in Melbourne and importing classic vehicles for a living. He knew the ropes, understood the bureaucratic process. You start by getting Federal permission to import, then move on to complying with the State requirements. Ultimately it was achieved. I 'sold' Penelope to him and subsequent to importation, he had 'on-sold' to our son Joseph. In due course we had a white-edged maroon number plate with Vic – Club Permit noted above our number 193J·H. We also had a VicRoads log-book entitling us to 45 riding days during 2016/2017. The club plate scheme enables low-use and hobby vehicles to venture out onto the highways for a fraction of the normal registration cost. Previously, you could only go out on your particular club's runs on prescribed and advertised routes. There was no ability to look out the window on a sunny day and decide to pop around the peninsular on your 1912 Alldays & Onions auto. Fortunately, this had recently been changed to just being a given number of days and the 'where to' not needing to be publicly notified. You just fill out your log-book and travel accordingly.

One of the main reasons for choosing Melbourne as my entry point was having two of our four kids living there. Both Kitty and Cam, and Joe and Jess had produced grandkids to add to the pull. October 2016 was like a 'perfect storm' was being unleased – one I couldn't really ignore. The

Australian Panther Owners were having a rally, grandson Arthur was having his 2nd birthday and the Australian MotoGP at Phillip Island were all happening over successive weekends. There was also the renowned Motorclassica taking place at the world-heritage-listed Royal Exhibition Building during this time. Motorclassica stands on the world's stage as Australasia's largest and most prestigious *concours d'elegance* and exhibition of classic, exotic and prestige cars (and motorcycles). I could do it all ... family stuff mixed in with self-pleasure.

The 2016 Panther Rally on South Australia's Fleurieu Peninsular was such a delight for us. We had a nice ride there from Melbourne, initially via The Great Ocean Road. Aussies trumpet this coastal ride with much fanfare, whilst Kiwis often refer to it as *'The Pretty Average Ocean Road'*. It is OK, but now severely speed-restricted and cluttered with slow-moving 'maggots' ... which is a bikers' term for the ubiquitous lumbering white camper vans that are a blight on many of the best riding roads. After a cool escape from Melbourne and a moderately interesting first morning, I lunched in the gentle spring sun on the deck at an older hotel in Apollo Bay. The break was welcome and the food and beer suitable. I looked over and down at Penelope with some pride. She looked great and had performed impeccably. A couple of locals wander over and we talk 'old bike' stuff for a while. I can't delay too long as I know I have to put 550 km beneath our eager spinning wheels this day ... and I've only banked 200 or so. We're mostly clipping along at the old mile-a-minute pace when we can. Adding to the delays on the ride had been the many areas being cleaned up after a severe weather event only weeks earlier. This meant roadworks at regular intervals. It was pretty evident that the road had taken a hammering. Although we kept to the coastal route for the afternoon, the actual sea-sightings were pretty infrequent.

It was a novel and enjoyable experience to overnight in the old Mt Gambier Gaol, which was now a family-run backpacker accommodation.

Mt Gambier is South Australia's second largest town although its population is less than 30,000, so not huge. It is known for its geographical features, particularly its volcanic and limestone maars, with the most notable one being the crater-formed Blue Lake right on the edge of town. The peak of the dormant volcano was actually the first place in South Australia named by European explorers. It was sighted in 1800 by Lieutenant James Grant from his survey brig, and named for Lord James Gambier, Admiral of the Fleet.

I spent some time aimlessly wandering the night streets of the burgh but didn't really feel very sociable … and was happy with my own company, scoffing a pretty average pizza late in the evening. The town seemed to be full of hoons in loud cars appearing to be a whole generation out of sync with modern society. I watch the police interact with a hopelessly drunk young woman. The term 'legless' seemed so applicable to her zig-zagging stagger. Fortunately in this instance the men in blue had a gentle touch.

Looking ahead, you always envisage quaint and welcoming eateries, serving just what you feel like at the time. Sadly, life is rarely like this and Mt Gambier didn't present anything next morning that appealed on my breakfast radar … and neither did Tantanoola or Millicent. I'd hit the road quite early so as to fit in a photo opportunity up at the look-out above town that enables views of the Blue Lake. Posing done, we set sail. The road and riding was now pretty boring and my focus was on just keeping on, keeping on. I paused roadside for one break and made bad choices for a late brekkie and subsequently a late lunch at forgotten small towns along the way. The late brekky was a choice between Janet's Takeaway … a fry-up place that didn't look like it had anything that would be good for my arteries, and a gift shop selling 'great' coffee. Roy Orbison singing "Only the lonely … " drew me in. This was a bit of a mistake. I was the only customer. Although Cyndi Lauper hit me with her 'best shot' it wasn't enough to make me want to linger.

I am never too cut-up when my choice of meal and eatery proves to be a dud, as I have always espoused that the meal 'doesn't have to be the best one of your life ... and in fact would be a shame if it was, as that means you would never reach that pinnacle again!' I prefer the scenario of eagerly looking forward to the next one as it will probably be better than average one you have just put out.

The afternoon was hot and Penelope a little bothered, so we pause at a layby for a shady rest and think. I look over at Penelope and can't help but quiver a little with pride. Gently loaded with leather saddlebags I made twenty years ago, she looks magnificent and I can't understand how there was a time in my youth when I thought Panthers of her ilk looked awkward and a little ugly. She has been upgraded a bit and now runs handlebar-end blinkers and a cigarette lighter charging outlet ... so hopefully I can charge the batteries of my camera and phone while we ride. A kiwi couple with van towing a trailer with a Harley on it wander over and soon I am slugging down the proffered Yenda low-alcohol 'Session' Lager and enjoying a toasted sandwich. Good generous folk and not the last side-of-the-road engagement that makes me humbly happy. I treat Penelope to a different spark plug and press on through uninspiring going ... very un-Aussie-like pine forests and very Aussie-like straight roads.

The hours dragged by and with a bit of difficulty and help from an information centre in a small spot whose name I don't recall, I zigged and zagged my way cross-country after leaving the main highway at Tailem Bend. Fortunately, as I flagged and was beginning to squirm with discomfort and boredom, we encountered increasingly more inspirational and undulating countryside. Late afternoon I fortuitously found McLaren Vale and the campsite 'donga' I was booked into. A donga is what non-Aussies would call a cabin. I'd smashed out the 1,000 km in two pretty good days. The delightfully rural McLaren Vale (pop 3,000) is the centre of the wine region of the same name and is about 35 km South of Adelaide. The rally is to kick off with an event in neighbouring McLaren Flat (pop 1,100) which is only a short distance away.

The Friday night BBQ was always going to be a weekend highlight. It would signal the start of the rally and reconnect the widely-spread Aussie Panther owners and introduce the new ones and those like me who had not attended their annual gathering before. I already knew quite a few by repute. I think that deep down we all like having our egos stroked a little occasionally, and so it was that I was was welcomed to Mick and Jane Clark's lifestyle property with not a little fanfare ... and Penelope and I revelled in our moment in the sun. I'd corresponded with Jane but not met either of them before. I am quietly pleased to discover their relative youthfulness, as the membership of the old-bike clubs that I belong to is aging, slowly but relentlessly ... with seemingly no apparent way of attracting the young blood to arrest the decline. Jane is petite and oozes energetic vibrancy, whilst Mick is tall with an aura of competency and confidence. A few familiar faces step forward and we are greeted with hugs and handshakes. From Sydney is David Lewis, the co-ordinator of the Australian register and probably the marque's Number One fan and advocate. I'd met him a couple of years earlier when I was over to look at a job opportunity. On that occasion my financial coffers were low, and kindly, Jordan Princip, another Pantherphile, had offered me a spot on the floor of his rental property which was between tenants. Not only providing me with a spot to lie on, he'd then gathered up David and we'd shared a nice night out, gently imbibing Aussie ales and putting the reality to the names I had known for some time. It is good to see Jordan and David again as I have a strong sense of kinship with them. Our Panther world is like an extended family and international boundaries are never a barrier to this. Club magazines and internet forums enable strong relationships to form even across vast oceans.

From the UK were the current and the immediate-past presidents of the Panther Owners' Club, Tom Norman and Grahame Sherbourne. Now retirees, they are out in the antipodes holidaying with their wives and they make a fuss over both of us, demanding photos with Penelope. An erudite, silvered, perky Scotsman, I'd met Tom Norman in 2007 at the club's rally outside of Cleckheaton while I was in the UK promoting The Last Hurrah, and we'd bonded in a field. I'd not met Judith at the time, and sadly she was under the weather a bit for the period of the Australian rally and wasn't able to fully participate in all the activities as enthusiastically as she would have liked. Grahame and Barbara are from the Manchester area and I'd stayed with them on that 2007 sortie. Grahame is an ex-metalwork teacher, robust and barrel-chested ... and a Panther man to the core, with a shed-full back home. He and Tom have been great chairmen of the club, and wonderful advocates for the marque. Barbara is an eager pillion and a

**THE BIG SIT**

central part of many of their adventures ... a great crew and it truly is a high-point (and honour) to see them again.

There are numerous Panthers proudly disporting themselves in the early evening sun. One is the beautiful *June*, an early 1950s Model 100 of Dan Leather's from Darwin. Dan is another one of our younger members, naturally gregarious, I warm to him immediately ... he also is the future of groups like ours. He had trailered June in from Darwin, more than 3,000 km away after only coming ashore from his marine engineering role on the Tuesday night. I hope that Penelope and June will become friends ... we aim to make it to Darwin in the years to come. Dan has been very engaging over the aether and is keen for me to visit. He's disappointed that it won't be for at least a couple of years. He lets me know that he could walk to Darwin quicker than I am planning. Mick and Jane have their friends manning the BBQs and helping to dispense conviviality. For many regulars it is an annual re-establishing of friendships. One couple have brought their 1939 500cc Model 95 across from West Australia and there are several Queenslanders present. Because of the big distances most attendees make this a holiday adventure.

There were about 20 Panthers of all ages that took to the road on the windy Saturday morning, initially led sedately by a sidecar outfit and directed by Mick's mates on modern machines who would woosh by and take up station on each corner or intersection. I laughed to myself when stopping at our first gathering spot at Normanville for a morning tea, as I realised we'd already lost two bikes to mechanical ailments. I projected ahead and could envisage a pretty lonely ending if the unreliability continued at the same rate. We'd also soon run out of back-up trailers etc. The Fleurieu Peninsular is a superb riding playground with numerous routes available to enjoy and be challenged by. Late morning we visited a private collection of desirable vehicles and memorabilia, before stopping to put on a public display and have a decent lunch break at Goolwa. This is clearly a well-known and liked spot. It has a steam train, a paddle-steamer, a micro-brewery and pub for us to enjoy. Our collection of bikes evokes a lot of interest and the usual "I've never heard of these before!" The line-up in the sun looks magnificent. After a suitable break, more of the peninsular is criss-crossed until we've done 250 km or so and we all retire to our respective accommodations until the night's social event at the local bowls club.

Our ride from Melbourne won us the furthest ridden award, which surprised me a little, but it seems most owners trailer their bikes from far and wide, then enjoy the rally rides over the weekend. The event was superbly organised, even if the weather was cool and windy on the Saturday while we explored the peninsular, and extremely wet and cold on the Sunday when we joined an annual vintage club run out and about to a vineyard. It had been nice putting faces to names and making new friends. Penelope even met a sibling that was possibly manufactured in the same week back in 1965. Their engine numbers were just a few apart and by that time Phelan and Moore were on their last legs (having been in receivership since 1961) and only making about three bikes a week of the 'heavy weight' variety like Penelope, along with some 'light weights' with the bought-in Villiers two-stroke engine.

Our riding back to Melbourne was to be done over three days which would prove to be colder than ideal but still enjoyable in parts. I wanted to loop a bit inland to sample the semi-outback small roads and to get across to Echuca on the Murray River to see the largest collection of working river-boats in the world.

And so it was that the Monday morning after the rally saw a leisurely start to my day's ride. There were farewells to be had in the camp and a final gather-up for a look around *The Old Tailem Town Pioneer Village*. This was a bit over 100 km East of McLaren Vale, so on the way for many of us. It is a worthy stop with lots to pique our interest. Established by a Peter Squires in 1982, Old Tailem Town is said to be Australia's largest pioneer village. Privately owned, it now features over 110 buildings arranged in streets like a village. The buildings have either been transported there in one piece or taken apart and then put together again insitu. Furnished within their periods, many with original artefacts, it is a snapshot of the past and shows the story of life for settlers in South Australia, mainly through the early part of the Twentieth Century. It is a good place to wander around in the watery sunshine of a spring morning and note all the stuff we can recall from our own backgrounds. I chuckle when I learn that despite being quite a sizable local tourist attraction, there is no Eftpos payment facility … strictly cash, an arrangement that meets the approval of a busload of senior citizens who enter before me.

Later, I drop into the local motorcycle shop in Tailem Bend to get a spare spark plug for Penelope, then head away along the Mallee Highway

B12. After the joys of the previous days' riding it is dull with the road arrow-straight. Clearly we have moved away from the wine-growing region and now the land is used for other arable purposes and big silos point to grains being grown. The place names are all alien to me and Lameroo, Pinnaroo and Boika give me mild amusement as they are so unlike anything I would encounter in New Zealand. The settlements along the highway are often little more than sign posts. Finally, after a fairly gruelling day without many highlights, I roll into a small town, and to my joy spot a magnificent example of one of my all-time Aussie favourites – the back-country pub.

The Victoria Hotel in Ouyen (pop 1,050) is archetypal … enormous, two-storied with a wide veranda and the ornate cast-iron filigree ornamentation still present. It is cheap and cheerful. I share a beer and a yarn with a displaced Irishman who had fetched up in the area quite a few years earlier. He fills me in with an overview of the town's reason for being and present status. By happenstance, a little later whilst having a pre-evening-meal stroll around the town I encountered the Dickies, David and Joanne from the rally. They were heading home to New South Wales.

**THE BIG SIT**

Actually, I had briefly met them a few years earlier in NZ when I was escorting a group of International Panther owners around the South Island. They were heading the opposite way going to a 'warbirds' gathering. I remember being slightly stressed whilst trying to organise and get all the Brits (and one German, one Irishman and one Canadian) on the road and heading in the right direction. I know I never gave due focus to these bystanders who clearly wanted to interact with us all ... being that they too were Panther owners. Now, finally we were able to have some quality time together over a meal and a few beers. An entertaining evening followed that counted as one of the highlights of the adventure. Just a simple night with people you know you will like, given a chance.

Next morning I dog-leg off the highway I was following, to take in the first 'outback' road of my adventure. It is one-vehicle-wide and straight, lined with low scrub ... and empty. I get a small thrill of anticipation. These are the sorts of road that I hope to explore as I chunk my way around this huge island continent. I know that I am not being very intrepid, but the unknown and unfamiliar give rise to a small frisson of enjoyment all the same. My puerile persona gets another gentle tweak as we flit through Mittyjack, Chinkapook and Nyah. I amuse myself for some time mindless calling out ... "Nyah, Nyah, Nyah!". It fills in the time and gives me something to do. This side road gets me across to the environs of Swan Hill where I pause for a morning tea with rally-met Mark Bail and look at all his toys. As well as being a Panther owner, Mark has an eclectic collection ... tractors, a Model T Ford, a Morris Minor, a 400 hp kit-car, a Harley etc. His Panther had been one of two to rock the socks off the UK visitors at the rally. Among the rarest of Panthers, it is a 500cc model with an engine that whilst sloped, is not as inclined as the 'normal' ones. The Model 95 was produced only for a couple of years right on the cusp of World War 2. It is thought of as being the pinnacle of Phelan & Moore's designs, but production was curtailed by the hostilities and never recommenced.

Common Panther folk-lore had it that there were four known examples in existence and only a couple that would surface from time to time in the UK. To the surprise and delight of Tom and Graham, there were two M95s at the rally, both running and in impeccable show-condition. After my cuppa with Mark, I get on to the B400 which will take me the 150 km across to Echuca,

Via the magic of texting, I've let a few friends know where I am and where I am heading. I get a great response from Janet from St Anaud, NZ. She sends through a message telling me to not miss the Catalina Museum on the way. I am so glad she did as this turns out to be a bit of a highlight … as well as getting me in from out in the cold for a while. After losing 16 'flying boats' to the Japanese bombings of Darwin and Broome in 1942, the authorities looked for a safe haven for servicing and 'parking up' their remaining aircraft. They needed an inland lake which could take aircraft landings no matter which way the wind was blowing. It also needed to be reasonably near the infra-structure to build and maintain it. The near-circular Lake Boga in Victoria was found to be ideal and quickly commissioned as the *No. 1 Flying Boat Repair and Service Depot.* It remained in service for the duration of the war, being de-commissioned in 1947. During the Depot's wartime life, their personnel undertook large volumes of work. 416 aircraft were serviced, repaired, restored, rebuilt or overhauled. These aircraft included Catalina, Dornier, Sikorsky KingFisher, Sunderland, Walrus and Martin Mariner. In the five years of its life, there were more than 1050 aircraft arrivals/departures and an estimated 800 test flights (plus associated "unofficial aerobatics"). In addition to RAAF aircraft, many allied flying boats used the Lake Boga Depot for repairs, including those of the United States of America and the Netherlands.

During its heyday there were more than 1,000 ground-crew and support staff making it all happen. After decades of neglect, the sole remaining plane, a Catalina, was restored, and in recent years an impressive museum built to house it and many other artefacts from the base etc. I spend a pleasant couple of hours wandering among large radial aircraft engines, and the big chunks of flying boats displayed. The period photos are great and the Catalina most impressive. Finally, I figure it is time to leave the relative sophistication and warmth of the museum and take my place once more on Penelope. It is not nice outside, but then again every day on two-wheels has to be seen as a great one.

Echuca appropriately displayed her river-boats, several paddling around like over-size ducks, and I was impressed ... but the afternoon drizzle made me disinclined to stay and play. I'd been looking forward to Echuca but I am cold and down on enthusiasm. The thought of hunting out a backpackers and finding somewhere to stash Penelope for the night looms too large to contemplate and I decide to ride for another hour or so. Before heading out I meet a Kiwi couple with a family connection to Panthers. An uncle has a pre-1920 P & M, which is quite exciting. Phelon and Moore rebranded their bikes as Panthers in 1923 but prior to that, from their beginning in 1904 they had been known as P & Ms. We chat for a bit and they get a good photo of Penelope and me. I then headed on for a while and holed-up in a pretty average hotel/motel in the small town of Tongala (pop 1900), treating myself to a similarly average meal and a solitary evening. One small interaction at the gas station gave me pause to think. In the coffee area I noted a sign on the wall – 'You must love that house so much ... you've bought it twice!' The business was clearly run by a 'petrolhead' judging by all the motoring memorabilia on the walls and his interest in Penelope. He engages me in collegial bonhomie but soon is railing about his recently departed wife. He didn't mean departed as in 'passed away', he meant 'gone' as in 'pissed off to somewhere else'. After a 30-year marriage, she had "gone odd after menopause". He'd had to sell quite a few of his toys to buy back half the house ... which he clearly thought he already owned. He oozed presumptive bitterness, condemning all womankind in a few vitriolic utterances. I have nothing to add, no comments to give ... but it disturbs me, and I reflect in the quiet hours that follow, how much I love my own spouse ... as I am sure he did his once. He seemed to think the path he had ended up on was the same one for all of us men. I gently mourn for him.

The next day is only memorable for me leaving my Kindle plugged into the unit's power source ... but in due time it was returned to me. I also had my French Scorpion helmet fall off Penelope's seat whilst the visor was open and the swivelling mechanism broke, rendering the helmet more-or-less useless. I could no longer swivel the visor up, or clip it in place in its riding position. This is a shame as the helmet is probably the most comfortable one I have ever had. Weeks later, I source another one from Europe.

The final day's ride back to Melbs was cold and dull. Cold and dull tends to lead to long periods of sitting in a state of semi-torpor ... eyes open, brain set to 'rest'. I remember riding past an interesting old brick building which advertised pies ... but it was on the other side of the road and by the time the brain was aroused and in a cognitive state ... we were hundreds of metres down the road and unwilling to face the mental and physical efforts needed to chuck a 'Ueee' and go back. A little subjugated voice kept whispering "I would have loved a pie!" for many miles. Later, the cold drives me into a diner advertising 'all day big breakfasts'. Sitting on a window seat, warming in the early afternoon sun, I recall an evocative photo from years gone by. With my crew on a winter adventure I had taken a shot through the window of the Luggate Diner in the deep south of our South Island. The result showed our old bikes lined up outside, with the reverse writing of the diner's name on the window adding interest to the photo. I try the same ... its ok, but there isn't quite the same feel to it with just Penelope outside.

My welcome back into Melbourne was warmer than the ride had been. I was happy to be stopping, and happy also because Steph was flying in to be *Numero Uno Grandma* for the weekend. Our time with the family was to be short but as always very enjoyable ... even if a fair bit of the time would be spent going from one side of town to the other because of the geographical separation of the kids. Actually Steph and I have never minded much, as Melbourne has so many transport options. That combinations of buses, trains and trams always gives us variety and also quality time together exploring and enjoying 'The Big Smoke'. Often we'll stop en route and have coffee and a general gawp at the intriguing masses of humanity that big cosmopolitan centres consist of. The weather for Arthur's party on the Saturday was forecast as pretty crap, so the gathering in the park was changed to be a small at-home celebration. Because a lot of preparing was to be done on site and in the kitchen during Saturday morning, this was seen as a good time for me to drop in to the Royal Exhibition Building whilst coming across from Preston in the North-East of the city to Kensington which is in the West. This got me out of the way and into the magnificent downtown Victorian Royal Exhibition Hall to wander amazed and intrigued by the 500 or so exotic vehicles vying for the prestigious awards on offer. This is no ordinary car show and I felt a bit out of place in my old waxed-japara, oilskin motorcycle gear. The 'players' in the game all seemed to have tweed jackets with leather elbow patches. Bejewelled, elegant consorts, and champagne flutes were never too far away. The building and the contents were breath-taking in the way that you wish all your friends (and family) could be there to see what you are seeing. It was a magnificent precursor to a lovely family day.

We're loving our grandchildren, just lamenting that they don't live in New Zealand. The tyranny of distance does make each visit special and memorable though. The birthday celebration is low-key and no one goes home or to bed in tears, which is always a bonus when small children and inappropriate food is involved. I love watching Steph watching our offspring, now with offspring of their own. Steph was such a natural mother and being around wee ones is just like re-setting the clock. She is in her element. It is also a time of poignant hope for us, as Arthur's mum, the lovely Jess, is still fighting the ovarian cancer found during her pregnancy. She is about to try a fairly extreme diet which involves a lot of Brazil nuts I seem to recall. There is a lot of laughter as she feeds what seems to be kilos of nuts into a blender. Jess is hugely appreciative of the care that conventional medicine is providing … but still willing to also give something slightly kooky a go.

The family appear to half-heartedly disapprove of me disappearing on Sunday to take in the Australian MotoGP. I tell them it is good to have quality not quantity sometimes with grandparents. Steph's visit is so short, it is only fair that she should be the focus, and I can be off doing the stuff that silly old grandpas do. It is a longer, colder ride than I realised out to Phillip Island. By the time I reach the circuit itself, well over two hours have passed. I am cold but eager for the spectacular entertainment that these events bring. It doesn't disappoint even though my favourite riders don't star on the day. The ride back to Preston is even colder and harder. Australia in the springtime has surprised me a bit with the temperatures being a lot cooler than I had anticipated. I had a couple of light merino wool tops along with me but I know I am at least one layer short and should have been better prepared.

So after about 3,000 trouble-free km Penelope was tucked up in the garage of Kitty and Cam in the northern suburbs of Melbourne and left to await my return.

There's one last anecdote from 2016's ride. On the Monday we duly made our way out to the Tullamarine Airport in the early morning. There we were pleasantly surprised to see old classic-bike friends from Wellington, Phil and Anne Hoare, along with Phil's twin brother Geoff. After a warm greeting, Phil and Geoff look at each other and laugh. "It was Des and Penelope!" one of them exclaims. It seems that on the way to the MotoGP by bus, one of them had looked out the window and espied a Panther distinctively thumping its way along the highway … a rare sight on any day, but particularly on a day when the road was cluttered with the modern sports-bikes of the road-racing cognoscenti. "Just like Des's!" "Yeah, and from from what I can see of the old duffer riding it … it even looks like him." Of course with most of my visage hidden by the full-face helmet I now wear, all they could see was wisps of a white beard and the corpulent outline of a generic oil-skin-clad rider. It's a small world … sometimes.

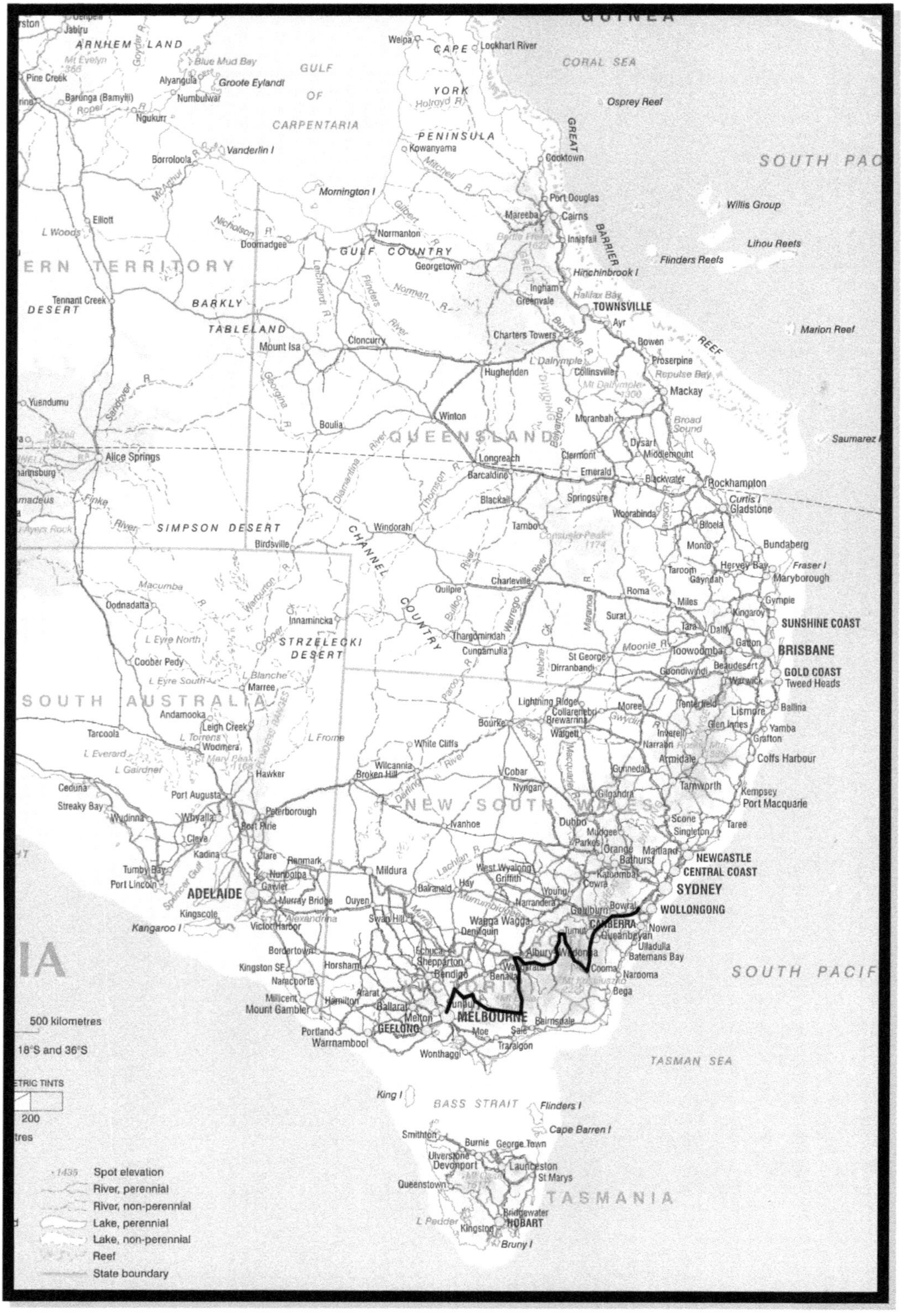

Jabiru
ARNHEM LAND
Pine Creek
Barunga (Bamyili)
Blue Mud Bay
Groote Eylandt
Alyangula
Numbulwar
Ngukurr
Roper R
GULF
OF
CARPENTARIA
Weipa
CAPE
Lockhart River
YORK
Holroyd R
PENINSULA
CORAL SEA
Osprey Reef
GREAT
BARRIER
REEF
SOUTH PAC
Vanderlin I
Borroloola
McArthur R
Kowanyama
Mitchell R
Cooktown
Mornington I
Port Douglas
Cairns
Mareeba
Willis Group
Elliott
L Woods
Nicholson R
Gilbert R
Normanton
Doomadgee
Innisfail
Lihou Reefs
Flinders Reefs
GULF COUNTRY
Georgetown
Hinchinbrook I
ERN TERRITORY
Tennant Creek
DESERT
BARKLY
TABLELAND
Norman R
Ingham
Greenvale
TOWNSVILLE
Ayr
Marion Reef
Mount Isa
Cloncurry
Charters Towers
Bowen
Proserpine
Hughenden
Collinsville
Mackay
Yuendumu
Sandover R
Georgina R
Boulia
Winton
Moranbah
Broad Sound
QUEENSLAND
Alice Springs
Longreach
Barcaldine
Clermont
Emerald
Dysart
Middlemount
Blackwater
Rockhampton
Saumarez
Finke
River
SIMPSON DESERT
Diamantina River
Thomson R
Blackall
Springsure
Woorabinda
Curtis I
Gladstone
Biloela
Birdsville
Windorah
Tambo
CHANNEL
COUNTRY
Monto
Bundaberg
Hervey Bay
Fraser I
Maryborough
Taroom
Gayndah
Macumba
Oodnadatta
Charleville
Quilpie
Roma
Miles
Gympie
Kingaroy
SUNSHINE COAST
Surat
Tara
Dalby
Innamincka
L Eyre North
STRZELECKI
DESERT
Thargomindah
Cunnamulla
St George
Dirranbandi
Toowoomba
Gatton
BRISBANE
Coober Pedy
L Eyre South
L Blanche
Marree
Beaudesert
Goondiwindi
Warwick
GOLD COAST
Tweed Heads
SOUTH AUSTRALIA
Andamooka
Leigh Creek
Lightning Ridge
Collarenebri
Brewarrina
Moree
Tenterfield
Lismore
Ballina
Tarcoola
L Torrens
Woomera
L Frome
Bourke
Walgett
Inverell
Glen Innes
Yamba
Grafton
Narrabri
L Everard
L Gairdner
White Cliffs
Coffs Harbour
Wilcannia
Broken Hill
Hawker
Cobar
Gunnedah
Armidale
Ceduna
Streaky Bay
Port Augusta
Nyngan
Tamworth
Kempsey
Port Macquarie
Wudinna
Whyalla
Peterborough
Port Pirie
NEW SOUTH WALES
Ivanhoe
Dubbo
Scone
Taree
Cleve
Kadina
Clare
Renmark
Mudgee
Parkes
Singleton
Orange
Bathurst
Maitland
NEWCASTLE
CENTRAL COAST
Tumby Bay
Port Lincoln
Mildura
West Wyalong
Griffith
Katoomba
ADELAIDE
Gawler
Nuriootpa
Murray Bridge
Balranald
Hay
Young
Cowra
SYDNEY
Kingscote
Kangaroo I
Victor Harbor
Ouyen
Swan Hill
Narrandera
Goulburn
Bowral
WOLLONGONG
Wagga Wagga
CANBERRA
Nowra
Queanbeyan
Ulladulla
Batemans Bay
Deniliquin
Tumut
Bordertown
Echuca
Shepparton
Albury
Wodonga
Kingston SE
Horsham
Bendigo
Benalla
Wangaratta
Cooma
Narooma
SOUTH PACIF
Naracoorte
Bega
Ararat
Millicent
Mount Gambier
Hamilton
Ballarat
Melton
MELBOURNE
Bairnsdale
500 kilometres
Portland
GEELONG
Moe
Sale
Warrnambool
Traralgon
18°S and 36°S
Wonthaggi
TASMAN SEA
King I
BASS STRAIT
Flinders I
200
Cape Barren I
Smithton
Burnie
George Town
Ulverstone
Devonport
Launceston
St Marys
Queenstown
TASMANIA
L Pedder
Bridgewater
Kingston
HOBART
Bruny I
Spot elevation
River, perennial
River, non-perennial
Lake, perennial
Lake, non-perennial
Reef
State boundary

CHAPTER TWO

# MEANDERING TO A MUSTER

I said I'd be back and true to my word, 26th Oct 2017 saw me pumping up tyres and uttering gentle encouragements. Penelope seemed to sense my eagerness and after just a couple of kicks she appreciatively burst into life with a thudding bark. I'd planned to spend a week tinkering and fettling whilst also putting in the requisite time as Koro with the family, before heading off with local Panther identity John Ferguson. Oil was changed, wheels were swapped (front for back) to even out tyre-wear that was already evident … a portent of things to come … and minor adjustments were made. We happily did battle with cross-town traffic several times to ensure that both grandsons shared their weird old grandpa and his weird old motorcycle.

It hasn't been the greatest of times for the family since I stashed Penelope. Jess sadly lost her battle with cancer in May. I wasn't there to see her waste away and my last recollections are of a still rubenesque, fun-loving, young mum. Steph made a couple of trips across in the last while and was there for her passing along with Joe, her dad Wayne and our Hannah. The funeral was as expected, sad but also a celebration of a loved life, well-lived. Joe and Arthur are a tight unit and will face the tough times ahead, best they can with what support we can give from afar. One so young and vibrant shouldn't be taken. It is hard to countenance that there are those who would say that it is 'God's will'. This same God they would purport to be kind and forgiving.

It almost seems wrong to write that there were also some pretty good times in our year, particularly the month we spent in France in the middle of the year with Number Two son Steve, wife Maud and offspring Jude and Nelson. We dodged our winter and had an enjoyable time riding around Beaujolais on the R65 BMW that we sometimes refer to as our Goldilocks bike – not too big, not too small, not too fast, not too slow, … just right! We are quite happy that with the modern family, and the modern car with mum, dad and two kids in car seats … there is no room for grandparents. They have to take the moto … what a shame!

John, or Ferg as he is known had promised me back-roads and old country pubs. It seemed we had similar leanings in this and early Thurs morning 2nd Nov 2017 I was eagerly out the door filled with excitement and anticipation. Although the day was wet and cold, I was borderline euphoric … another adventure was underway! The plan to be at the rendezvous spot early to fuel-up and have a coffee before Ferg arrived went out the door when Penelope inexplicably spluttered and died on me among the rush-hour traffic. Somehow a bit of aimless tinkering and a swap of spark plug got me going again.

However, soon we were in convoy making our way in a north-east direction out of Melbourne. Ferg's 1938 Redwing Deluxe was Phelan & Moore's luxury Panther with a specification which included linked brakes, twin headlights and a Smiths eight-day clock. The booming exhaust note was a delight to follow, although possibly not all onlookers would agree and clandestine nocturnal visits to your paramour would not go unnoticed. I soon found that Ferg and his outfit could maintain a steady 75-80 kph on the flat, soar to 90 on the downhills and slow to as low as 40 on steep uphills. We had about 500 km to cover in the day so whilst I was enjoying the zigging and zagging, we always kept up a steady progress when able. Ferg was proving to be a guide par-excellence, giving me all

MEANDERING TO A MUSTER

sorts of interesting things to look out for and often pointing to them as we passed. One that he missed though gave me an almost adolescent pleasure. We passed a sign to *The Paps*. The elderly, and readers of old books will know that paps was a racy description of women's breasts. *The Paps* are a pair of hills that meet that description … amply.

Despite previously being a bit of a paragon when it came to reliability, on this first day Penelope was definitely one of *The Donald's* Weakest Links. She had developed a hiccupping stutter and whilst we still could maintain a speed sufficient to track along behind Ferg most of the time … it was frustrating and a little embarrassing. At our first fuel and coffee stop at Bonnie Doon of *The Castle* movie fame, the tools came out and it was found that hanging about not being ridden, had not agreed with Penelope. Significant amounts of rusty detritus from her petrol tank had clogged the banjo filter on the carburettor and she was suffering fuel starvation. It was here after the 'adjustments' and a coffee that the sun came out and we

THE BIG SIT

were able to shed our outermost layers. This stop also gave rise to an embarrassing situation where I was unable to start Penelope. I had been ill (on my death-bed earlier in the week) and was still lacking in strength and vitality. After a few feeble ineffectual kicks, Ferg came over and gave her a lusty boot in the guts and she responded appropriately. I hid my embarrassment best I could and we headed off the promised delights of the Mansfield to Whitfield portion of the day's ride. Ferg had urged me to go ahead to fully enjoy the twists and undulations on my own, at my pace, which he correctly surmised would be a bit quicker than his pre-war outfit. Matter-of-factly, Ferg had told me it was one of Victoria's top rides. It was in reality better than that. This was one of the most enjoyable rides I could remember … ever, anywhere. I struck it with no traffic going my way, although dozens and dozens of bikes were encountered going the other way. Usually too busy flicking the old girl left and right to wave, I know we all felt somehow enjoined through a telepathic kindred spirit. It was a Thursday and we were out playing, thinking little of the wage-slaves in front of shimmering computer screens. Finally, the 65 km of pure bliss was over and grinning like a galah I pulled into the Whitfield Hotel to wait for my guide.

A solitary beer was enjoyed with an above-adequate lunch (chef's chicken pie) while we debriefed the ride so far and Ferg gave me a great version of Ned Kelly's adventures and miss-adventures. Soon we were off, heading for Beechworth, the delightful old gold mining town. I'd first heard of my fearless leader in one of our Wellington Classic Motorcycle Club member's accounts of an annual ride he did from Melbourne out to Beechworth … on old and frail vintage bikes as a guest of the afore-mentioned Ferg. These were often hilarious sagas filled with plenty of mechanical mayhem and more. I'd also enjoyed the delights of Beechworth twice before and whilst we would have loved to stop again and tarry, there were more delights ahead … and besides … we were on a mission.

Our subsequent afternoon stop may have been brief, but I'd spent the last few kilometres trying to decide how to pronounce Yackandandah and was delighted when Ferg pulled over and I could ask. This was a smaller, possibly even more quaint, old gold-mining settlement which seemed to have the right balance between fawning on tourists and getting about the business of modern-day life. I was also loving the stops because I could ask Ferg about things that I'd noticed along the way which had given rise to a question in my mind. Never was he stumped whether it was flora, fauna or history. He was also undemanding and enjoyable to be with. Already he was a trip bonus.

Google, when consulted later told me that Yack has a population of under 1,000 and is also noted for a poem published in the 11 June 1857 edition of The Melbourne Punch called *The Lass of Yackandandah*

"Let poets sing of English girls,

Their beauty and their candour;

Give me a sweeter nymph than all,

The lass of Yackandandah."

"She draws a cork with such an air,

No mortal can withstand her;

She turns a tap, and turns our heads,

The lass of Yackandandah."

I wondered if this hottie of a barmaid had also inspired *The Paps*.

The last 150 km to Corryong were a bit of a slog as end-of-day rides often are, especially on old dungas. Finally, we rolled into one of the last towns in Victoria and after a lap of the main street we checked into the only hotel we could find. Ferg has travelled extensively both for work and pleasure. I was delighted to find that like myself he always looks to dine out rather than dine in. I think it is being defeatist and too easy, just to go through to the dining room of your accommodation. There is not even the slightest component of hunter-gatherer in that. So after a beer, then a clean-up etc we ventured out for a bit of exercise and to look for a meal. Disappointingly, we had over-estimated the delights that Corryong would have on a Thurs night, and soon were skulking back into our lair for the night, asking if the kitchen was still open.

Being that we had 600 km ahead of us, an early start followed next morning. It dawned a pretty average day. Whilst refueling before we left, Ferg made some half-hearted enquiries about the direction we were heading. The elderly pump jockey seemed to confirm our intended route and once more we optimistically headed off, leaving a raucous cacophony behind us in the early morning stillness. Soon there was rain and misery. Actually the misery bit is only relative because you wouldn't be a life-long motorcyclist if wet and cold impacted on the joy of being out and about on your moto. Since arriving in Australia a week earlier there had only been one warm day and mostly the temperatures were pretty consistently 8° overnight with day-time running to 15°. Today we'd challenge that. We were soon in New South Wales … tick! The morning's ride to a coffee break was spectacular and interesting. There were challenging twisting downhills and almost endless climbs that had the mighty outfit down to 2nd gear and breathing heavily. I'd not thought of Aussie having this sort of terrain. In 'heat of the moment' … a particularly inappropriate phrase given the clemency at the time … Ferg misinterpreted his Tom Tom and we took a spur road up to Cabramurra, the village that serves as the headquarters to the Snowy River Scheme's hydro dams etc. This was a fortuitous deviation as there are only so many times that you can tell yourself you are having fun. It was 4° and the rain was persistent, seemingly with no respite. The coffee may have been average but in the circumstances, sitting in front of a big gas fire with my paws wrapped around a big mug … it was heaven-sent. It would have been easy to stay all day in this mountain-top haven, warm and dry within a café of sorts. Subsequent Googling told me not only that Cabramurra was Australia's 3rd highest settlement at 1488 m but that it was about to be dis-established as a township and the permanent residents moved out.

As Kiwis we are parochially proud of our Southern Alps and the wonderful soaring passes that traverse them. Dismissively we usually think of Australia having nothing to rival them ... just a flat red continent with roadkill the only challenge to your straight-line riding ... yet here I was many hundreds of metres above NZ's highest public road, sitting in a café looking out at the ongoing deluge. Ultimately there was no alternative but to gird our loins and go back out into it. In the murky, borderline-sleety conditions, we wound our way successively down and up and over more staggering hills conquering the Main Divide at over 1500 m before finally breaking out into the lush foothills. This corresponded with leaving the rains behind, so when Penelope's stuttering hiccups worsened to a silent glide and embarrassing halt ... it was in watery sunshine. This time the carb filter was clear but there was no petrol flowing from the tank. Ferg suggested consecutively blowing back through the fuel lines with one tap closed and one open. Not a pleasant task but my huffing and puffing was rewarded each time with a satisfactory bubbling in the tank showing I had cleared the blocking crud away from the outlets ... at least temporarily. Petrol flowed again and spirits lifted. The fast flowing road out of the foothills onto the plain brought us to Cooma and lunchtime. It also brought us to hustle and bustle. The pub was full of motorcyclists and bikes were evident everywhere in town. We had timed our arrival with *The Snowy Ride*, a big cancer fund-raiser which attracts more than 2,000 riders and raises hundreds of thousands of dollars for a worthy cause. Their big ride was the Saturday so we would see a constant flow of two-wheelers all afternoon as we continued on our relentless quest to make it to the rally site before dusk. Although only of relatively modest size (<7,000 pop), Cooma is the main town of the Monaro district and I took juvenile joy when riding along the evocatively-named Monaro Highway leading out of town noting that we passed ... going the other way of course ... more than one Holden Monaro. In addition to hosting *The Snowy Ride*, Cooma was the site of a big auto show for the weekend so all afternoon we witnessed the passing of most models of car that the Australian Motor Industry had ever made. My favourite was an almost-fluoro pink Holden Torana XU1 from the early 1970s – the car that impecunious adolescents had sinful night-dreams about. Google, being the know-all bastard that she is, tells me it was an original colour called *strike me pink*.

The afternoon saw us dip into our third state for the day as we skirted Canberra and couldn't avoid going into the Australian Capital Territory ... and now I think the train-spotters are going to tell me it is not a State but a Territory. I understand their pedantry, but I claim it anyway. When suitably away from Canberra and past the unusually named Queanbeyan we stopped for a simple but nice break in a slightly quirky café in Bungendore. Interestingly, the immediacy of interacting with the café proprietor and and the delights of getting my coffee and snack, meant that I forgot to quiz my resident font (of all knowledge) about the huge solar farm we had passed back a bit before Canberra. The downside of a big day's itinerary on a slow ride means that there will be times when you go by things of interest with the thought lingering ... "I wish I had time to stop and find out about that!" (The Royalla Solar Farm was developed by a Spanish company, is made up of 83,000 solar panels and has the capacity to power more than 4,500 ACT homes - Google)

Also in the afternoon, which had warmed up a bit, we suddenly turned off onto a side road which was gravel. I was unsure if this was Tom Tom directing us onto 'the shortest route' or a cunning shortcut that Ferg knew about. Now it seemed that his old outfit had gained 10 horse power and had lifted her skirts up and begun to run like hell. Penelope and I are happy on gravel but do always take a few km to become relaxed and confident. "I'll stay out of Ferg's dust" was my fibbing justification for falling back a bit during this adjustment. Being a very minor road there was absolutely no traffic, except for one juvenile yokel in a battered ute who suddenly appeared dangerously close at my right elbow before pitching it sideways across my bows into the corner I was slowing for. Slewing all over the road, he then chased after Ferg, followed him for a while then most aggressively repeated the derring-do pass he had made on me. "What a Dickhead!" were some of the first words we both uttered later when we finally ended our day. We were booked into the Bundanoon Hotel in the Southern Highlands of New South Wales, and we knew the informal gathering for Friday night was going to be held at the property of Jordan and Carol at Penrose. This appeared to be 10 km or so out of town. It was a pleasant surprise to simultaneously spot a hand-stencilled leaping Panther on a core-flute sign. I think we both chuckled at the discreet lack of words or arrows on the sign. Intuitively we turned to the direction the panther was leaping and at the next bifurcation in the road there was another panther … still leaping but this time to the right.

And so it was that after a bit more than 1,100 km of back-road adventure, we thudded into a haven of Phelan and Moore's finest, resplendent under a sizeable corrugated lean-to. Panther owners are always proud of their handsome steeds, but I think there was no one there more proud than Ferg and me. Our bikes were not the shiniest and not even as shiny as when they left home. I think we probably both stifled a self-satisfied smirk as we realised we were the only ones to ride to the gathering … and what a ride.

Although Jordan and Carol had made it clear that this year's Panther 'do' was to be a 'muster' not a 'rally', I still couldn't help but think of their place as Rally HQ, and what an ideal spot. I'd met Carol last year in McLaren Flat and instantly warmed to her quiet Welsh ways. They share a rural property with others, presumably of the same ilk, and we were able to use some of the common areas and buildings for the social gatherings. Ferg

**THE BIG SIT**

and I were greeted almost as conquering heroes, and it was great to see a lot of the faces from last year beaming at us as we peeled off layer after layer of clothing. The place was a hive of activity as preparations for the BBQ were well underway. Carol had a small coterie of friends as seemingly willing helpers, rushing to and fro with large bowls, tureens etc filled with appealing-looking side dishes to accompany the meats. After the initial meet and greet, look at the other bikes, we were soon yesterday's news, and sent off to book into the pub. It was decided that to enable us to enthusiastically participate in the evening, we should leave our steeds to cosy-up to their kith and take a generously offered car away to town, and later a sober driver would deliver us back. So it was that we freshened up, had a quick reviving beer … or was it to gird our loins for the night to come? Anyway, in time we were back among the similarly afflicted, gnawing on chops, snarlers, meat patties etc, telling lies and oozing bonhomie best we could. One of the bonuses of having quite a few 'trailer sailors' is that there are often cars about to ferry folk around. So it was that David and Robyn from Sydney took us home and Laurie and Susan returned us in the morning for breakfast … lovely people all of them.

There's something quite evocative about the bringing into life of a dozen or so single cylinder classic bikes. The staccato roar and distinctive thumping bark, progressively builds and often becomes firstly syncopated and then mixed to become one invasive sound, as one after the other of these treasures are coaxed into action. As with any family outing, there are the recalcitrant who refuse to go. Sadly, today there were two bikes that never really wanted to come out and play, one being possibly the prettiest of the group, a 1934 Model 100 with a striking two-tone green petrol tank … maybe she was freshly restored and a little shell-shocked about leaving the workshop to be put out amongst crass show-offs like Penelope.

The later model Panthers are known to smoke a bit and even though I have incorporated most of the known cures in Penelope, including the use of a Rover V8 car piston, we were captured by Leigh Turner, blowing a 'puff of blue' as we fired up. It took a while but ultimately all those that were going to go … were going. Next mission was to fuel-up, another exercise in herding cats.

Finally, we were strung out along the highway following Jordan and Carol, heading for a special morning tea. We'd all been given a route description but it was so much easier just to keep someone ahead in sight, hoping that that someone also was following the right leader. Of course when you organise an event like this, not only do you want the rides to be pleasant for the participants but also the stops need to be pretty damn good too. Needless to say Jordan and Carol had excelled themselves. Although we largely followed behind them like a mother-duck with all the ducklings strewn out behind … running to keep up, every corner of note had a leaping panther fixed to the most proximate post. We undulated, and twisted and turned and 'oohed and aahed' to ourselves. One instance gave rise to way, way, more than that though. I was a couple back from the lead and we dipped down on a minor side road which had hedge rows excluding any views of the surroundings. As we approached the railway crossing at the bottom of the dip we passed the ubiquitous sign saying 'Look for Trains'. Ahead I saw Carol almost leap off the pillion seat as they crossed the tracks. When, in turn we each got to the point where we could similarly look down the line, our hearts leapt in our chests ... there was a train right there ... only 20 m away with its big blazing light giving the situation real gravitas. It took a moment or two to realise that the train was not actually moving, and I wonder if the driver just parks up there to scare people if he is a bit ahead of schedule and has a couple of minutes to spare. Worked with us!

Even though our departure had been fractured and seemingly shambolic we arrived on time for the 11.00 am morning tea appointment at the charming Burrawang General Store which dates from 1867 and now is an arty, boutiquey café. Fully timber-lined, it is resplendent with lots of old signage and memorabilia from its colourful past. We had all of the upstairs to ourselves and it was a great opportunity to further mix with the other players along for the weekend. The service was leisurely and random which only added to our enjoyment. No one was in a hurry as we had not all that long before had a fulsome breakfast. I can't recall what I had but I remember noting that I seemed to have made the best choice, as it was an exquisite morsel.

Our second riding chunk for the day was a little less interesting and did involve one small piece of town riding in Moss Vale with a turn-off without a leaping panther for guidance. Seemingly we all made it ok as ultimately all bikes were present for the lunch break, which was just that ... a break. This was a great option. We parked our bikes on the green opposite the historic Berrima Ladies Gaol (still operational) and were told to be back ready for the off at 2.00 pm. This gave us a couple of hours to wander about this lovely little village and enjoy either visiting the various attractions like the old courthouse, the Surveyor General Hotel (est 1834) or the cafes, old churchs etc.

The village of Berrima, now with a population of not much more than 600 was once a major settlement known officially as The Town of Berrima and most of the civic buildings were built before 1840. This again brought home to me how much older than NZ Australia is settlement-wise. The Southern Highlands of New South Wales are quite a way from coastal Sydney and yet they were establishing town plans and carrying out major construction in the 1830s, a decade before the first settlers' ships were even arriving at NZ's untouched shores. Being quite replete from the leftover BBQ brekkie and the earlier-mentioned exquisite morsel from Burrawang, I didn't meander off to the cafes with the main group but instead took some time away on my own to look at some of the early-settler architecture, and to catch up on some emails on the way-smarter-than-me smart phone I now was travelling with (Steph had put my trusty old Nokia through the wash in France ... my fault).

The village was quite a delight with a mix of the freshly-restored almost-twee, rubbing shoulders with the builders' dream doer-uppers. Not for the first time I thought how much Steph would have enjoyed the old stuff we were amongst. I often muse on her throw-back leanings and how she would have been great as a pioneer woman, being as she seems to relish deprivation and has nothing but disdain for the comforts and labour-saving accoutrements that most of her gender aspire to. I smile because I know which of the two cottages included here she would be gushing over.

A short afternoon ride takes us to a private vehicle collection. This was so wonderful because it made so many of us feel normal and to reaffirm that our 'saving for posterity' was not really hoarding and our families had nothing to worry about at all. The owner was not on site this day but had made the two large ... and I mean large, sheds available for us to explore. To say the contents were eclectic is the biggest understatement you could imagine. Here were Bentleys, Cadillacs, a Baby Austin, Nashs, a hydroplane, aero parts, an E-type Jag, a Studebaker, a double-decker bus, a Renault 750 etc. The collection was random and a lot of the stuff was being worked on judging by the items strewn over the floor. Many of the items individually would have a real value if finished. The slightly smaller second shed clearly had the stuff that wasn't being worked on. The two sheds were on a rural block with a low-level typical Aussie farmers' house also on the spread-out site. We were told this was just the guy's weekend retreat where he came to play with his toys. I don't think any of us were too surprised to learn his wife had left him. It takes a special type of woman to endure a hobby this vast.

As can be imagined, a lot of fun was had here ... and a cup of tea with biscuits. It was also a good spot for a photo of the bikes and riders who were on the 2017 Panther Muster ... with Panthers. There were others on lesser makes who rightly remained behind the camera. From here it also wasn't a long ride back to HQ. John and I took our bikes home to the pub this time though and after a bit of difficulty and shifting of a lot of demo materials etc we managed to get them tucked up for the night in a garage a level below us. Management had been a bit blasé about finding room for us because they thought we were coming on bicycles. All was sorted in the end.

The day had remained cool but no real rain had eventuated. It had been fun chasing Jordan and Carol along, noting that our late-model 120s were very evenly matched on the uphill climbs. I must confess that it had been a deliberate ploy to get to be second-in-line and fill their mirrors. On the Friday night I had re-connected with Tony, a big, burly, bearded character

**THE BIG SIT**

from Victoria who for this weekend would be riding a spare Panther of Jordan's. With enthusiasm he recalled how the previous year on the Fleurieu Peninsular he had enjoyed our spirited riding when he followed me on his BMW 800 while we both pushed along quicker and quicker. Earlier that day our ride had been quite processional with an older couple in a sidecar leading the way very sedately. Penelope just couldn't handle going so demurely through the countryside, as she is a bit of a larrikin at heart, so for the afternoon we chased the marshals who would jet ahead to position themselves at intersections and turn-offs. We had a lot of fun ducking and diving, vainly trying to keep up with the modern bike ahead. Similarly, today, initially I could see Jordan was adjusting his pace for the following sidecar outfits which are not as sprightly as the solos. On a bit of a straight we made our move up into position close behind them. Of course Tony also covered me thinking there might be some fun to be had.

So it was that Jordan could see a couple of bikes looming large in his vibration-blurred mirror, and adjusted his speed accordingly, not realising that we were stretching out and away from some of the followers. There were some minor repercussions as at the evening's social event Jordan was told he had been going too fast for some of the group and to go a bit easier for the Sunday's ride. I'd been happy to engage in this bit of fun because I knew we all had instruction sheets as to where we were going and had leaping panthers on all the crucial turns. I am a big fan of everyone riding their own ride, at their own pace.

Bundanoon means 'place of deep gullies' which is quite apt. It has a population of under 3,000 and has experienced cycles of boom and bust during its history. I now chuckle as I learn that it was formerly known as Jordan's Crossing. Being almost within commuting distance of Sydney has seen the area boom again with an older, more affluent influx. There is not a wide range of suitable evening eateries for the organizing team to choose from but the Bundanoon Pizza Restaurant proved ideal for our group. For most this is an annual catch-up with other admirers of the Phelan and Moore-produced motorcycles. These are real fans who in many cases have travelled big distances to get there and re-establish the ongoing camaraderie that so obviously exists between them. These gatherings have been held for many years up and down the East Coast from Queensland to South Australia and the attendees are like family, what we would call whanau. This year the Watts family from Queensland have their son Riley riding a Panther for the first time. Many of the crew have known him since he was a small child and enjoyed seeing this transition.

As always with these gatherings, lies are told, stories and memories shared, all helped along with a lot of laughs. We have a few supporters along who for one reason or another were unable to have their Panthers at the 'muster'. I am sure that seeing so many others out on their pride-and-joys will have triggered that next burst of energy needed to finish their project bikes and join next year.

Sunday morning was programmed as a more leisurely start with just a 35km ride in the hills to another suitably-chosen morning tea café, where we would have our last gathering and then disperse every which-way. This gave Ferg and I time to check out, load up once more, park the bikes in the main street and go off to a small cycle shop café for breakfast. There was also time to linger in the local Makers' Market which was just that. It was in their hall and had no store-bought stuff at all, just the creations of the local populace. Opposite our bikes, an old duffer with a WW2 'Blitz' army truck was selling wooden artefacts. Together we made quite a sight.

Our ride to *The General* at Canyonleigh was just as we had come to expect here in the Southern Highlands of NSW, green and undulating ... so unlike the Big Red Continent I had pictured ... but that would come later. Maybe I was becoming satiated, but this was just another lovely café in a lovely setting, with time spent communing with affable friends. It was becoming time for some hard-tack rations, I was going soft. The luxury of it all was seductive. I needed to get on to a regime of *'glass of water and a look out the window'.*

It had been a great weekend run by genuinely nice people and assisted by their equally lovely friends. I hope this won't be my last Australian Panther Register's gathering. Ferg and I were now to head in opposite directions. He would take a more direct route home and ultimately make it safely by Melbourne Cup evening ... too late for the race though. He'd been a great companion and I am sure this won't be the last time we adventure together.

For me it is time to head north, hopefully to sunshine and warmer climes. This year in my kit I have included a tent and sleeping bag. These are kept in a canvas swag I have made specifically for the ride . I roll up the whole 'kit and caboodle' and attach it to the carrier with Andy Strapz' 50 mm wide elastics of the 'Piggy back' variety. These allow me to keep my waterproofs on the outside of the load and be able to get them off without disturbing the load. Excellent devices that I can't recommend strongly enough.

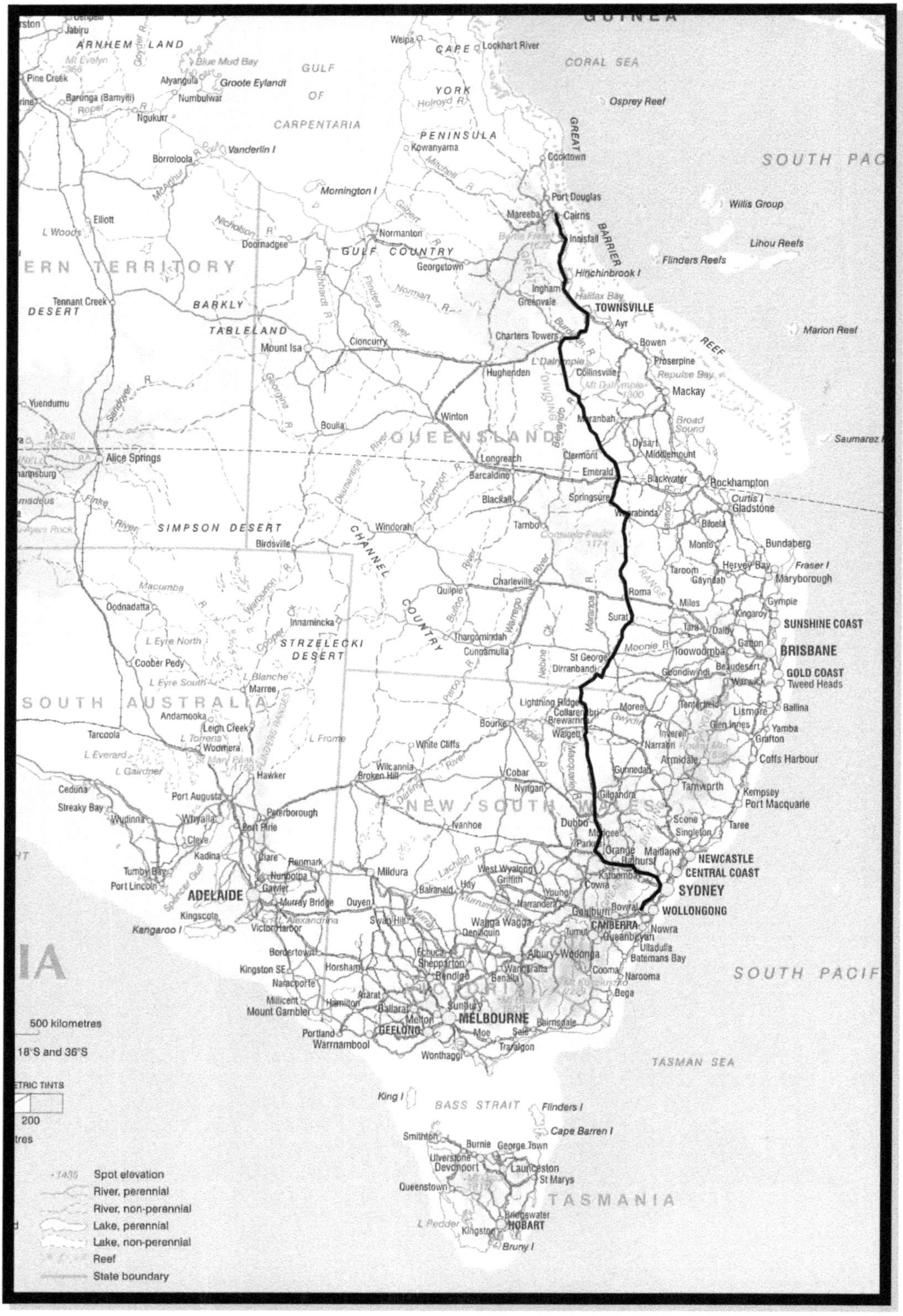

GUINEA
CORAL SEA
Osprey Reef
SOUTH PAC
Willis Group
Lihou Reefs
Flinders Reefs
Marion Reef
Saumarez R
GREAT
BARRIER
REEF
Jabiru
ARNHEM LAND
Mt Evelyn
Blue Mud Bay
Pine Creek
Alyangula
Groote Eylandt
Baranga (Bamyili)
Numbulwar
Roper R
Ngukurr
Weipa
CAPE
Lockhart River
YORK
Holroyd R
PENINSULA
GULF
OF
CARPENTARIA
Borroloola
Vanderlin I
Kowanyama
Mitchell R
Cooktown
McArthur R
Mornington I
Port Douglas
Mareeba
Cairns
Elliott
L Woods
Nicholson R
Doomadgee
Normanton
Gilbert R
Innisfail
Bartle Frere 1622
GULF COUNTRY
Georgetown
Hinchinbrook I
ERN TERRITORY
Ingham
Greenvale
Halifax Bay
TOWNSVILLE
Tennant Creek
DESERT
BARKLY
TABLELAND
Norman R
Leichhardt R
Flinders River
Ayr
Bowen
Burdekin R
Charters Towers
Mount Isa
Cloncurry
L Dalrymple
Proserpine
Repulse Bay
Hughenden
Collinsville
Mt Dalrymple 1300
Mackay
DIVIDING
Yuendumu
Sandover R
Georgina R
Winton
Moranbah
Broad Sound
Boulia
QUEENSLAND
Belyando R
Dysart
Middlemount
Alice Springs
Longreach
Clermont
Barcaldine
Emerald
Blackwater
Rockhampton
Curtis I
Gladstone
Finke
Diamantina River
Thomson R
Blackall
Springsure
Woorabinda
Dawson
Biloela
Ayers Rock
River
SIMPSON DESERT
Tambo
Consuelo Peak 1174
Monto
Bundaberg
Windorah
Birdsville
CHANNEL
COUNTRY
Bulloo R
Warrego
River
Charleville
Maranoa R
Taroom
Hervey Bay
Fraser I
Gayndah
Maryborough
Macumba
Quilpie
Roma
Miles
Gympie
Oodnadatta
R
Warburton
Cooper Ck
Innamincka
Surat
Kingaroy
SUNSHINE COAST
Tara
Dalby
L Eyre North
STRZELECKI
DESERT
Thargomindah
Cunnamulla
Nebine Ck
Moonie R
Toowoomba
Gatton
BRISBANE
Coober Pedy
L Blanche
St George
Dirranbandi
Goondiwindi
Beaudesert
GOLD COAST
L Eyre South
Marree
Warwick
Tweed Heads
SOUTH AUSTRALIA
Lightning Ridge
Moree
Tenterfield
Lismore
Ballina
Andamooka
Collarenebri
Brewarrina
Gwydir
Glen Innes
Yamba
Leigh Creek
Bourke
Bogan
Walgett
Inverell
Grafton
Tarcoola
L Torrens
Woomera
FLINDERS RANGES
L Frome
White Cliffs
Narrabri
Armidale
Coffs Harbour
L Everard
St Mary Peak 1165
L Gairdner
Hawker
Broken Hill
Wilcannia
Darling
River
Cobar
Macquarie
Gunnedah
Tamworth
Ceduna
Nyngan
Kempsey
Port Augusta
Gilgandra
Port Macquarie
Streaky Bay
Peterborough
NEW SOUTH WALES
Wudinna
Whyalla
Port Pirie
Ivanhoe
Dubbo
Scone
Taree
Cleve
Mudgee
Singleton
Kadina
Clare
Parkes
Orange
Maitland
NEWCASTLE
Renmark
Lachlan R
West Wyalong
Bathurst
CENTRAL COAST
Tumby Bay
Port Lincoln
Spencer Gulf
Nuriootpa
Mildura
Griffith
Katoomba
Cowra
Gawler
Balranald
Hay
Young
SYDNEY
ADELAIDE
Murray Bridge
Ouyen
Murrumbidgee
Narrandera
Bowral
WOLLONGONG
Kingscote
L Alexandrina
Swan Hill
Goulburn
Kangaroo I
Victor Harbor
Wagga Wagga
CANBERRA
Nowra
Deniliquin
Tumut
Queanbeyan
Bordertown
Echuca
Albury-Wodonga
Ulladulla
Batemans Bay
Kingston SE
Horsham
Shepparton
Wangaratta
Cooma
Naracoorte
Bendigo
Benalla
Mt Kosciuszko
Narooma
Millicent
Ararat
Bega
Mount Gambier
Hamilton
Ballarat
Sunbury
Melton
MELBOURNE
Bairnsdale
SOUTH PACIF
Portland
Warrnambool
GEELONG
Moe
Sale
Traralgon
Wonthaggi
TASMAN SEA
King I
BASS STRAIT
Flinders I
Cape Barren I
Smithton
Burnie
George Town
Ulverstone
Devonport
Launceston
St Marys
Queenstown
TASMANIA
L Pedder
Bridgewater
Kingston
HOBART
Bruny I
IA
500 kilometres
18°S and 36°S
ETRIC TINTS
200
tres
1435 Spot elevation
River, perennial
River, non-perennial
Lake, perennial
Lake, non-perennial
Reef
State boundary

CHAPTER THREE

# CAIRNS OR BUST

My travel plans were still pretty fluid at the time of The Muster's end. I needed a bit of time to do some minor maintenance on Penelope, but I did need to start making some hard decisions. Originally I had planned a gentle wandering northwards, with a focus on quality over quantity. Too often my big rides were exactly that … just big rides with no time to look and listen, gaze and gawp etc. Usually work commitments created time constraints and there was rarely the relaxed, often aimless meandering along that had been such a big component of our first youthful adventure together. In 1976/77 Penelope had valiantly carted Steph and me from New Orleans to Buenos Aries, taking almost a year to do so, as we stuttered our way along, zigging and zagging without an itinerary or calendar. The ride finished when we ran out of money … not time. So this year I had boldly only bought a one-way ticket to Melbourne, because I didn't know when, or even where I would be returning to NZ from. "I'll probably spend all of November slowly getting up to Brisbane … having a good look around".

Of course life doesn't always follow a smooth path, and I started to think that Cairns would be a better destination. It might be another 1,700 km but I had no pressure to get there quickly … yeah right!

Not long before my departure to Melbourne in late October, I had received a call from the Building Research Association of NZ (BRANZ) asking if I was interested in co-presenting a nation-wide roadshow for them. I had done one a few months earlier, and was aware of a similar series of seminars coming up, but it was on a topic I knew nothing about.

I knew that they already had specialist presenters on-board so had not considered it an option that I would be called upon. Now, seemingly work commitments were going to prevent the BRANZ in-house subject-expert from doing it, and the fall-back person was in the middle of cancer treatment. It had been suggested that as a *'talking head'* I could slot in yet again. It would once more be 21 venues spread over 7 weeks.

What a dilemma ... a well remunerated gig, versus an adventure! One brings in money and one pours it out ... mmmmm! Back when I conceived the idea of progressively riding around Oz over a period of years, I naively presumed health and wealth would play ball, but I didn't bother to think it all through fully ... as it was just a fantasy-land dream in my head. Our daughters assert that I suffer from 'terminal optimism' and worry that it will get me into trouble one day. My real job had finished at the end of July and we had spent all of August in France seeing the new addition to the line-up of grandchildren. Now I had no obvious income other than the government pension.

"I'm away all of November. When would we need to start?"

"Oh, the first one will be Napier on the 20th Nov."

"Bugger!"

Ultimately, I'd agreed to take my presentation-loaded computer with me to learn and rehearse my bit and to be back in NZ for a run-through and briefing on 18th Nov. So my month of tootling along was now severely truncated and only 11 days remained. Damn ... better get on with it then!

My afternoon following the many farewells and offerings of accommodation up-country etc was just an easy ride of less than 50 km to the village of Robertson where I was to reconnect with an ex-work colleague and her husband. I had enjoyed the crazy vibrancy of the heavily-tattooed Jedda in the work environment, and equally enjoyed the all-too-few social interactions with her and husband Mark. Mark is a car-trimmer and this is a field I had dabbled in decades ago, so along with cars and motos, we also could talk about compound-feed, walking-foot Singer 132K6 sewing machines … and did. I'd been disappointed when Jedda's role in our expressway project finished and they decided to return to Australia. I was now excited to be able to catch-up with them, even if only briefly as they were both working during the week in Sydney, necessitating a pre-5 am departure from home on Monday mornings. That didn't stop us going out for a meal at the notable Robertson Hotel and sharing quite a few wines. Robertson sits on a plateau at a bit under 750 m and is renowned for its rainfall and potatoes. Fortunately, the heavens didn't open during our evening perambulations to and from the pub … but a spectacular night of rain followed, just to give me a sample of what can be dished out. Demonstrating her omnipotence, 'Her upstairs' also threw down thunder and lightning all night, something that would continue next day for most of my ride.

I'd arranged that I would have my maintenance time at David and Joanne Dickie's place in Orangeville, half a day's ride away. So after a leisurely lie-in, wake-up and stretch, I came to the realisation that the precipitation was not going to stop, and I would just have to go back out and suffer. Quite a few months earlier I had sourced a suitably sized, spiral bound, Road Atlas of Australia. I love maps and the like, so it gave me considerable joy in the planning stages of my trip. I then put it away safely … so safely of course that when time came to go to do the ride, I couldn't find the atlas. Never mind, my smarter-than-me smart phone has Google Maps and it was no problem to work out how to get to the Dickie's. The problem was that the phone would keep rotating the map as I moved it … it doesn't seem to understand 'page north'. So it (I?) was at times confused as to which way to go. That is my excuse for wandering lost and lonely in the pouring rain on Monday morning. I sort of knew I was going the wrong way but some of the riding was glorious, especially coming down off the plateau. Randomly and to my surprise during the ride I came across one of yesterday's coreflute panthers ... so backed up and removed it for later reinstatement on my shed door. Still disorientated and going completely the wrong direction somehow I ended up out on the coast at Wollongong, then skirted the edges of Sydney before heading inland again and finally finding Orangeville and the lifestyle block that David and Joanne live on with David's elderly mother. I had probably doubled the mileage needed for the day ... but no one was counting.

I'd spent a night with them in Ouyen the previous year so had got to know and like them a lot. They have raced sidecars for many years in both classic and modern guises with Joanne as the swinger. Joanne also has a couple of road-going outfits that she rides and for the muster had used her big Suzuki to tow a trailer with their early 1950s Panther on it. David rode to Bundanoon on the immaculate R100RS BMW they had bought new and toured Europe on 30+ years earlier. It is not for me to show pictures of their toys ... but in addition to the 2 old Jaguars and 2 Panthers there were beautifully-presented exotica everywhere to salivate over. There was the house double-garage for the car and bikes in current use ... and a 5 bay shed for the other toys.

David and I whipped off Penelope's petrol tank and sluiced it out best we could and also ascertained that the reason the lights were not working was a dud battery. A quick trip to the local provider put that right. A lovely meal and night followed. The spare room I was put in, had a bookcase filled with books covering David's hobbies relating to warbirds and all sorts of automobilia. Voraciously I dipped into many, all the time knowing there was not time to read anything properly, and tomorrow was an early start and a proper day's ride. Cairns would never be reached if I didn't start putting in the hard yards.

A convivial early breakfast was had and in cool but clear air I was soon humming down the rural backroads that would lead me across to the main highway that would take me north-west away from Sydney through

the Blue Mountains to the legendary motor-racing circuit of Bathurst which I had decided Penelope had to lap. Annoyingly, things still weren't 100% and a bit more roadside tinkering took place on the way. The Blue Mountains were surprisingly enjoyable even though I was now on a major arterial highway. The day and my spirits were warming. Hunger drove me to stop at a roadside fuel and food outlet. I should have toughed it out as the fare was appalling, simply awful, by far the worst of the trip. The legendary race circuit of Bathurst was of course delightful. We just took our time but still loved going up and over the mountain section and down Conrod Straight. There was no time to dally at the museum there, but I had previously enjoyed it a few years back. Arbitrarily I'd set Dubbo as our goal for the day. I had decided that to go north, I would stay quite a long way inland. Dubbo is more or less the edge of the NSW outback and the furthest south and east that the legendary Australian 'road-trains' can come. Finally, I had been able to shed a few of the 4 layers of merino that had been keeping me from a state of complete rigor. The ride from Bathurst to Dubbo was pleasant and the rolling hills fell away behind me and I could feel that a different Australia was opening up for me. Dubbo (pop 38,000) is a real hub for transhipping and is by far the biggest town in the area and in fact the nearest town is 150 km away. It was hot and I was pleased to find a pub with a spare bed and cool refreshments. This is the intersecting point of the Newell, Mitchell and Golden highways so if I did it wrong in the morning I could end up in Sydney, Melbourne or Broken Hill.

I posted this the next night on Facebook from Lightning Ridge.

*Today has been one of those 'Des Days' ... the ones you have now and then. After dossing in Dubbo, I was up and away quite early, looking forward to my first day without 4 layers of merino on. I went with just one and a short-sleeved shirt. The first morning stint was nice and cool with Penelope humming along sitting on 60 mph/100 kph. This was ok as the trucks are governed to 103 or 105, so they only creep up slowly. So after a nice breakfast ... I took a wrong turn ... being the observant man that I am, after a while I felt the sun was in the wrong place and realigned myself ... but 15 km and 15 km back make 30 km from the tank ... that you have already guessed would result in us running out of petrol 10 km from a town. So I abandoned Penelope and took my wallet, helmet and passport to town with nice old couple going there to go to the dentist. A ride in a Kenworth got me back and 'service was resumed'.*

*The day got hot and Penelope's apparent fuel starvation problems came back but although she stuttered, she still kept up the 100 kph progress. About 35 km from Lightning Ridge I sensed a 'tightening' and declutched and coasted to a halt. Penelope was pulsing with heat although the piston was not seized in the bore. Yesterday ... when it was cold ... I had put a hotter plug in as the B7HS had looked oily. Silly, silly boy. Highway B55 does not have lots of traffic but after a while a mufti cop comes along and asks a few questions ... do I have camping gear ... yes ... have I water ... yes, but maybe it is getting low. He tossed over a bottle and told me he had a sweep crew coming through this evening and if I was still there they might be able to get me to town.*

*After a significant lie down, I reckoned Penelope was never going to get any cooler, or me hotter. A few kicks later and we were off at a much reduced pace on a colder plug.*

*Now holed up in a cabin trying to do some work-work, as the Dubbo hotel didn't have wifi. I think I will stay here tomorrow and am cogitating whether to richen up the mid part of the carb action by moving the needle a notch. In theory she will run cooler but sootier.*
*What a buggeur, as she had been going so well!*

I was enjoying the new countryside, being as it was now so different from the earlier days. Gone were the green hills and winding roads and it was now it was just Penelope and me trying to manage our insecurities ... and inadequacies. The roads were straight, scrub-lined and largely empty, with just the occasional intriguing side road and dusty drive off to some hidden farmhouse. One off the intriguing side roads would have taken me to Come-by-Chance. It was 48 km away and I don't really have the time to investigate. I pose Penelope by the sign and scoff a muesli bar.

I was very relieved to make it to Lightning Ridge after such a drama-filled day. I book a cabin for 2 nights. It is a small settlement a few kilometres off the highway and is a centre of opal extraction and in particular the rare black opal. It seems to have three or four holiday parks yet only one shop and two daytime cafes. My dusty camp included a bar and eatery that just passes as adequate, probably only because of the young French charmer who takes my order both nights. My cabin is over-priced but is somewhere to hole-up and pretend to do work. My morning coffee shop is real old-school, lacking in charm or sophistication, run by an archetypal out-back Ocker couple ... the coffee is ok though. One of the daytime cafes has some semblance of class, and I do have a nice Caesar Salad there for lunch, mentally congratulating myself for finding a non-fried repast. I also chuckle to myself and think of home and family, knowing that I would still get the lecture from one of the food-Nazi daughters on how a Caesar Salad is not actually healthy and all that lettuce just contains water and little goodness. Overall Lightning Ridge does nothing for me as I am not going to fork out good money for an opal experience. I briefly rub shoulders with a car group who are on an annual outing from the coast somewhere, but they are car-focused and Penelope has no attraction for them.

I have been offered all sorts of bolt-holes to go to and leave Penelope if things are not going too well and some are quite tempting. Graeme and Glenys Watts are very keen for me call in and stay. In addition to their love of Panthers, they also are into Citroen 2CVs which have a strong appeal for me. I note though that they are over 600 km away in a slightly backwards direction ... and one of my other perceived failings is that I don't like going backwards. Also dismissing a Brisbane offering, I decide we will press on best we can. Penelope may be now drinking oil like a dipsomaniac ... but she is still willing and seemingly able. Again I crib from my FB postings –
*So the first day after overheating, Penelope has begun with a successful 120 km to Dirranbandi. I have kept the speed down to 90 kph on a whiff of*

**THE BIG SIT**

*throttle. It is a lonely road out here. One car going the other way in first 60 km and nothing spotted going my way in the whole 120 km. After a short break we'll try for St George to refuel with the aim of getting to Roma. We are now in Queensland and in a different time zone.*

The driver of a big road train carting huge tyres dismisses my awe and tells me he carts bigger. His truck with two trailers is carrying 10 tyres. They are arranged two abreast of each other and look to be about 3 m in diameter. The wider and taller ones only go one behind the other. He is driving from Perth to Mackay, a real long-haul (I check later to find it is about 5,000 km one way). There is not a lot open in Dirranbandi so I just take a break and pose Penelope in front of an old traction engine of sorts and do a 'selfie'. My 'followers' on FB have been poking the borax at me for not smiling, so I gamely try one. Reasonably pleased with the result and the progress so far, we decide it is 'up and at them' again. The day has got a lot of km in it yet. More FB postings from the day -

*This nice little café (The Timber Crate) in Surat (pop 400+) has charming service, good enough coffee, nice home-made pie and ... for me ... a funny occurrence. When my food came I put the paper I had been reading on the seat next to me with the spine facing the gentle cooling breeze. Part-way through the pie, a sudden wind from the other direction just took the paper and blew it away down the main street, way too fast for me to catch any of it. Standing embarrassedly there like a real plonker, I noticed that the papers had stopped moving. I started forward as fast as I could manage when suddenly another big lot of wind came and blew all the paper back to and past me. A couple of old dears were also outside and they sprang into action too. Between the three of us we caught every page. Very dramatic. You have to take your exercise any way you can get it.*

**THE BIG SIT**

*Well, the day is done ... pretty damn good with not a lot of stammering from Penelope. When it gets too intrusive we stop for a rest and that seems to work a treat. We've made it to Roma which is quite a big little town of 7,000 inhabitants. It is at the crossroads of three main roads and has the biggest cattle sales in Aus. Grains are big employers as are the energy companies with several fields nearby. I've been promised the delights of live music downstairs tonight. Pretty good room for $65.*

The Commonwealth is a pretty standard back-country pub and I was happy enough at the fare (The Lightning Ridge cabin (donga?) had been $85 a night). When we rolled into town and rode slowly around the centre, I spotted The School of Arts Hotel, a very appealing and ornate classic pub that I thought would do me a treat ... then I saw the chalk-board offering budget rooms from $120. Thanks, but no thanks!

On my evening walk later, I read the sign up close and found it was $120 per week! Still I was happy enough with where I was. I have a philosophy about overnight stays and the angst that often surrounds finding your bed for the night ... it doesn't have to be the best stay of your life, and in fact it would be a shame if it was, because that would mean you would never attain the same level again. As mentioned earlier, a similar criteria is applied when it comes to eating out. If you seek perfection all the time, you will often be very disappointed ... and of course we know where every meal ends up anyway. The Nike slogan often comes into play – Just do it!

I am getting into a bit of a routine. The days are long, hot and they are not easy. A lot of the time I am feeling more than my 68 years. I have a sore shoulder that is seemingly frozen, my heart condition inhibits strenuous activities, my iron levels are a little low and the week I left home I had to seek medical advice about a daunting occurrence diagnosed as Benign Positional Vertigo. I've got exercises to try and dislodge the crystalline build-up that causes the crazy spinning head in the night but it certainly has not fixed it yet. My hernia is grumbling away in the background, as it has for the last 25 years. I think of my mum and her refrain in her last years of "growing old is not for sissies!" I quickly balance that with another of her gems "every day above ground is a bonus" and smile. I must confess to being a little lonely, mainly missing being able to share some of the delights with others. I don't like travelling or riding in big groups but I do like having one or two with me to be able to turn to and say "What a boring day", "Man, did you see the size of that harvester?", "the road-kill is fresh today", "What a crappy dust-hole Lightning Ridge is", "I'd love a corner or two", "Are we nearly there yet?" etc.

Although the riding is straight forward, the view repetitive and mundane, every day is still a new one. Unlike 'normal' life, every vista is fresh. We've not been there before, so there is no familiarity, no 'Groundhog Day' events. We may not be trekking across frozen wastelands snacking on failing Husky dogs or rowing the Atlantic ... but we are having an adventure, possibly the envy of some of our peers. Once again I reflect that a lot of folk, when they hear of our plans to ride around the Big Red Continent, either say "Wow, you lucky bastard!" or "That'll be so awesome!" Both proclamations are askew. There is no luck involved ... there has been sacrifice and a decisive action to make it happen. Luck is when you win Lotto ... or a stranger bequeaths you a Brough Superior SS100 ... both very, very long odds and unlikely to happen. As for the awesomeness, yes there has been some already and there will be more to come, but mostly there is the tedious necessity of sitting on a motorcycle for hours and hours on dull, straight roads with nothing but your thoughts to accompany you. That in itself necessitates a certain level of resilience and patience.

I've always treated long rides like work. You get up early and ride until morning smoko, when you have a break. Then you ride until lunchtime and after lunch you do another stint before having a short break mid-afternoon, then you go till knock-off time. After you have done 5 or 6 days ... you have a 'weekend' off. My breaks in the day usually involve getting in the shade and reading. Although the roads are straight, deserted and long, there are regular shelters, some big, some small. Some rest areas have toilets and space to park the road-trains. On this part of the trip I have been reading an old Inspector Wexford book – slow and dated, but good enough. I've got mandarins and a box of muesli bars that I ration out in a ratio of two to one.

*So after Roma – a real mixed bag of a day. On the road by 7.00, we flew along in cool conditions, revelling in our sprightliness. Detouring into the little village of Rolleston to get gas, in the absence of a cafe, I helped the economy by supporting the pub with a toasted sandwich and a pot for lunch … you can tell I am almost fluent in road-speak. An Aus-Brit fair burst in, all excited because he had also popped in for gas and spotted Penelope whilst driving by, initially telling the missus it looked like an old Ariel. Then he spotted the sloping cylinder. "A Panther" he cried, telling me he'd had one back in the UK. Instantly, he was back to his youth and loving it. He'd also had a Watsonian sidecar on his and was further thrilled when I showed him photos of the Goddes' one from our 'muster'. Mind you, he admitted that he and a mate attempted to ride to the races at The Nurburgring … didn't make it to the ferry.*

*The afternoon was the flip-side and the heat brought back the stuttering – still can't ascertain if it is fuel starvation. An honest 500+ km day with more worries as my rear tyre has worn out.*

I had fetched up in Clermont, an uninspiring town of a couple of thousand unfortunates … not that I see or meet many. There are a couple of hi-viz-clad hard-looking men drinking outside the pub having a smoke, and not much by way of clientele inside. I like the old hotels but tonight I am directed to the concrete-block motels out the back. A walk 'downtown' finds nothing of interest, just a couple of closed shops and another motel. I suspect this is a town falling on hard times. Clermont's *raison d'etre* was gold, then copper and now coal. Being ill-informed, opinionated and possibly unfair, I don't see coal as a future for anywhere. There is a trainee barmaid on and she looks fairly life-worn, although tattoos can do that to a woman. There's not a lot she can practice on as for most of the evening there are only a couple of us in. An unwatched big-screen tv blares away in the corner broadcasting the Rugby League World Cup. I am the only person in for a meal and I have a lovely corned-silverside and salad meal, washed down with two glasses of red wine as a day-well-done reward before retreating to my cell.

*More FB – Oh dear, what have Dunlop done to our K70 tyres. They have been a staple since the 1960s and are a good all-round tyre, suited to both front and back. They took Penelope all the way from Beijing to Arnhem on one set. You could always get 10,000 miles from a rear. We first became suspicious when Bruce Sharman couldn't get across from Perth to Sydney on his epic Distinguished Gentlemen's Ride. Seeing I had done about 3,000 km last year ... I checked the wear in Melbourne before I left this time. There was indicative wear already on the rear so I rotated the wheels, as you can on late-model Panthers. Now with less than another 3,000 km, the rear is shot and shouldn't be ridden. The middle stability groove is gone completely ... it is canvas next. The likelihood of finding a skinny 19" tyre out here is pretty unlikely. Another 900 km???*

Another early start saw us humming along the highway at 100 kph in the cool, singing songs and pretending Penelope's rear tyre was meant to be smooth ... and that she wouldn't start stuttering when it got hot. The night in Leo's Hotel (motel) had been ok after all, no better, no worse than some of the preceding ones. I was pleased their motels had solar panels on the roof. The sky is still blue, the road is still straight and pretty lonely. Out on this remote arrow-straight tarmac ribbon I reflect on life, I write new short stories in my head, I finally get past Chapter 11 on my long-neglected novel ... and I swerve around road-kill from time to time. I often lament the fate of the numerous kangaroos and wombats I pass every day. So often they are left in the most unbecoming positions. As a Kiwi I am so unused to encountering such substantial obstacles. Flat hedgehogs and the occasional possum are the only blights on our road surfaces. I was totally unaware of the size of wombats … they grow to a metre long, weigh 35 kg, and live underground. How come I never knew that? More amazingly they do square poos. How come I never knew *that*? I am a man of trivia … however, once-known, never forgotten.

On one of my straight empty stretches, I come to a road-works red light. Obediently I stop and wait. It doesn't take me long to realise that it is a weekend and I can see a small fleet of parked-up diggers, loaders and the like. You'd think they would turn off the lights when they went home on Friday. I saw nothing that would require the traffic (what traffic?) to be one-way etc. Just another out-back anomaly to muse upon.

For entertainment I sometimes toot the horn in random patterns and turn the handlebar-end blinkers on, firstly to one side then the other, gently amused because I can watch them from my position and check their flashing. Occasionally I stand up and stretch. This always brings a reflective smile because back home in my other life, I am so often on long rides with Steph and when I stand she always kneads my appreciative buttocks … probably to the amusement of other road-users.

Another thing I do on these interminable stretches is an oldie but a goodie. I shut my eyes and count. I've done this since I was a lad bored silly on the straight roads of the Wairarapa and Canterbury. When young and gung-ho I could maintain a full 10 seconds. I remember being surprised on the straight roads of Iran in 2005 on *The Last Hurrah* adventure that I could only get to 6 or 7 counting slowly, then it was a panicked rush to get to 10. Now, with not a soul in sight, on straight, straight roads I can do no more than 5 without involuntarily opening my lids. Age-related wisdom maybe?

I've seen very few motos out on the highway and the ones I have seen have been going the opposite way. So it was with some pleasure I spotted an at-rest, laden-for-adventure bike in a layby as I came in for my afternoon break. A younger-than-me, middle-aged couple were already brewing-up on the shady table and socially I stop nearby and go over for a chat. They were heading home to Emerald, a town I had passed through the day before. Picking up on my accent, the husband (why am I so crap at noting down names?) dropped into the conversation that although he had been in Aussie for more than 30 years he was a Kiwi by birth. Of course this led on to the Spanish Inquisition and it turned out he grew up in Martinborough, the little town in the Wairarapa that we had spent 12 years in. That started the Spanish Inquisition Part 2 and I learned that Steph and I knew so many of his childhood mates, had known his brother, father etc. He knew our house … and told me of the Martinborough Primary School reunion and how he and Christine (remembered that one) were returning for it early in 2018 and staying for a week in the area. I told him that at one stage we had all four kids in Martinborough Primary. They did me a tea and we had a most sociable time chatting about all sorts of things. They were semi-retired and had ridden their Yamaha around 'Big Red' the year before, the 'Full Lap' as it is often called. All too soon we had to go our separate ways. I realised afterwards that it had been many days since I had engaged in any social interaction other than asking for food, shelter, sustenance etc. It had been a highlight, made especially so because they were such nice people.

This was another day of needing to be on my toes keeping an eye on my fuel, as again I note with amusement that the roading authorities let you ride 20 km out of town then tell you there is no fuel for 200 km. I ponder on the logic and wonder why the purveyors of this important ingredient for our tripping, don't have signs each side of town saying 'Last fuel for 215 km' etc. I have a normal range of around 300 km in the tank and now also have the 5 litre container I was forced to buy when I didn't get it right a few days back. The towns are pretty evenly spaced, so as long as you remember when you last filled, it is no major problem. Old motos like Penelope don't have the luxury of fuel gauges. Sometimes between towns there will be a 'road-house' which just is a stopping place for resting and refuelling, usually with some sort of ability to provide basic food. Today I stop at one called Belyando Crossing. It has two pumps and an area for camping. They do an adequate toasted sandwich and being as I am a customer I am allowed free use of their toilets.

I am pretty happy with progress although I am getting through oil at an alarming rate and I still haven't really got a clear solution to Penelope's stuttering which may not be fuel starvation now as there is not as much muck coming from the tank and blocking the carb-top filter as earlier in the ride. She loves the cool mornings and it is only when things get hot that the 'missing' returns and slowly becomes intrusive. I wonder about the magneto which provides the spark but know that it is a new electronic device with very little that can go wrong.

Anyone who rides knows that it is a very tactile experience. You are touched by whatever environment you are passing through. Along with being able to feel the road racing by only 200 mm beneath your feet, you suffer the effects of the wind, the rain, the dust, the fragrances, the insects, even the loneliness. When it is hot, you are hot, when it is cold you are very cold. If the day is absolutely calm, on a naked bike you are sitting out in a 100 kph gale when you are cruising. Now I am not complaining as I think that the joy of motorcycling is a most wonderful thing because of all these intrusive influences. I ponder on this today because at one stage I am passed by a luxurious silver Lexus 4 x 4. This glittering capsule with tinted windows just creeps by and I mentally compare our current status. I am battling the afore-mentioned hot 100 kph winds and Penelope is thrumming with exertion and road-surface-induced vibration. My unseen companion in his 50+ years newer conveyance is sitting in air-conditioned comfort, the cruise-control is set for 108, the Mark Levinson surround-sound system gently playing music which is bluetoothing from his iPhone … he'll be dipping into a box of scorched almonds or sucking on a Werther's Original butterscotch toffee. There will be no sense of speed nor any feeling of intrepidness. At journey's end, he will emerge fresh as a daisy, he won't be bug-splattered and drained emotionally or physically. But hey … who wants to be that man? Not me! Not me, not now not never! His Lexus will never be his friend and faithful companion. I give Penelope a thankful pat.

I reach the mining town of Charters Towers in the late afternoon. It is Sunday and almost-civilisation. This is the biggest settlement we have come to since Dubbo. It has a population of about 8,000 and is quite a hub of excitement. Steph and I have stayed here before and I almost turn off to the old hotel we were happy in … but I am thinking … if I can stand another 140 km I would be out at the coast and then only a half-day from Cairns. Maybe out at the coast I could find a moto shop with an ultrasonic cleaning bath and we could have a go at cleaning Penelope's carburettor properly, so a cure can be effected or that device can be eliminated from being the cause of her malaise. After a short break, a refuel and an oil top-up we decide to join the traffic leaving the hinterland. Soon the terrain changes, I can see hills. We undulate ... something we haven't done for days and days, maybe thousands of kilometres. If my bum wasn't so tired and sore, it would be a good ride. The surroundings become verdant and lush, the air almost moist. Townsville (pop 180,000) comes as bit of a shock and I realise that I don't want to go into such a big town, I can see high-rise buildings. Fortunately, we are able to skirt the metropolis although we still have to endure a few sets of traffic lights and a motorway. After an age I spot a camping sign and turn off. Our day is nearly done.

The holiday park is hyper-clean and spruced up beyond a level I would normally countenance. I consider breaking out the tent to justify carting it along and ask the pleasant young woman in the office if the threatening rain clouds will deliver. "Probably, we've had a couple of showers today. It's that time of year … you never can tell". I look over at the inviting cabins and ask about vacancies. She launches into a spiel about how they have all been done up. I wearily capitulate and hit a new high of having to hand over $100 for the night. It's a reward I tell myself, knowing that we've done well to get this far in so few days. Maybe the quality has been missing but we've both shown a level of resilience that perhaps some would have doubted we still had. True to her word the cabin is first class and appointed beyond the level of my needs. I walk across to a Chinese restaurant for an evening meal, do a little work and book a ticket to Wellington for Thursday and a flight home to Golden Bay for Friday night. I am pretty happy with the results so far.

Almost there! Just one more push and Cairns will ours for the taking. Again I see little point in re-writing or plagiarising my Facebook postings of the time.

*Breakfast starts with Rumble Coffee beans from son Joseph, ground each time and put through the Aeropress. This coffee is a single origin Columbian one with notes of milk chocolate, dark berries and toffee … so the card says. The Townsville to Cairns leg was always going to be different. The landscape dramatically changes to tropical rainforest-clad hills layering back into the distance in lines of differing hues. The immediate vista ridden through, is all cultivated with sugar cane and banana plantations. The countryside is verdant and now filled with evocative odours. It is as far removed from the outback as could be imagined. There are regular settlements and traffic. Penelope seemed to sense the occasion and flew along in the early morning stint needing to be held back on occasion. More than once I had to tell her that 100 kph was fast enough and just because the signs said 110 … that wasn't for her. This day was to be less than 400 km so could savoured and enjoyed in a more leisurely way.*

Penelope's stuttering would return once she got hot and it was interesting that when at one stage we caught up with the end of a rain shower and the ride was suddenly cool ... the stuttering stopped. For the first time in my motorcycling life I hoped the threatening rain-clouds would find me and deliver succour.

My early start to our last day got us to Ingham in one quick chunk, and as I still harboured hopes of a carb clean, we stopped by a motorcycle shop in the main street. I park Penelope in front of the main entrance, close to the ramp to the workshop and go in, expecting a little interest in the oddball pairing that had fetched up at their door. Sadly, our interaction was pretty short and sharp.

"Morning, does your workshop have an ultrasonic parts cleaning bath?"
"Yes it does!"
"If I take my carb off and strip it, could we put it through the bath?"
"No mate ... way too busy ... couldn't get to it for 3 days!"

It is a small surprise that a motorcycle shop shows way less interest in us than the general public do. I am not expecting to be feted or heralded in any way, but their total lack of interest in a fellow two-wheeler is duly noted. Maybe I had been quickly clocked as not being someone who was going to spend money in the shop buying a bike, and as one just passing through, I could be dismissed offhand. We move on, only slightly disheartened. The temperature is nigh-on perfect and we're getting along quite well.

We're at the seaside at Cardwell by 9.30 and I take a proper break. An adequate coffee was sourced from a caravan and I wandered about, stretching my legs and being amused by the black cockatoos that I hadn't seen before. An intriguing pie cart had a line-up of punters. The proprietor had the most wonderful banter and a hand painted menu listing about 30 varieties. I was tempted by many of them but felt it was a bit too early in the day. I compromise and have a chicken and veggie pastie, reasoning that you have to keep up your vegetable intake when you are on the road.

More of the same follows for our second session of the day and we're at Innisfail in time for a lunch at a modern tavern. I select an outside raised deck to be my spot for the repast and refreshing pint of chilled lager. I don't choose the spot to look down on Penelope as a watchdog, I just enjoy looking at her resolute loveliness. She looks great … travel-worn but obviously still up-for-it. An old-bike fan tracks me down and we chat for a while. It is not intrusive, just a man with an interest. He also likes to ride his classic bikes on adventures so loved seeing Penelope all loaded up. The Victorian number plate always stimulates interest and admiration.

There is nothing of particular interest that sticks out on the last 100 km or so that made up our post-lunch finish to this year's leg. I do stop and photograph a 'bridge' over the highway for possums. They are protected

**THE BIG SIT**

here in Australia, whilst in New Zealand millions of dollars are spent each year culling them because they are seen as one of our biggest pests due to their impact on native birdlife. I know the end is nigh for the year. Mid-afternoon sees the ride done and dusted. The pot at the end of the rainbow is there for us and we gratefully take it. It has not been an easy 4,000 km but life is not all roses.

And the most wonderful part of the success. Truly the best of old friends Jo and Russell left the key out for me … in the beer fridge. Jo was part of a coterie of winsome Queensland Physical Education teachers who boarded the MV Australis in Jan 1972 which I was already on, having set sail on my OE from Auckland. Luckily her group and my group all became friends, flatting together in London. Later that year we played rugby against Russell and invited him back to the flat party. The rest is history. Time does not dull our bond, our interactions are often decades apart but still glorious.

Thank you Penelope, thank you Australia, we'll continue next year.

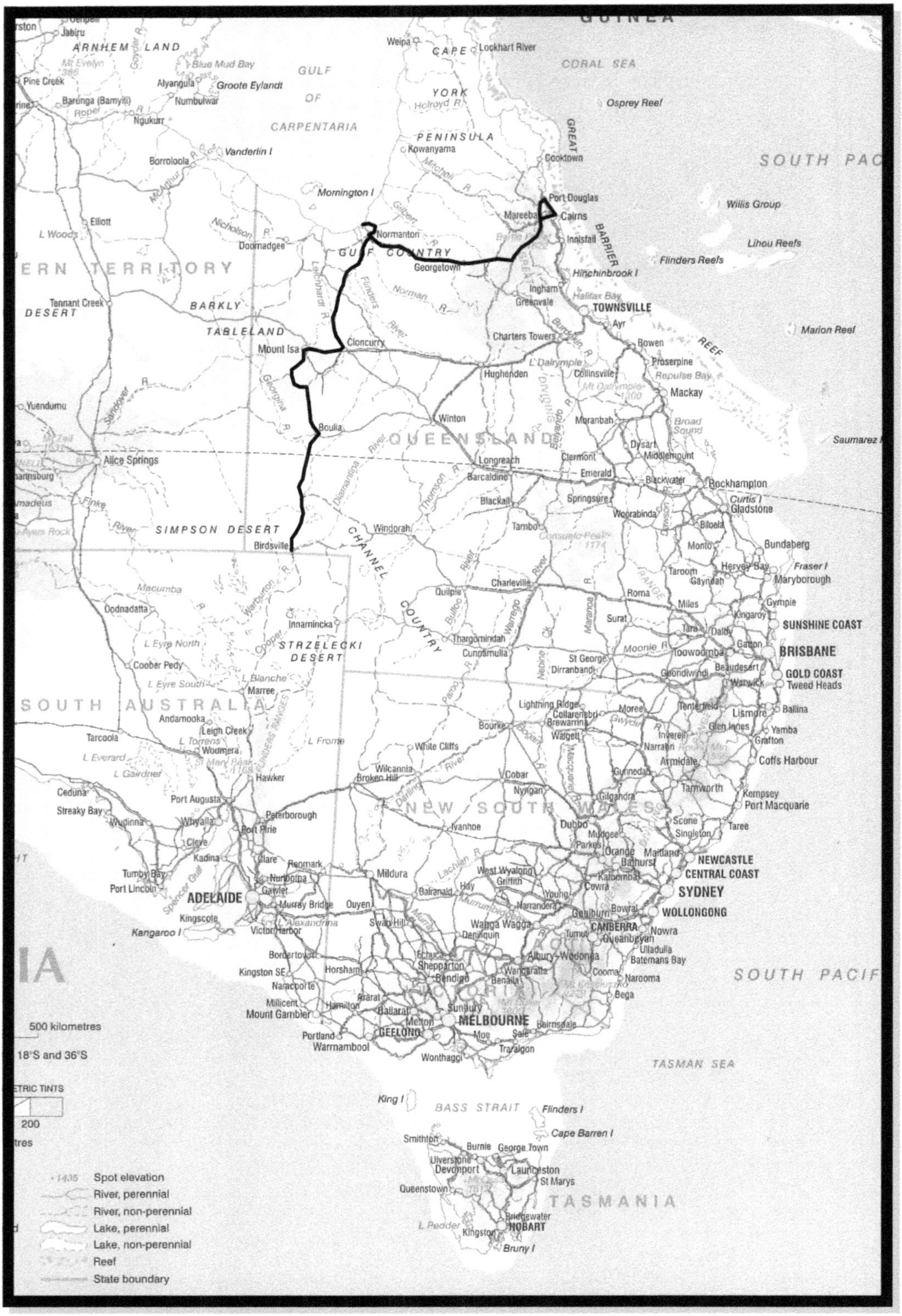
ARNHEM LAND
GULF OF CARPENTARIA
CAPE YORK PENINSULA
CORAL SEA
GREAT BARRIER REEF
SOUTH PACIFIC
Jabiru
Pine Creek
Alyangula
Groote Eylandt
Blue Mud Bay
Numbulwar
Barunga (Bamyili)
Ngukurr
Vanderlin I
Borroloola
Weipa
Lockhart River
Holroyd R.
Osprey Reef
Kowanyama
Cooktown
Mornington I
Port Douglas
Willis Group
Mareeba
Cairns
Elliott
L Woods
Nicholson R.
Doomadgee
Normanton
GULF COUNTRY
Innisfail
Lihou Reefs
Georgetown
Flinders Reefs
Hinchinbrook I
Ingham
Greenvale
Halifax Bay
TOWNSVILLE
ERN TERRITORY
Tennant Creek
DESERT
BARKLY TABLELAND
Ayr
Marion Reef
Charters Towers
Bowen
Mount Isa
Cloncurry
Proserpine
Repulse Bay
Hughenden
L Dalrymple
Collinsville
Mackay
Yuendumu
Winton
Boulia
Broad Sound
QUEENSLAND
Moranbah
Dysart
Middlemount
Saumarez
Alice Springs
Longreach
Clermont
Emerald
Barcaldine
Blackwater
Rockhampton
Blackall
Springsure
Curtis I
Gladstone
Woorabinda
SIMPSON DESERT
Windorah
Tambo
Biloela
Birdsville
Monto
Bundaberg
CHANNEL COUNTRY
Taroom
Hervey Bay
Fraser I
Maryborough
Charleville
Quilpie
Roma
Macumba
Oodnadatta
Miles
Gympie
Innamincka
Surat
Kingaroy
SUNSHINE COAST
Thargomindah
STRZELECKI DESERT
L Eyre North
Cunnamulla
Toowoomba
Gatton
BRISBANE
Coober Pedy
St George
Dirranbandi
Goondiwindi
Beaudesert
Warwick
GOLD COAST
Tweed Heads
L Eyre South
L Blanche
Marree
SOUTH AUSTRALIA
Lightning Ridge
Collarenebri
Moree
Tenterfield
Lismore
Ballina
Andamooka
Leigh Creek
Bourke
Brewarrina
Walgett
Inverell
Glen Innes
Yamba
Grafton
Tarcoola
L Torrens
Woomera
L Frome
White Cliffs
Narrabri
Armidale
Coffs Harbour
L Everard
L Gairdner
Wilcannia
Broken Hill
Cobar
Nyngan
Gunnedah
Tamworth
Hawker
Ceduna
Port Augusta
Gilgandra
Kempsey
Port Macquarie
Streaky Bay
Wudinna
Whyalla
Peterborough
NEW SOUTH WALES
Port Pirie
Ivanhoe
Dubbo
Scone
Singleton
Taree
Cleve
Mudgee
Parkes
Orange
Maitland
Kadina
Clare
Renmark
Bathurst
NEWCASTLE
CENTRAL COAST
Tumby Bay
Mildura
West Wyalong
Katoomba
Port Lincoln
Gawler
Balranald
Hay
Griffith
Young
Cowra
SYDNEY
ADELAIDE
Murray Bridge
Ouyen
Narrandera
Bowral
WOLLONGONG
Kingscote
Goulburn
Swan Hill
Wagga Wagga
Tumut
CANBERRA
Queanbeyan
Nowra
Kangaroo I
Victor Harbor
Deniliquin
Ulladulla
Batemans Bay
Bordertown
Echuca
Albury-Wodonga
Kingston SE
Horsham
Shepparton
Wangaratta
Cooma
Narooma
Bendigo
Benalla
SOUTH PACIFIC
Naracoorte
Ararat
VICTORIA
Bega
Millicent
Hamilton
Ballarat
Sunbury
Mount Gambier
Melton
MELBOURNE
Bairnsdale
500 kilometres
Portland
Warrnambool
GEELONG
Moe
Sale
Traralgon
18°S and 36°S
Wonthaggi
TASMAN SEA
ETRIC TINTS
King I
BASS STRAIT
Flinders I
200
Cape Barren I
Smithton
Burnie
George Town
Ulverstone
Devonport
Launceston
St Marys
Spot elevation
Queenstown
TASMANIA
River, perennial
River, non-perennial
Bridgewater
Lake, perennial
L Pedder
Kingston
HOBART
Lake, non-perennial
Bruny I
Reef
State boundary

CHAPTER FOUR

# CAIRNS TO BIRDSVILLE

Interestingly, over the preceding 18 months or so I have become more adept with my smart phone, enabling me to be way more active in sharing my road-trip with friends on Facebook in real time. This sort of creates a diary-like record which is not something I have ever managed before. There is a stream-of-consciousness immediacy to the writing that I don't see the need now to diverge too much from. I'll add content and comment, and if I do it without changing the font type ... you'll not notice. To complete the subterfuge I will remove the daily dates and try to smooth the reports into normal text. The often derided Facebook has become a tool to keep me connected with family and friends. I must admit that I do enjoy the quick reactions and encouragement that a posting engenders. I love the ego-stroking from the onlookers who make me feel intrepid and bold ... although I know it is all relative. Being able to 'talk' to my audience on a daily basis is such a contrast to the adventures of our youth when letters were sent and received ... often with a turn-around time of many weeks, sometimes months.

The 2018 leg of the adventure began in Melbourne with the welcoming of Grand-daughter Nina, Number Five overall and definitely a keeper. I then rejoined Penelope in Cairns where she has waited patiently under several layers of spider-infested tarps. Due to the issue last year where she possibly nipped-up, I had a new piston (Rover V8) for her. After breaking a lens of my glasses and laying-in the wrong-size back tyre, as well as some general mechanical ineptness ... delays resulted. Being with wonderful old friends and being in the tropical paradise of Far North Queensland (FNQ) with no itinerary means that delays are not really a problem, they just prolong the pleasurable time you are having ... drinking beer, dipping in the pool etc ... and a week is only a week. I've been myopically slow and clumsy, enjoying the now. I've had a short interaction with the local old bike club where I screened my *Last Hurrah* movie on the Sunday afternoon. I don't think they knew how to take me. It was pleasant enough but hardly memorable.

Finally, on June 5th 2018 we move, and ride out of Cairns – bedding in Penelope's new piston. I've decided on a loop up onto the Atherton Tablelands as a 'sea trial'. On a typically sunny afternoon I rode up the stunning Captain Cook Highway along the magical North Queensland coast, past Port Douglas and then up another motorcyclists' dream-road to Mt Molloy where I hunker down in a $40 room at the historic hotel which constitutes the hub of this community.

I reflect that my second shake-down day was a bit mixed with a couple of minor disappointments and some good riding to get both of us ready for the days ahead. The night in the Mt Molloy Hotel was great for a cheap and cheerful place. The host was welcoming and the winsome barmaid from Upper-state Michigan, charming. $40 including brekky has to be ok. I hoped to post a map-record of each day but I forgot to turn on my phone's new tracking app until Mareeba, which I found to be devoid of a decent cafe (since been told it is in a side-street) so my ride-record is only partial. Here, on the main street, Penelope wouldn't go until I treated her to a new spark plug … don't know what that was all about. Just being irascible I think. As this year's ride will be in the tropics I have forsworn wearing my waxed cotton motorcycle-specific riding jacket and replaced it with an ex-army camouflage cotton jacket with lots of zip open gussets. It won't have the same level of protective qualities but will be much more comfortable in the heat, and it has lots of capacious pockets to carry phone, snacks, tools, books and the like. I like it a lot and quickly have a 'regime' where everything has a given place to be and I know exactly where that place is. This year I have also added a flexible five litre fuel bladder to our luggage. This straps on the back and should give me about 400 km range.

The Tablelands are great to ride through as the air is cooler, and the countryside exotic and varied. Bananas, sugar cane, peanuts, mangos, avocados and coffee are all abundant. I stopped at Herberton because for some time I had been seeing signs to a 'Spy Camera Museum' as well as a local history/mining museum. Sadly, the Spy Camera man was away, presumably spying, and his place was shut for the day. The other museum though was a delight and very extensive and interesting. Herberton was the first town to be established on the tablelands and mining of tin and copper etc was carried out right from the early days.

The ride down to the coast was also relished, knowing that soon bends and undulations will be just a memory. The leg from Innisfail back to Cairns which I had done last year is still pretty dull and it was nice to be back at the Mothership for the night. This was enjoyably spent watching State of Origin rugby league with Jo and Russell.

I only tarry for the one night. Balmy weather, a pool and convivial company is beguiling but I've an adventure to have … and I need to dry out. Having a can of XXXX in my hand at all times is becoming a habit, one I need to shake.

First day away is a another mixed one! Of course it was FNQ-sunny and with a soaring heart I headed off to take the third of the four roads up to the Tablelands behind Cairns. First however there was the 'tank' museum

**THE BIG SIT**

to visit. What a stunning complex with more tanks than the Battle of El Alamein. Huge halls of them and a big extension planned for September to house another 35 tanks including a Panther. I can't recommend it enough, if you are into this stuff.

The ride through dappled-sunshine avenues of trees on a winding climb meant another dose of morning-euphoria. Such fun but once again when Penelope got hot, she started to stutter. This is confusing me as the coil on the electronic BTH magneto has been changed even though they (BTH) only know of one failure in 12,000. The HT lead has also been changed and the tank cap breather dealt to. I will richen up one notch tomorrow and see if any different.

Still a great day was had with a nice break in Mareeba while the local Brit-bike artisan fiddled with Penelope's tank cap. He owns three BSA Gold Stars that he has made the cranks for. Initially he was quite stand-offish and cool towards me, but as our time together unfolded and I was seen to know a lot about his interests and our shared love of old stuff ... we bonded.

So progress was down on planned but the tent was soon up and pizza consumed in Innot Springs – a tiny dot on the road out to Georgetown. The pub had a singer belting out Willie Nelson, Don McLean, Elvis, Roy Orbison etc so I knew all the words. A cool night follows and a lack of a foam pad inhibits comfort. For some reason I had made the decision back home, that as we didn't have foam pads or Thermorests etc back in the day, that I wouldn't have one here either. I felt I would soon toughen up after a few sleepless nights. I really should surround myself with folk who are smarter than me, to stop me from making poorly thought-out decisions.

No map was produced because the old duffer again forgot to push go on the Riser app!

So just like the shambles that was the Burke and Wills expedition ...

1 inch forward. Despite some loving attention Penelope is still showing signs of hesitancy. Does she have sixth sense and know what I am planning for her? Currently she is taking the joy out of the ride and if she doesn't soon conform to her reputation, I really will be forced into doing a Basil Fawlty on her.

We're done with corners for a while now, so there is no chance to practice counter-steering. I was surprised to find State Highway 1 became one lane for quite big chunks after Innot Springs. One lane really is just that … one strip of tar-seal that you fight over. It meant taking to the gravel when on-comers were encountered. Good practice though for the roads to come. I have also seemingly passed the opportunity of capturing a sign for the 'Believe it or NOT' file. Back in the rainforest I passed signs warning of 'Tree Kangaroos crossing'. Unlike Drop Bears that Aussies try to trick you with … these appear to be real. Stopping for photos is often a real mission and regularly I comment to myself "That'd make a good photo … the folks back home would be interested in that … " Sometimes there is a car up your bum or the decision-making process takes too long and you're loathe to haul up and turn around. The Facebook crowd get what I give them. It is not everything and often not the most memorable sights of the day.

I decide against aimlessly limping along and stop at a holiday park in Georgetown. I take a cabin and attack Penelope with spinning spanners. I even threaten to tweak her nipples to see if that gets a reaction. She used to be so reliable and I hate to see her reputation being impugned. I decide to remain in the area for another day to explore a bit and give Penelope a chance to redeem herself.

After looking at the truly world famous mineral collection in Georgetown we had a ride out to Forsayth which is where the Savannahlander classic train terminates its three-day journey from Cairns. Sadly, Saturday wasn't the day it turns around. I did however get some practice in on corrugated gravel roads and that showed up that I needed to adjust the steering-head bearings.

The peregrination continued albeit slowly. A couple of steady days got us to Normanton which is the 'big' town in the Gulf area. It even has an airport and 2,500 pop which makes it huge compared with Innot Springs (100+) and Georgetown (250). It looks to be a spread-out charmless frontier town, although as I pulled into the Purple Hotel, three cowgirls looking like they were in the cast of McLeod's Daughters were leaving. There's something beguiling about wholesome country girls devoid of make-up and meaningless frippery supposedly designed to attract.

So we have now more or less reached the Gulf of Carpentaria ... a long way from Melbourne. A feature of Normanton's main street is the fiberglass replica of *Krys the Savannah King. Krys* was a two tonne salt-water crocodile measuring over 28' (8.6m) long. This was shot by a woman croc-hunter in 1958. It is absolutely enormous and for me it was the width and general mass that overwhelmed me. Sobering to think these prehistoric beasts lurk in the sea nearby. With some trepidation Penelope posed for a photo ... although suitably distanced from her. Salt-water crocodiles ... or 'salties' as the locals call them are a real threat and recently a New Zealand woman was taken from a beach just north of Cairns while having a late evening walk with her friend.

I have now definitely decided against camping at the Burke and Wills Camp 119 on the advice of every Aussie I have met. *"You don't camp by the mangroves up here son! Crocs have been protected for over 40 years now and are at epidemic levels!"* I will go there though, as it has for some time been one of this year's goals ... to go as far north as Burke and Wills went.

I do a bit of maintenance on Penelope and am hopeful of a good run going forward. At least the oil leaks have been stemmed and the stuttering has lessened. The riding is dull but still of interest because everything is different from home. I've seen kites fighting and been raced by pink and grey galahs flying right beside me in a square-four formation. I've now seen wedge-tail eagles and had Skippy hop across the road in front of me. The Brahma cattle often stand resolute until I am 20 m away. All the while, the tarmac ribbon stretches out endlessly to the horizon and beyond.

Penelope is still bringing joy to the world and is such a conversation starter. Most people come over to look at the BSA, Norton or Matchless, but to date only four folk have told me they owned one years ago. Most poignant was back at the Mt Molloy Hotel when an elderly, seemingly semi-vagrant man sidled up to me, and took out a small note book. Mute, and unable to talk, he penned me a note telling me he had a Panther when he was 16 and had paid $100 for it. It was a special moment of kinship brought upon by Penelope. She really is a star.

Ay Karumba!

I decided that unlike Burke and Wills, who determined at Camp 119 that the water in the nearby mangroves was salty, and so declared their mission a success and turned for home ... I would feel a bit of a fraud if I never actually laid eyes on The Gulf of Carpentaria. So it was that I made my way out the 70 km or so to Karumba. The sea and sky were both picture-perfect blue and I am pleased to have gone to the beach. With the graphic image of the giant Krys still fresh in my consciousness, I am stunned to see a couple of youths down in the shallows immediately in front of a sign proclaiming WARNING ACHTUNG Crocodiles inhabit this area – attacks may cause injury or death. Keep away from water's edge. I take a photo but squeamishly move away to ensure I am not present should a re-run of Jaws take place. Being at The Gulf would also give me the opportunity to see the elusive 'Green Flash' which supposedly can be seen on a clear evening as the sun sets from a west-facing landmass. For a split second as the last of the sun disappears into the ocean ... it can be seen ... or not! The Victorians did Green Flash tourism out into the ocean on sailing boats. Yet again ... I am still not sure I have seen it.

I have seen the regal and fascinating brolgas though.

Penelope is still presenting with a stutter after about an hour of riding and in Mt Isa I will definitely seek out someone with ultrasonic cleaning capability to give the carb a real going over. Otherwise she is still her delightful self and I wouldn't wish to be on anything else.

Normanton to Karumba is a real short day, so I spend a bit of it under a tree reading. I am sure the 'readers' will be envious and the 'non-readers' should be! Currently I am re-reading the Harper Lee classic *To Kill a Mockingbird*. Her prose is so good I feel I should share a snippet. It is set in 1935 and told through the eyes of 8-year-old Scout.

'... *Aunt Alexandra was positively irritable on the Lord's Day. I guess it was her Sunday corset. She was not fat, but solid, and she chose protective garments that drew up her bosom to giddy heights, pinched in her waist, flared out her rear, and managed to suggest that Aunt Alexandra's was once an hour-glass figure. From any angle, it was formidable.*'

Of course it could be I have been away from home too long. I am also starting to like Grey Nomads ... but they deserve proper coverage and that will be another day.

The camp at Karumba Point is the site of yet another serendipitous, warm-and-fuzzy moment brought on by Penelope. After my 'green flash' quest, I lingered at the beach-side bar-and-grill, enjoying the tropical evening. Ultimately, I decide the day is done and I return to my nylon shelter. As I approach, from the darkness beside a hedge, appears a figure, who greets me with "I know you are Des ... I've already met Penelope!" I am of course speechless and surprised. Ian then introduces himself. His brother-in-law Steve, back in Sydney is a Pantherphile, so the marque is not unknown to him. Of course, when Ian espies a Panther, obviously out and about, on Victorian plates ... he rings with the news. *"I've just seen a Panther, all loaded up ... up on The Gulf!"* *"That'll be Des and Penelope"* comes the answer, *"Go talk to them!"* Ian and partner Gail are Grey-Nomading the winter away in the warmth of the north. It is a convivial interaction that I savour.

Of course a lot of this ride is reflective, but some of the ride is also about learning and seeing, and meeting new people. In the camp I'd met and enjoyed the attractive, vibrant young-retiree who is part of the crew needed to service the camp during the busy season. She has a bus she lives in, and family way down south. She's in the sun for the winter and working part-time in the camp keeps the costs down. I see her again in the early morning and she has her little Honda CT110 Postie-bike all loaded up with fishing gear and she is about to go for her daily dose of relaxation before work. In the course of a general chat she mentions about needing to catch the tide as it only comes once a day. She putters off and another guy and I look at each other and agree that tides come twice a day, namely every 13 hours and she doesn't know what she is talking about. This surprised us a little as she oozed an aura of competence. I subsequently learn that

**THE BIG SIT**

there are a few big gulfs around the world that do indeed only have one tidal cycle a day. In addition to the Gulf of Carpentaria, these are the Gulf of Thailand, the Persian Gulf, the South China Sea and even the Gulf of Mexico. It is always good to learn ... and never be too adamant about what you presume you know.

It is nice lazing about, but boredom sets in pretty quickly. I am not one to disport myself, mostly unclad, under the burning orb that is the sun up here in the tropics. I am not trying to become 'bronzed Tim Bradley'. My gaelic background precludes that. There was a time in my youth when a tan was desperately sought, and as my freckles joined up I almost could fake it, but now I find it much more preferable to keep a cotton covering over my delicate whitey-pink flesh. Besides, we've still got a long way to go no matter where I decide to finish this year's ride. I'll never complete the circumambulation of Big Red if I don't put in the hard yards.

So an early start on June 12th saw Penelope and me thrumming along from Karumba Point (Outback by the Sea) back to Normanton again, to have a train ride. The morning was cool and the colours sultry. When we turned away from the rising sun, a beautifully graphic shadow was found to be racing us. I waved, and the figure waved back ... I gave a thumbs-up and so did he. Penelope gave her best in trying to vanquish this shady rival ... to no avail. We were seemingly matched for speed and endurance. What a sight we made, haring along, leaving a trail of rolling thunder behind.

The Gulflander is an art-deco Queensland-built train from 1951. It is operated by Queensland Rail from Normanton and is powered by a 100hp six cylinder Gardner diesel, which drives through four-speed gear box to the rear wheels. The carriages date from a year or two newer, and came from NSW. The railway itself only goes down to Croydon and does not link to Forsayth where the Savannahlander comes to from Cairns. The 200 km gap was never completed. I'm just taking the morning excursion and the guide gave a good commentary pointing out Kaypok trees, turpentine bushes, koolabahs etc and showing us where the water level was 12m over the rail bridge in 1974 causing the area to be evacuated and cut-off for three months. The Normanton Railway Station also had a fascinating vintage Railmotor which came out from the UK as a bus in 1931. It runs on alternate days to the Gulflander.

Fun though it is playing with trains, there was still Burke & Wills Camp 119 to visit. By the afternoon it was suitably hot, which added to the aura of the place. You do end up shaking your head at the stupidity of the politicians who put together such an over-large team, with no outback experience, who then blundered along in the wrong season, constantly making poor decisions. Bravery is never a good alternative to knowledge and skill. I am glad I didn't camp there as it was pretty bleak and is quite remote. It is deserted and I do a short video on my phone, reading out some of the provided information.

The Burke & Wills expedition had set off from Royal Park, Melbourne at about 4 pm on 20 August 1860 watched by around 15,000 spectators. The 19 men of the expedition included six Irishmen, five Englishmen, three Afghan and one Indian camel drivers, three Germans and an American. They had 23 horses, 6 wagons and 26 camels. They took a large amount of other equipment, including enough food to last two years, a cedar-topped oak camp table with two chairs, rockets, flags and a Chinese gong; the equipment all together weighed as much as 20 tonne.

It was six months and 3,250 km later that they reached the environs of The Gulf. At this point it was just Burke, Wills, King and Gray. They'd told the balance of the men involved in the final push to wait back at Cooper's Creek for 13 weeks. Under the leadership of William Brahe, this group actually waited 18 weeks before reluctantly setting-out for Melbourne via Menidee. They left some supplies buried at the foot of a tree with a clear, dated inscription carved into the tree instructing them to dig. In a happenstance of extreme bad luck, Burke and co staggered into the depot barely nine hours later. Gray had already perished four days back, three weeks after getting a thrashing from Burke for stealing some porridge. The surviving trio dug up the supplies that had been left for them and rested a bit. Wills and King wanted to follow the way back taken by the rest of the expedition but Burke determined that they wouldn't catch the others and should go another direction to a settlement at Mount Hopeless. This was the closest known place of help to where they were. It was 240 km away to the south west. Burke buried a note telling of their intentions but neglected to make any changes to the message on the tree trunk.

Meanwhile, while returning to Menindee, Brahe had met with another part of the expedition led by William Wright, belatedly trying to reach Cooper's Creek with their supplies. The two men decided to go back to the depot to see if Burke had returned. When they arrived on Sunday, 8th May, Burke had already left for Mount Hopeless, and the camp was again deserted. Burke and Wills were 56 km away by this point. As the mark and date on the tree were unaltered, Brahe and Wright assumed that Burke had not returned, and did not think to check whether the supplies were still buried. They left to rejoin the main party and return to Menindee. Six expeditions were commissioned to find the missing men including two by sea. Burke and Wills both perished around the end of June 1961 and whilst King was able to live with a group of Yandruwandha aboriginals willing to give him food and shelter, he was in an extremely poor condition. In return for their succour, he shot birds to contribute to their supplies. He was found on the 15th September and survived the two-month trek back to Melbourne, but never really recovered his health and died still a young man of 33, nine years later.

All in all, a momentous cock-up ... and the telegraph followed the route taken by McDougal Stuart a year or so later ... but that is another story.

But back to me, after leaving The Gulf, I holed up in a donga at the Burke and Wills Roadhouse (AKA Fourways) 200 km south of Normanton. The body needed a break after a few nights in the tent. My theory that after the first sleepless night you are so knackered that you subsequently sleep well, is not proving to be as correct as it once was. Again I hear the shouts of "Harden up Princess!"

I have sourced some CRC carb cleaner and have applied suitably to some of Penelope's possibly gummed-up orifices. Mt Isa tomorrow

So just another day ... living the dream ... nothing much to report at all. The $75 night in the donga was bit of a nightmare with many attacks from unidentified insects/creatures. I was not sure if getting the air conditioner to work just blew them into my cell but whatever ... I spent most of the night cowering under the doona (Oz-speak for coverlet, eiderdown, duvet etc). The corned riverside had been great though, as was the early morning coffee. Roadhouses don't do haute cuisine but neither are their portion sizes of that ilk. Usually you are served by young travelers who have washed up and need some work. Good scheme.

The 180 km down to Cloncurry were straight and dull relieved by a 30 min chat to the Traffic Controller at a Fulton Hogan (a Kiwi company) bridge job, but the 120 km or so across to Mt Isa was surprisingly interesting and undulating. Mt Isa looks like the mining town it is. I saw no heritage buildings or things of interest. Possibly I was selling the town short, but walking through the town near the pretty good museum complex, I came across a small group of blind-drunk aboriginal women, one with no top on, fighting and yelling. My tent site is double the usual $10 but I think that in my tent, I can better keep out the critters than the donga did the previous night.

The local Yamaha shop assisted with a thorough clean of Penelope's carb using a special unguent which seemed to dissolve all the varnish and crud. The shop boss-lady had been keen to book me in for workshop time in a week's time and it had taken a bit of old-duffer persuasion to let me action things on the day. In the end they were happy when I did most of the work and they only charged me for 30 mins. I decided to do a big local ride the next day before heading south.

There were lots of Grey Nomads in the camp, some with some very good gear. I am finding it an eye-opener that many have just relocated their lives for a period and even have their pets with them … cats, dogs, birds etc.

I've got a big call to make … do I head down The Birdsville Track to South Australia? (bike shop guy says NO!). The Birdsville Track is a serious out-back route and not to be taken lightly. I'm only too aware that we're not really a suitable pairing for a ride like this. Many thoughts go through my head. I know the real out-back explorers consider it soft … it is just a long empty dirt road. Is gung ho a compliment, or a derisive and cautionary observation? Should I really be so dismissive of bike clubs that have a back-up trailer on rides around the block. Will pride come before a fall? Is being 'terminally optimistic' a good or bad thing? My trial ride went well, so spirits are up, later I crawl into my tent, still undecided but deep down knowing what my direction will be. The morning shows that the feedback from my FB posting confirms that my friends seem to know I will stubbornly resist the easy black-top route.

Riding from town I reflect on Mt Isa? Mum used to say "If you can't say something good about someone … then don't say anything!" Mt Isa is a town of 20,000 people with a whooring great, ugly mine complete with smoke stacks, in the middle of it … yep, right in town! Copper, lead, zinc. World Health Organisation studies show lead levels in local kids to be many times the recommended safe limits. it is also seemingly a totally franchised town with every multi-national represented … and nothing else except machinery repair places. Oh and the good bit? 18 km from town is a beautiful man-made lake with a sealed two lane cycleway all the way there. Was that ok mum?

I'm happy to put it behind me, surprised that there were a few long-termers in the camp who are wintering-over there … but as the old saying goes 'there is now't so queer as folk'.

Of course, with the little inner boy still wanting praise, wanting to impress, there was probably little doubt as to whether I'd take the roads the 'Norms' use. Is it a deep-down insecurity that wants me to have my fan-base go "Wow, I knew he'd not let us down. Go Des!"

My first day heading south from Mount Isa gets me to Boulia. It's an early finish to the day as we quickly put 300 km behind us and I am in no rush to get to Birdsville because we had quite a bit of rain a couple of nights back and the red clay needs to dry and harden. Moving off the centre tar strip onto the dirt margins has been a bit scarier today after I learned early in the piece that the dryness was only skin-deep … with a very slippery sub-base. It should be two more days for us before it is completely unmade roads and by then the track should have hardened up again. Now that I am heading away from the 'main' road, I have to plan my days. There is very little out here and settlements seem to be about 250 - 300 km apart to sell petrol and food. This means I either only do a short day or graft out a big one

And the day's ride to Boulia? Well our shadow was back and looking great on the red road-margin. We'd missed him on the cloudy day from Fourways to Mt Isa. It is surprising what having a mate along can do for your spirits.

Being that I don't have any 'sounds' plugged in, I do a lot of musing, wondering about a lot of what I am seeing etc. I'd love to have David Attenborough up as pillion so he could tell me things. I realise I know so little about my surroundings. How long do ants live and do they build more than one ant-hill in their lifetime? Why are there thousands of small pointy ant-hills in some places and huge ones in others? Are they by different sorts of ants? Who decides when an ant-hill is finished? Is there a superintendent or project manager who says "That's it boys … job done! Have a couple of days off and we start Monday over by that dead coolibah tree. It's a Roger Walker job so should be interesting, probably will leak and things won't fit … but hey, we're just the workers."

I do love the road signs. Occasionally there is one that says 'Drive on the left in Australia'. What an over-abundance of words! Or I suppose it could be a shortage of words and the sign should say 'Drive on the left in Australia, NZ, UK, Japan, Pakistan, India, Fiji, South Africa etc, etc'. I think by memory there are more than 70 countries that drive on the left, so potentially a big sign. Other signs advise on road etiquette. For instance, there is one showing that a road-train should stay on the narrow tar strip and oncoming cars etc should take to the dirt shoulders. Another tells that there is a parking spot One km ahead to stop at and drop dust before entering town. The word town is gilding the lily a bit as it will be just a clutter of workshops to service the surrounding area. It will be linear, with a tiny population and include a watering-hole for locals and travelers alike. I can't help but chuckle as I pass a big sign facing away from me … and the back side has had SCROTE emblazoned on it.

Boulia is a settlement of about 300 and I am driven into my tent by the millions of flies, swarms of them wanting to cling onto my skin!!!. One of my reasons for not being a great believer in an omnipotent one above, is that nobody but absolutely nobody would create flies. The caravan park is on the edge of town and later I walk back to the roadhouse to find food. I encounter a broken camping trailer sitting in the middle of the road. The 'A-frame' draw-bar has snapped off and it is now pointing to the sky, well and truly dead-in-the-water. The family are sitting forlornly at the side of the road wondering how they were going to get all their gear home etc. A cop car is there and I wonder where he has come from. I learn later that most of these outback camping trailers are designed in Australia, but fabricated in China.

I am served by a young Italian girl and I pass the observation that she is a long way from home. Grimly she responds "I am a long way from anywhere!" I get the impression she is just toughing out her three months' remote work which enables a priority visa application.

Another empty but interesting day follows and I fetch-up at the little settlement of Bedouri (pop 122). I am pleased to see that it has a hotel and remarkably … an information centre. I chat with the middle-aged woman manning (should that be 'womanning') the iSite. She is an outsider, a 'blow-in', but loving the remoteness and difference of being 'outback'. Her partner works for the roading-gang and they have very little costs by way of mortgage etc. There is little or no entertainment, but they don't miss the East Coast city life at all. A young French couple serve me in the bar when I indulge in a mid-afternoon pre-dinner beer. We're all looking forward to the night's rugby on the TV which will pit both our nations' finest against each other. As it happens, right at the crucial time, there is a mini-influx of people and the French lad spends most of the game cooking meals. A young middle-aged Māori woman from Gisborne shares a beer and a quick explanation of how she has ended up in the area. A teen-mum, she'd never travelled, until, with her daughter safely through to adulthood, she answered an advert for a station cook. Her first-ever flight got her on the way to a remote Aussie experience. She was with a hard-looking jackaroo, who after slugging down a couple of beers, indicated to her disappointment, that they couldn't wait any longer. They had 40 or 50 km to go to get back to the station and had to be off the road before the kangaroos got active at dusk. I think they had brought an injured station-hand into town so he could be taken away to receive better medical help.

It is a real bonus to get to watch the All Blacks v France rugby as it is a bit of a minority sport in most of Australia and not always on channels that the bars I have been in can source … or want to show. It is quite an easy win to the All Blacks on the night partly as a result of the French having a player out for most of the game. I stay for a few more beers and later I couldn't help myself when a Snooty Adelaide Matron – an ex-teacher, told the German barmaid that the wine was pronounced *MER-lo* not *mer-LO* in Australia. The German had got the pronunciation from the Frenchies she was working with. I told the S.A.M. that I thought Aussies pronounced it *MER-LOT* … she didn't get the joke.

After my night in field at the end of the settlement, I take some early morning exercise by going for a walk along a stop bank. I notice a well-outfitted Land Rover Defender parked up apart from the few other campers. I see some smoke and with surprise, spot what looks like a Kiwi Thermette. Intrigued I sidle over to confirm what my usually-not-so eagle-eyes have settled on. I am right, and I am invited to share a morning cup of tea. They are a couple from home who had sailed a yacht to Australia in 1979 and have now explored more or less every track, trail and desert that Aus has. I ask if they get stuck. "Yep, lots … but we have all the gear to get unstuck." They have a winch at both ends as well as the obligatory sand-mats etc. They're a self-deprecating pair, obviously very self-sufficient and adventurous. Their whole rig is tuned for the job in hand. There is a place for everything and everything is in its place.

The *Thermette* is a wonder of simplicity that warrants an explanation. There is a cylindrical spacer about 125mm (5") high where a fire is made under the boiler unit which is about 300mm (12") high and of the same diameter on the outside with an inside that tapers down to the 50mm (2") chimney that projects through the top of the *Thermette*. This makes a conical water jacket which is top-filled through what is the pouring spout. A couple of fold-out wire handles complete the

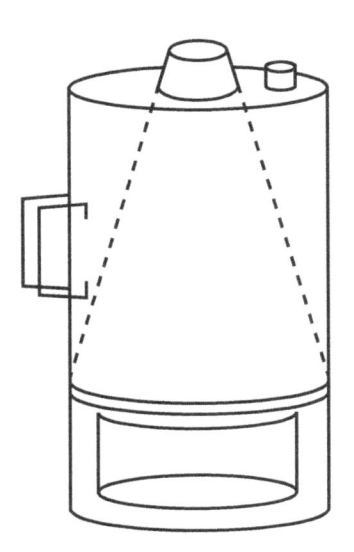

**CAIRNS TO BIRDSVILLE**

package. Because the water jacket completely surrounds the fire and goes from a thin point which heats quickly (and hot water rises), it is incredibly efficient as the tapered chimney makes the fire and smoke pass through quickly, creating a low pressure area which draws more air in through the bottom and so further feeding the fire. A small fire is started using almost anything, then once under way it is top fed through the chimney. Leaves, twigs and small broken branches can be poked in. In an amazingly short time enough water for 12 cups of tea is boiled. When finished with the fire can be extinguished with a small splash of water. This leaves just a small 4 inch blackened circle to show that you have been there. This wonderful device was invented by a John Ashley Hart in 1929 and patented in 1931 originally being promoted by the slogan *'the more the wind the quicker it boils'*. In 1939 The NZ Goverment asked Mr. Hart to waive the patent rights and got approval to make and supply their troops in the North African deserts. From this came the nick-name *Benghazi Boiler* and the reputation as the quickest boiler there was. Every sixth soldier was issued with one. Later still, apprentice plumbers were required to make one as part of their demonstration of sheet metal skills. Ministry of Works trucks always had one behind the seat for the road-gangs to do a brew-up on. A Kiwi icon, it is still made and sold today. The older, copper ones are in high demand on the internet auction sites.

Once again I cross the Tropic of Capricorn, and this time there is not a soul in sight as I pose beside the needle-like marker. I prop my phone up against a small rock and scuttle into the shot after pressing the 'selfie' button. A pretty average photo results with a dramatically sloped horizon … but it is a record. Not long afterwards we cross below a raised part of the land-mass. It is a fairly substantial hill just a few kilometres off to the right. A sign-post makes me aware of a look-out and I make this detour my early afternoon break. It is here that I read all about the wonderful barren land that is lying below me. This is the Channel Country, an enormous flood plain (over 200,000 km2) which a local may only see filled once in their lifetime. In 1990 the waters were 500 km across and easily seen from space. Amazing life-forms are resurrected on these rare occurrences. The flood waters flow inland from the north and the east, beginning 700 km away and taking three weeks to flow slowly to this enormous basin. The dry and dusty plain lying below me belies this phenomenon. It is hard to comprehend that when the floods occur, everything in my sight, the sunburnt land off to the horizon and beyond would be under water.

It has been a few good days from Penelope with only a few hiccups at one stage. The tweaking in Mt Isa may have worked, although the days have never got hot, so I am not yet trumpeting from the roof tops yet. She's getting 51 mile per gallon (5.5 Litres per 100 kilometres) which is only average. I'm back on the middle notch of the needle ... for the anoraks out there.

I'll let my Facebook posting tell the next bit of the story.

Finally!

*Woah ... I have reached the end of the world ... the Birdsville Hotel. Man and machine are going well and attracting a lot of attention ... partly because we are 'unsupported'. What does that mean ladies? Is it a good thing or should I be irked?*

*The last couple of days have been interesting in a dull way. Increasingly the Grey Nomads being encountered are rufty-tufty with amazing outback gear. Also I am encountering lots of hardened bush-bunnies doing the adventure desert crossings, of which there are numerous. These are the sorts of people who think The Birdsville Track is for wusses*

*After putting up my tent in Birdsville I ventured out 35 km to Big Red, the biggest sand dune in Aus. This ride confirmed that my range on the main tank is less than 270 km and that we are not very good in sand ... and when we lose confidence on corrugations and slow, we end up being smashed by the endless destructive jolting. The right technique requires the muy grande cojones of the young, enabling a speed to be maintained sufficient to keep the bike planing over the corrugations, so enabling a smooth passage. The age-shriveled Molloy Miniatures seemingly preclude this practice most of the time.*

*The Big Red visit also showed how precarious our ride is. The day is not far off being done, and what visitors there have been ... are gone ... back to Birdsville for a cool one. At the foot of Big Red I strike soft sand and bog down, rear wheel spinning ineffectually. I am suddenly up to my rear axle and Penelope stands vertically in the sand on her own. I walk away to gather my thoughts and plan the extrication. I am not sure how serious this is. I am alone and the afternoon is silent. I can see across the desert away towards Birdsville, and there are no tell-tale vehicle dust trails coming my way. I know I am not really equipped for this. I have no shovel, I am not strong and young anymore. I am aware though, that if I fail to get out and on to hard ground, I* am still not yet really in trouble, as the cool of the morning is a popular time for visits and help will come … it could just be a 18 hr foodless, bedless wait. Let's not be too over-dramatic here.

I decide that I'll have one shot at pushing and paddling while the wheel spins. It is always a precarious time in soft sand … your wheel can 'dig a hole' … or can 'grip and go'. I go back and fire Penelope up. I know my effort will need to be controlled and reasonably short, as my heart condition precludes an all-out burst of eye-popping effort. I stand alongside, feed out the clutch and push. The rear wheel spins and initially there is no forward motion. I yell encouragement and my pledge to be measured goes out the window. There's suddenly a little movement and within a couple of metres we are making reliable progress across the carpark. Without stopping I leap aboard and continue with my feet paddling, still shouting, panting like an old steam train. We regain hard ground and head away, pretty relieved and thankful. My chest heaves and my heart pounds for quite some time as I head back for a deserved libation.

Big Red is also the site of one of Australia's most unusual events. They hold an annual three-day rock concert there. The crowd camp below the dune in their thousands to be part of this adventurous happening. It is 1,900 km from Sydney, 1,600 km from Brisbane, 1,200 km from Adelaide and a mere 700 km from Mt Isa. So no matter where you come from, it is a hell of a long way to go to get there, and it is not on a sealed road. For many it is like a pilgrimage, something you must do once in your life.

I've had a good night in the pub with a family crew from Tasmania who have just finished some epic desert/dune crossings coming through the Simpson Desert. One of their vehicles now has a bent chassis and probably now only has scrap value. They still think that the adventure has been worth it. Word has clearly gone around that I am the old duffer with the old bike and I am getting a lot of congratulations. One guy sees me in the food queue and as he passes just utters one word … "Legend!" The Birdsville Hotel is a meeting place of the adventurous. I feel a little bit of a fraud ... I've only been fully on the dirt for the last couple of days. I have also been trying not to let on that inside my city-soft exterior lurks a core of marshmallow. Meanwhile, I'll wallow in the adulation ... it is not often thrown my way.

I've been amazed that whilst I've barely encountered more than a dozen cars a day for the last while, here in Birdsville the hotel is full and buzzing. I know Birdsville can be got to from all four points of the compass but none of them are all that easy. It is such a surprise to find that there are so many people out and about, challenging themselves and their equipment. Tales of woe and expensive gear failure are heralded.

It is like being in a different world. Most of the vehicles spread out in the camping paddock sport racks with jerry-cans, sand mats, ropes and other desert-travel paraphernalia. Nearly all have tall whip-aerials with a fluro flag atop so they can be seen from a distance if they are in a dip and also if they

## THE BIG SIT

*are charging a dune they are spotted earlier from the other side. They've all got monster, great chunky tyres and wax has never been near any of them. Laid out alongside these desert waggons are swags, those archetypal Aussie one-man bed and tent combos. This is not like the holiday parks of the outside 'ring-road' of Australia. This is for the one-percenters.*

*I hope to start the day tomorrow with the famous camel pie from the Birdsville Bakery. It is a big test tomorrow ... the longest day, and the first of the actual Birdsville Track. I am just a little daunted. I may do a quick needle move to try and improve mpg as there is a bit less 'anticipated fuel surplus' than previously calculated. There are other travelers heading south on the main route and feed-back from those coming north is that track is good.*

*An achievement of the last couple of days on straight roads before I left the seal is that I have taught myself to ride with my left hand operating the throttle. It took a while!*

Darwin
Palmerston
Jabiru
Batchelor
ARNHEM LAND
Daly River
Pine Creek
Katherine
Barunga (Bamyili)
Blue Mud Bay
Alyangula
Groote Eylandt
Numbulwar
Ngukurr
GULF
OF
CARPENTARIA
Weipa
CAPE
Lockhart River
YORK
PENINSULA
Kowanyama
CORAL SEA
Osprey Reef
Cooktown
Borroloola
Vanderlin I
Mornington I
Port Douglas
Cairns
Mareeba
Kalkarindji (Wave Hill)
Elliott
L Woods
Nicholson R
Doomadgee
Normanton
GULF COUNTRY
Georgetown
Innisfail
Hinchinbrook I
Flinders Reefs
Lajamanu
NORTHERN TERRITORY
Ingham
Greenvale
TOWNSVILLE
Tennant Creek
TANAMI DESERT
BARKLY
TABLELAND
Mount Isa
Cloncurry
Charters Towers
Ayr
Bowen
Proserpine
Hughenden
L Dalrymple
Collinsville
Mackay
Yuendumu
Winton
Boulia
Moranbah
Dysart
Middlemount
Papunya
Alice Springs
QUEENSLAND
Longreach
Barcaldine
Clermont
Emerald
Blackwater
Hermannsburg
L Amadeus
Yulara
Finke
SIMPSON DESERT
Birdsville
Windorah
Blackall
Springsure
Woorabinda
Tambo
Biloela
Monto
Taroom
CHANNEL
COUNTRY
Quilpie
Charleville
Roma
Miles
Surat
Macumba
Oodnadatta
Innamincka
STRZELECKI
DESERT
Thargomindah
Cunnamulla
St George
Dirranbandi
Toowoomba
Goondiwindi
VICTORIA DESERT
L Eyre North
Coober Pedy
L Eyre South
L Blanche
Marree
L Maurice (Carie-Thulka)
SOUTH AUSTRALIA
Andamooka
Leigh Creek
Lightning Ridge
Collarenebri
Brewarrina
Walgett
Bourke
Moree
Inverell
Narrabri
Armidale
Tamworth
Gunnedah
Tarcoola
L Torrens
Woomera
L Frome
White Cliffs
NULLARBOR PLAIN
L Everard
L Gairdner
Wilcannia
Broken Hill
Hawker
Cobar
Nyngan
Gilgandra
Ceduna
Streaky Bay
Port Augusta
Wudinna
Whyalla
Peterborough
Port Pirie
NEW SOUTH WALES
Ivanhoe
Dubbo
Scone
Singleton
Mudgee
Parkes
Orange
Bathurst
Maitland
NEWCASTLE
CENTRAL COAST
GREAT AUSTRALIAN BIGHT
Cleve
Kadina
Clare
Renmark
Tumby Bay
Port Lincoln
Mildura
West Wyalong
Griffith
Katoomba
SYDNEY
ADELAIDE
Murray Bridge
Ouyen
Balranald
Hay
Young
Cowra
Narrandera
WOLLONGONG
Kingscote
Kangaroo I
Victor Harbor
Swan Hill
Wagga Wagga
Deniliquin
Goulburn
Bowral
CANBERRA
Queanbeyan
Nowra
Tumut
Ulladulla
Batemans Bay
STRALIA
EDITION 2
Bordertown
Kingston SE
Naracoorte
Horsham
Echuca
Shepparton
Bendigo
Benalla
Wangaratta
Albury-Wodonga
Cooma
Narooma
Bega
Millicent
Mount Gambier
Hamilton
Ararat
Ballarat
Melton
Sunbury
MELBOURNE
GEELONG
Bairnsdale
Portland
Warrnambool
Moe
Sale
Traralgon
Wonthaggi
100 200 300 400 500 kilometres
ction with Standard Parallels 18°S and 36°S
TASMAN SEA
NTS
BATHYMETRIC TINTS
0 1000 500 200 0 200
and depths are shown in metres
King I
BASS STRAIT
Flinders I
Cape Barren I
Smithton
Burnie
George Town
Ulverstone
Devonport
Launceston
St Marys
Queenstown
TASMANIA
Bridgewater
HOBART
L Pedder
Kingston
Bruny I
Road, principal sealed
Road, principal unsealed
Road, secondary sealed
Road, secondary unsealed
Road, minor sealed
Road, minor unsealed
Operational railways
Spot elevation
River, perennial
River, non-perennial
Lake, perennial
Lake, non-perennial
Reef
State boundary

## CHAPTER FOUR

# BIRDSVILLE TO ULURU

So I tell my FB crew.

Ok ... so what's up? What have you been doin ... same old, same old? Me too ... sorta. Corrugations, soft patches, sand drifts, giant potholes ... did I mention calamities?

So back up a bit. The night in Birdsville was a 1° cold one ... character-building when you don't have a snow-foam or Thermarest but that is all right (note the spelling - I was caned as a young one for spelling it alright). A not-very-early breakfast of a curried camel pie and coffee was had at the legendary Birdsville Bakery. Here I saw the most unsuited outback bike of all time ... way more so than a mildly eccentric old duffer's obsolete British banger. This was a Japanese sports bike, turbo-charged with nitrous-oxide-boost, shod with a knobby tyre on the front and the fattest, treaded hoop you have ever seen, on the back. This would have made all corrugations, sand drifts and the like disappear in an immense rush of euphoric ecstasy, all the while, the rider would be just a gnat's whisker from eternal glory. It certainly made the trail-bike riders look pretty wussy with their pretty, multi-coloured, scrawny, chook-chasers.

A couple of other local vehicles deserve to be recorded. One is Onslo a 1963 blue VW Beetle. Onslo is immortalised in a children's book of adventures and did actually cross the Simpson Desert. Sadly, Kelly Theobald, his young owner and the author of the book, was killed in a car accident in 2015. Onslo sits next to the gas servo, advertising the book and inspiring travellers. The other is the Simpson Desert Recovery Truck, a huge ex-German Army MAN multi-wheel-drive vehicle called The Monster. This truly is the biggest, meanest-looking thing I have ever seen. It seemingly can go anywhere and rescues dead 4 x 4s from the desert, hauling them up onto the enormous flat deck and churning its way back to base

Birdsville has been interesting and not disappointed. The sign announcing you've arrived gives a population of 115 +/- 7,000 and an elevation of 46 m. The people I encountered were quite unlike those I rub shoulders with on a daily basis ... imaginative, adventurous, resolute, interesting and often fun. The annual attractions of the area mirror these attributes. In addition to The Big Red Bash, The Simpson Desert Racing Carnival has meetings on successive weekends at Birdsville, Betoota (pop. 0) and Bedourie. These races are seen as a 'must go' for many from all over Australia. They are a fund-raiser for The

**THE BIG SIT**

Royal Flying Doctor Service and are often epic weekends. In 2010 the Birdsville races had to be cancelled because of flooding but the event still went on with the punters betting on 'ghost' races.

I'd fretted a bit in the night about my fuel range. It seemed I had needed to add fuel from my bladder at less than 270 km which equated to a range of only about 340. The distance to Mungerannie is 320. I consulted the lady in the gas station and she said "No worries mate! Roads good, go easy on the throttle, you'll be sweet. Birdsville only sells 10 litre containers … you don't want one of them."

I did follow her advice but also dropped the needle a notch on the carb. I was still concerned because the ride out to Big Red had shaken my confidence a bit. Getting stuck in sand with no one around was not something I wanted to repeat. There has also been stretches where I couldn't achieve top gear. Partway through the day I had a reassuring realisation … when I had run dry on my main tank I had only used the one fuel tap … so I still had the other side of the tank to use. Phew!

My day is empty of fellow man but full of nature. The solitude is a bit daunting but I know I am ahead of other intended south-bound vehicles. It just feels a bit lonely, although I am constantly excited by the ride. I talk to myself a lot … I talk to Penelope a lot. After all, she is the key to success here. We have a few breaks … and snacks. At one, I have just stepped away a bit from Penelope, when she does the unthinkable … she lies down. I get to her quickly as I am fearful of the precious petrol spilling from the tank. Fully-laden she will be a big ask to get upright, especially as she has fallen a little awkwardly. Just as I am plucking at the saddlebags, two 4 x 4s roll up. I hadn't seen a soul since leaving Birdsville … until right now when some added hands would be appreciated. I nod upstairs in case the Omnipotent One had a hand in this. I know some of my cuzzies maintain a direct-line and have been asking that I get special treatment. I would have got Penelope up on my own, but the help was not spurned.

Oh, did I mention calamity earlier on? I suppose a Des ride is not complete without one. Fortunately, the marionette master upstairs was seemingly still looking after us whilst chucking in a character-building challenge. Late afternoon we hit a pretty big, jolting bump and suddenly there is no connection between the throttle and the rear wheel. The engine roars but we go nowhere ... all drive was lost. We were dead-in-the-water. I know we can't be much more than about 1 km from day's end at Mungerannie. After waiting a while, maybe 30 minutes or so, I walked to the roadhouse/hotel. I know it is a real no-no to abandon your vehicle but I knew I was close and could even see a construction of some sort through some trees at the limit of my vision. Mungerannie has a population of 2 but 1 (the wife) was away. However, the host Phil, who looked like a well-fed Robinson Crusoe, had a couple of mates up to help out and Rhys towed me into the camp and I set up in the workshop.

**THE BIG SIT**

*The rear sprocket had parted company with the brake drum. When the original sprocket was replaced before our Beijing to Arnhem ride twelve years earlier, a new steel one was shrunk onto the cast-iron brake drum and additionally was held by 8 small cap screws. The shrunk-on grip had been lost and the screws had all sheared off ... not good. I'd not be able to get back any of the circumferential 'shrunk' grip, but replacing the screws would have to do. The crew gave me a battery drill and in my half-clumsy way I drilled out all the broken-off remains and did my best to re-tap the threads. I found eight suitable screws among the junk box and in the absence of any Loctite etc, I reassembled with a drop of super-glue and a prayer. Not being religious I don't think the prayer helped ... but you never know.*

*This had meant a 24 hr delay to my non-existent time-table, but it has to be said I had a great time broken-down in Mungerannie. Better than Busted flat in Baton Rouge, one of the songs I often belt out while riding. Kris K not Janis J. Being as this is the only source of food or petrol between Maree and Birdsville, there is a steady trickle of folk coming in to be re-provisioned. It is a quirky old roadhouse with several WW2 Blitz army trucks abandoned outside, giving a rustic ambience. There's a couple of signs to entertain ... one an Adelaide Metro 'Hail the Bus' bus-stop and another boldly proclaiming that MacDonalds are opening soon. Phil is a great raconteur and host. I would never have had the interesting and enjoyable times I had there ... if it was not for the breakdown. Quite a few beers and many laughs are shared in the short time I am marooned. I buy some fridge magnets and take away great memories.*

*I head off with my fingers' crossed that the repair will hold. I am not all that confident as only seven of the eight screws went in well. They look tiny to be providing the drive to a thumping single-cylinder engine. The road improves a little and the colours change. Sometimes the road is chalky white, sometimes an unusual green-hue and often a tangerine orange. After a time, I unclench a little and start to enjoy the ride and the day. A flock of previously-not-seen* birds entertain me by scudding by closely. Later research shows they may have been Inland Dotterels. I sing and reflect on how wonderful this week has been. It is a pretty special part of Australia and I feel pretty satisfied to have given it a crack and largely succeeded. There have been many times when the solitude has been almost overwhelming.

So the Birdsville Track is done and dusted. Reflections? 95% good surface. Penelope is wonderful on good gravel. Being long and skinny she tracks straight and true. The normal small corrugations were purred over at a good 75-80 kph. However, there are however occasional big potholes that launch you from the saddle, giving rise to an involuntary cry. There are also the soft spots and sand drifts which are sphincter-clenching seconds of terror. I read once where after a near-miss or super-scary moment you should do some strenuous exercise to dissipate the adrenalin that has suddenly accumulated in your body. Many times over the last 3 days I should have been jogging alongside Penelope to achieve this.

So she has been magnificent and although I had promised her today would be the last day of dirt roads, I have decided to forgo the fleshpots of Adelaide and shortcut across to Woomera via part of the Oodnadatta Track.

So we are in the historic Maree Hotel. All going well I should have cell phone coverage again in a couple of days. Keep safe!

*By the way we did 317 km on the main tank, one tap only at an economy of 69 mpg (4.1 liters per 100 km).*

The pub in Marree (pop 150) turned out to be an elegant old girl with lots of charm and several 'special-interest rooms'. One was a museum to Tom Kruse who delivered the mail to Birdsville for decades. A very entertaining movie played in the corner showing his amazing exploits. Another room was filled with exhibits relating to the explorer John McDougal Stuart who was the first to go South to North of Australia and make it back. A wiry Scotsman who liked a tipple, he successfully carried out six expeditions to inland Australia without losing a man. His sixth one was to find a route from Adelaide in the south to the top of Australia so it could be connected to the burgeoning telegraph network. His group reached the site of modern-day Darwin only a year or so after Burke and Wills reached Camp 119 on the Gulf of Carpentaria. Stuart was another to not have a long life and after going partly blind on the last expedition, he returned to the UK to write up his journals, passing away within a couple of years.

The Lake Eyre room had photos from the time Malcolm Campbell was based in Marree with his Bluebird car which after 2 years of struggles did finally crack the World Speed Record in 1964 on the nearby salt lake with a speed of 403.10 mph (648.73 km/h). Marree was also an important rail-hub for the legendary Ghan until the route was changed. So an interesting spot. A magnificent semi-art-deco locomotive displayed on the mail street is the principal attraction of the town … apart from it being the flying-off spot for scenic flights over the neighbouring salt lakes.

I had an interesting momentary fantasy interaction not long after my arrival. It was late afternoon and I was at an outside table in front of the pub, perusing my maps and savouring a deserved beer after my delivery from the trials and tribulations of the Birdsville Track. Penelope was beside me and we would have presented as a pretty worn, dusty duo.

Parked opposite was a large air-conditioned coach proclaiming *Adelaide Sightseeing*. Possibly 40 or so elegant suburban matrons had dined in the hotel and been summonsed back to their dark-windowed, comfortable conveyance … which was dust-free and possibly at the limit of their excursion. Any further would have the outback intrude and they'd soon be 'all shook-up'. I could see quite a few of them giving me the once over as they made their way across the wide road in dribs and drabs. I sensed that the more adventurous would love to throw off the conventions of their matron-hood and come ride with the dusty, beer-swilling outlaw. I reckoned that if one broke rank and made a dash for us, there'd be a cat-fight in the middle of the road. I told you it was a fantasy! I still reckon though, that there would have been more than one who would have liked to have taken a ride on the wild side. I suppress a giggle, because this posse of older womanhood have no idea how conventional and square I really am. Delusional Des?

The decision to do 'just one more' day on the dirt was taken because to go around to Woomera on the seal is 570 km but only 270 to pop up the Oodnadatta Track, hook a leftie after 75 km and whistle down through Roxby Downs … and back on to the tar. So I told Penelope that, and first-up there was no holding her. We fair flew along at an indicated 60 mph like we were in *The Charge of the Light Brigade*. It was invigorating and we were like a swashbuckling Hollywood duo cutting a thunderous swathe through the tawny countryside spewing out a dusty plume behind. Of course that didn't last … we hit a few big ones and soon calmed down.

At the turn-off we paused and had a break … not a Kit-kat but an oaty bar of some sort. While there, a BHP ute appeared and paused. Salutations were exchanged and then I said to the couple of young blokes. "What's the road like ahead?"

They grinned.

"Shit! Worst road in the whole region … we hate it."

Oh dear, nothing I could do about that. Man, were they right ... at times I was in 2nd gear being smashed by big corrugations etc and big soft patches. I persevered for another 60 km which was the halfway point to Roxby. This time I got out a mandarin. Lo and behold, the same ute appears.

"Told you the road was shit!" A shared chuckle saw them off into the distance.

The next excitement was being passed by an old Landcruiser (Two vehicles passed me in the day) and then finding it with a shredded tyre. Ira? ... was needing no help whatsoever and I watched and chatted. She is an opal miner from Marree and seemed to enjoy our interaction ... so much so that we parted with a hug.

Finally, all the excitement that has been our adventure through the real outback was over ... and we were back on tar-seal being chased along by shiny cars and trucks.

Woomera! What an odd place. It was built so the British could test their rockets during the Cold-war period. It was an excluded area and housed 7,000 military personnel. Now the population is 150 and the town is filled with displays from those old days ... rockets on every street corner almost.

I settle down in an old barracks after a night across the other side of town in the only hotel ... a sculless place, modern and vast. I cogitate in my bed later how tomorrow we'll aim for the underground town ... Coober Pedy. We both need a serious clean up. I've already had to get into the dirty laundry bag for extra clothing ... bit cold.

More from Facebook

*Ok, so later on I am going to tell you about George. George is that wonderful rarity who can truly be described in that phrase from our parents' day, as being 'salt of the earth'. But as we know in life there is no point in getting to the climax too soon.*

I awoke in Woomera, in my cold cell-like room and after putting on the kettle, thought ... do I want to go through the ritual of grinding the beans, Aeropressing the coffee and with the choice of mandarin or oaty bar, suffer a solitary, chilled breakfast? No, I decided it would be off to the town's only cafe in the I-Site. I paused for some more rocket shots, meeting a delightful young family taking time out with their three young daughters to loop around Aus. Rose, Ava and Mia were 11, 9 and 6 and were as lovely as could be. The brief, fleeting interaction warmed the cockles and gave the day a great start.

A pretty good long black, and a bacon and egg roll set me up well for a chilly but sunny day. The countryside was still outback ... still looking like a Karen Standke picture ... but it had changed. Now it had a sealed and white-lined road bifurcating the wide vista. It almost seemed like a sanitised, theme-park outback I was riding through. Now there were clean people in clean cars whistling along, looking out through clean windows at me ... I sensed, dismissively annoyed that I was holding up their 110 kph traverse of this Technicolor cake-tin-lid scene.

So ... what about George? Remember my bush repair back in Mungerannie? It took me through two days of the most remote countryside Australia has ... and then mid-afternoon today, the dream was interrupted ... again. Not a cry for attention, I promise you ... my disappointment was palpable. The dream was over ... maybe.

Expletives were expleted and we glided (glid?) to a halt in disappointed silence, still 50 km short of Coober Pedy. Of course there was no cell phone coverage ... but who was I going to call? Ghostbusters???

And ... along came George the shearer. Those of you who believe, will reckon you sent him ... just as you made sure our failure was not out-back, so to speak. For this I thank you.

George had a Falcon ute, the back chocker with a freezer full of meat, a BBQ, a swag, bags, billy, two dogs, shearing gear, Uncle Tom Cobbly and all etc. In the cab he had a new guitar and all sorts of stuff. In other words ... a fully, full load. Did he say to himself "I wonder if that joker needs a hand ... shame I have no room, otherwise I'd stop."

No, he hauled on the picks, did a U-eee and came back to ask if I was ok. Between us we totally unpacked his ute, and in a magnificent effort for a shearer with a bad back and an old duffer with a dicky ticker, hoicked Penelope up onto the tray. We then piled everything back on, with one dog right up on top and me in the cab with quite a load on my lap.

He was on his way to Alice Springs to his sister and was going to free-camp along the way. Delayed by me we are now in a caravan park. I've shouted him a cabin and tomorrow he will head on ... and I will look to find proper engineering expertise. Unlike Mungerannie with a population of 2, Coober Pedy is a mining town with 1,500 residents and already I am on the track of *the key man. I may be de-railed a bit by the weekend though, as it is Friday night.*

*So am I disheartened??? After a good BBQ and a few beers with my new mate, how can I be!*

*Never fear ... there will be more ... this is not the end. Kia Kaha.*

George moves on the next morning. It is a leisurely start as he has to get his alcohol level down to below what his ignition-linked gadget in the ute allows. Our repast together had involved quite a bit of the amber fluid, so it was mid-morning before he was confident to try a blow in the spout. I'd chuckled the night before when checking-in. The lady on reception indicated that they were a dog-friendly place and his dogs would be welcome in the units, but preferably not on the beds. George was affronted. "No way they're coming inside ... they are working dogs ... they stay outside!"

Getting engineering help proved a little harder than anticipated in a town filled with mining equipment. The only engineering shop has shut down and the guy is now just taking the money at a back-street co-operative that sells petrol. He is a bearded older guy, very brusque and not easy to crack. He tells me the only place that can help is back before Woomera ... the BHP Engineering Workshop at Roxby Downs. He tells me there is no one in town he would trust ... and he is not well enough to do the job. I think it is such an easy job if you have the equipment ... which supposedly he has. I've been given a couple of other names and I mention one of them. "Well, if I had to trust anyone in town to do the work ... he'd be the only one. Actually I am selling my operation to him." Slowly I get him onside and although I have to wait until Monday to get things happening ... there is now a plan, and things are underway.

"Are you a prospector?" asked the old guy in the RSL selling raffle tickets during happy-hour on Sunday. So my assimilation is going well. A day earlier the woman in the underground bookshop ... properly underground, not some place from my left-leaning world ... asked if I was a local she didn't know. Good not to stick out.

Hopefully on the overnight bus from Adelaide is the vital thread-tap to match the high-tensile 4mm cap screws which are going to be installed in fresh holes and so re-attach Penelope's rear sprocket to her brake drum. A drop of Loctite will complete the job and we'll soon be back on the road. Because the sprocket is steel and the brake drum is cast-iron, they cannot be welded together ... which is such a shame. We are just going to be relying on the little screws being stronger than last time, and in nice new freshly 'tapped' holes. It is not ideal but there seems to be no obvious alternative.

Coober Pedy is an odd little town which has notoriety because of the opals and underground constructions but it lacks a lot of day-to-day services. Apart from no engineering capability ... there is no barber. I'd thought of a good spruce-up ... a new visage to present to the world ... designer-stubble to my ears and Ross Kemp over the top. But no, Prospector Des I remain for now. Coober Pedy is also the centre of Mad Max tourism. The film was made around here and quite a few film-props remain as tempters to the numerous guided activities.

My time in the holiday park allows for observation of my fellow travellers. There are a lot of caravaners who seem to have just set off (Adelaide is only 2-3 days away) and it is obvious that on-the-road regimes and procedures have not been established. Teamwork is usually poor and uncoordinated. This contrasts with what I saw in Karumba on The Gulf. There, no matter where you have come from ... it is a long way and the teamwork is impeccable. The couples have all been on the road for weeks if not months and no one comes across as a 'newbie'. They know their roles and slip into them seamlessly without discord.

One day I saw a BMW adventure bike purr past us (without acknowledgement ... but that is ok), and head to the far end of the camp.

BIRDSVILLE TO ULURU

Later I go for a walk, thinking I could stop by for a chat. I see no sign of the bike and as I hadn't seen them ride out … I was surprised. The next morning, I happen to be down that way and see a tent partly unzipped … and there is the BMW. I chuckle and wonder what Penelope would think if I had a tent big enough that we could sleep indoors together. Needless to say I don't tell her.

There's been time for reading and time for reflecting. The Birdsville Track was pretty big for me and at the time I couldn't take it all in as there was so much to do in 'the NOW'. Looking back, I recall all the different colours and textures … the road alone threw up colours of green, purple, white, tan and the obvious outback red. There were flocks of galahs and white corellas, wedge-tail eagles, kangaroos etc … and the huge sky arching over us. The exotic nature of my surroundings always made me feel it was a special privilege to be there.

… and the reading? Now it is *A Town Like Alice*, one of my favourite Neville Shute's. Very non-PC, but a great story that brings a tear to my eye every time. Great portrayal of the Gulf area and the little towns I have been through.

Being marooned in a camp with a shop allows some indulgences that I normally don't succumb too. Most afternoons when the day has heated up, I treat myself to an iced confectionary and a chat with either of the two women who seem to 'man' the place … one is a reader and we often talk books. Just by the freezer with the ice creams, is a large poster from the South Australian Police and the Royal Flying Doctor Service. It shows an outback road and a crashed motorcycle on its side with the detritus of the event strewn everywhere. The words on the poster speak to me … as they are meant to … and I have to share.

We all know Dorothea Mackellar's iconic poem and right now you are standing smack bang in the centre of that *sunburnt country* we all love. What you might not know is that she wrote it for you. Yes, you. A middle-aged biker standing in *an opal hearted country* searching for his dreaming, that connection between *warm, dark soil and soul*.

She actually wrote it as a warning – one of the very first community service road safety messages to be produced anywhere in the world.

Don't believe me? Let's take a look.

Buried in *her beauty*, out in this *wilful, lavish land*, there lies some deep and lasting *terrors*. There are no second chances for those who make bike riding mistake.

Those *droughts and flooding rains* play havoc with these tracks and leave ruts and holes and corrugations that will throw you over your handlebars faster than you can say *sweeping plains*. So ride to the road conditions.

And beneath the hot gold hush of noon the roos and wedgies own these roads and they aren't getting out of the way for the likes of you. Neither will emus, cows, sheep, donkeys or camels. Slow down and don't play chicken with the wildlife – you will lose.

*Her pitiless blue sky? Far horizons? Wide brown land?* More clues. Come to grief out here and you are in for a long lonely wait for help to arrive. Better to stay upright in the first place. There is no view when you are flat out on a stretcher in the back of the RFDS plane.

*Core of my heart, my country. A lonely place to die.*

Smart woman that Dorothea. Ahead of her time.

Slow down. Take care. Drive to the conditions of the road. Might take a bit longer but all the best things in life do.

It is a sobering and powerful message but I feel the content is almost too much for the poster, big as it is. There are so many words that I worry that the click-bait generation will be overwhelmed.

The underground nature of Coober Pedy is quite amazing and very cool, literally and figuratively. The town is opal-focused and has had some wonderful historical stories of surprising strikes. One museum decided to put in a big post to support something or other and struck a $50,000 opal find whilst digging. The temperature underground is pleasantly the same all the year around, meaning it is a respite in the summer and a cosy nook in the winter. I become a regular at an underground café for my morning coffee. I swap "Kia ora" greetings with a Māori wahine from Hawkes Bay each day and share a few Kiwi-isms. She is still learning the ropes as a barista, but doing well. She is another who lives in a bus with a dog. I have yet another Kiwi experience when I seek out the post office. There on the counter to tempt you as you carry out your transaction is a display of Whittakers Peanut Slabs. Whittakers are chocolate makers from the Wellington region and the Peanut Slab has been a treat since my childhood. The woman serving me reckons that the staff spend a good portion of their wages every week dipping into the box, but can't bring themselves to ask management to take them away. Of course I also succumb to temptation, but rationalise my action as being that of a patriotic New Zealander.

Woop, woop! After 6 days there is a movement ... and no, I am not needing more fruit in my diet. Finally, late Friday morning I got my re-attached sprocket and brake drum back.

Earlier I'd checked out of my little cabin and made a small mountain of gear by Penelope. Of course when I came to put things back together I found the jobs I could have and should have done during my enforced break ... like securing the chain-guard properly. Bugger! Silly boy ... but expected somehow.

Anyway by 2 o'clock we were purring down the grey-top. We needed to leave because we were getting pretty comfortable there, making coffee-shop relationships etc. We were almost becoming institutionalised. There was not even the slightest unknown in our days. Hunter-gatherers we were no more.

You have to laugh because ... the nights are very cold and whilst my cabin had a big air-conditioning unit in It, I hadn't used it because we were months short of the hot times. Yep, I turned it on last night just to check it wasn't some sort of heat pump ... and after filling the room with dead bugs ... and the noise of a DC3 ... heat issued from it. I had toughed it out for no reason at all.

So we scuttled along to Marla which is a road-house with camping. Sadly, no cabins etc, so the tent is up again. I'd decided not to tent again until we re-reach the warm. Unfortunately, that game needs two to play and tonight the other side isn't.

I met a new hero though. Paul Wheeler is cycling from South-east Australia to Broome in the North-west. He has been on the road 90 days so far. We chuckled together at the small-house-sized caravans that some have in the camp. Later we convivially share a beer and tell a few lies.

Paul is towing a BOB single-wheel trailer and his logistical requirements are many. Whereas I carry four litres of water, Paul carries 10 … except for when he is 'off piste', then he carries 25 litres. For me there is always a roadhouse every day, even if they are 300 km apart. For Paul, who is not hurrying along, that might take four or five days. For him, every inch is earned. If he doesn't get out there and pedal … he goes nowhere. He is always looking for side-routes which don't have the traffic of the state highway. Sometimes he is weeks away from what we would call civilization.

Indeed, I had a good night with Paul. For both of us it was a rare evening of discourse. So often we spend our evenings alone in our tents. We also have a beer with a young guy with a Royal Enfield Himalayan which is a new 410cc adventure bike that I am quite interested in. He is loving it and has just done his first proper ride down the Oodnadatta Track. He is a local paramedic and spends a lot of time out at an aboriginal reserve, which I am slightly surprised to learn is hundreds of km away from the main road. Paul and I share our thoughts on solo travelling and our observations of our fellow road-users are quite similar … and at times a little scathing. Some of Paul's ride … like the Mawson Track out of Adelaide … sounds idyllic, but so much appears to be 'trial by bicycle'. Subsequently I follow his Facebook postings which are interesting and vivid. Ultimately he takes over five months to get to Broome. He really is a legend. I am also drawn to him because like me he is just an ordinary joker. He is not a super-elite-athlete but just a milk-man from down Adelaide-way.

We're closing in on the centre of Australia and not much more than a big day away from Uluru, the old Ayers Rock.

We punch out a quick 200 km quite early in the day much as you would expect I suppose. The horizons were initially so far away that I couldn't see them properly, yet I could identify intriguing rock formations etc. Then as the day warmed, the horizons closed a little as sun haze took away the distant vistas.

My thoughts raced ahead to the wonderful photos I would pose in front of the big red monolith now known as Uluru. Vainly I see it as part of a set. We have a wonderful photo of Steph & I on Penelope overlooking Lake Titicaca in Bolivia … an emotional one in the Chaco Desert of Paraguay with her frame broken … there is one at the top of the Karakorum in Pakistan, one in front of the Great Wall in China, some cool ones in NZ as well … and the Gulf of Carpentaria, Birdsville etc.

We still might achieve our goal but I become just a little hesitant to detour 600+ km for a photo. I'll share my concerns and why initially I bloused out. My default setting usually precludes turning around and going back. This has normally worked ok for me … never letting 'what if' be the dominant influence.

Those of you who have been following my path will know that in Mt Isa we gave Penelope's carb a good clean and she performed wonderfully stutter-free for the next 1200 km down to Woomera. When we left there we filled at the main road servo … and 20 km later her hesitation was back … and has been there in the background ever since, usually in the afternoons. But in the lead up to turning off to Uluru the stutter became more intrusive and I stopped to give us both a break. I decided to see if putting in another plug changed things … it had before. Woah, the plug body was a pale blue … things looked to be getting way too hot! I did put in another plug and it worked for a while. I had also discovered something potentially even worse. The oil is showing specs of what looks like aluminium but it is hard to tell … they also could just be little bubbles. Bubbles are ok, aluminium specs not so. I rub my fingers together and can't feel a gritty sensation. My close-up vision is pretty good, but not quite good enough. I try dabbing the oily fingertip with a rag, then looking for shiny residue. Not really conclusive, let's say they were bubbles.

Anyway with both these worries playing away in the background we turned off for Uluru … 260 km. We went about 5 km … then I suddenly lacked the fortitude to go on. Without a wingman to offer sage advice, I suddenly didn't know what to do. In the end I went back to the roadhouse on the corner (unpowered tent site $11, room $115) and was put out the back ... in the cold again.

But wait ... there might yet be a happy ending ... there usually is. I decided to richen-up the mixture again because of the possibly overheating spark plug and in doing so found the paper gasket against the cylinder head was incomplete and fell to pieces as I removed it. So a box of Uncle Toby's muesli bars was bought and a new gasket cut out using my Swiss Army knife. Is this the answer to the stutter??? Will we get to Uluru in the cool before the stutter comes back ... or have I cured that ... or will the engine be wrecked by the aluminium particles? If this was an old radio serial we'd be signing off with "I guess you'll have to come back tomorrow for more."

In 2006 I rode across the top of the US re-creating the *Zen and the Art of Motorcycle Maintenance* ride on correct period 1965 motorbikes. Daughter Kitty came along to film, just as her brother had with *The Last Hurrah*. I remember her saying before we started "What if nothing happens?"

In my life it seems that there is NO SUCH SCENARIO.

BIRDSVILLE TO ULURU

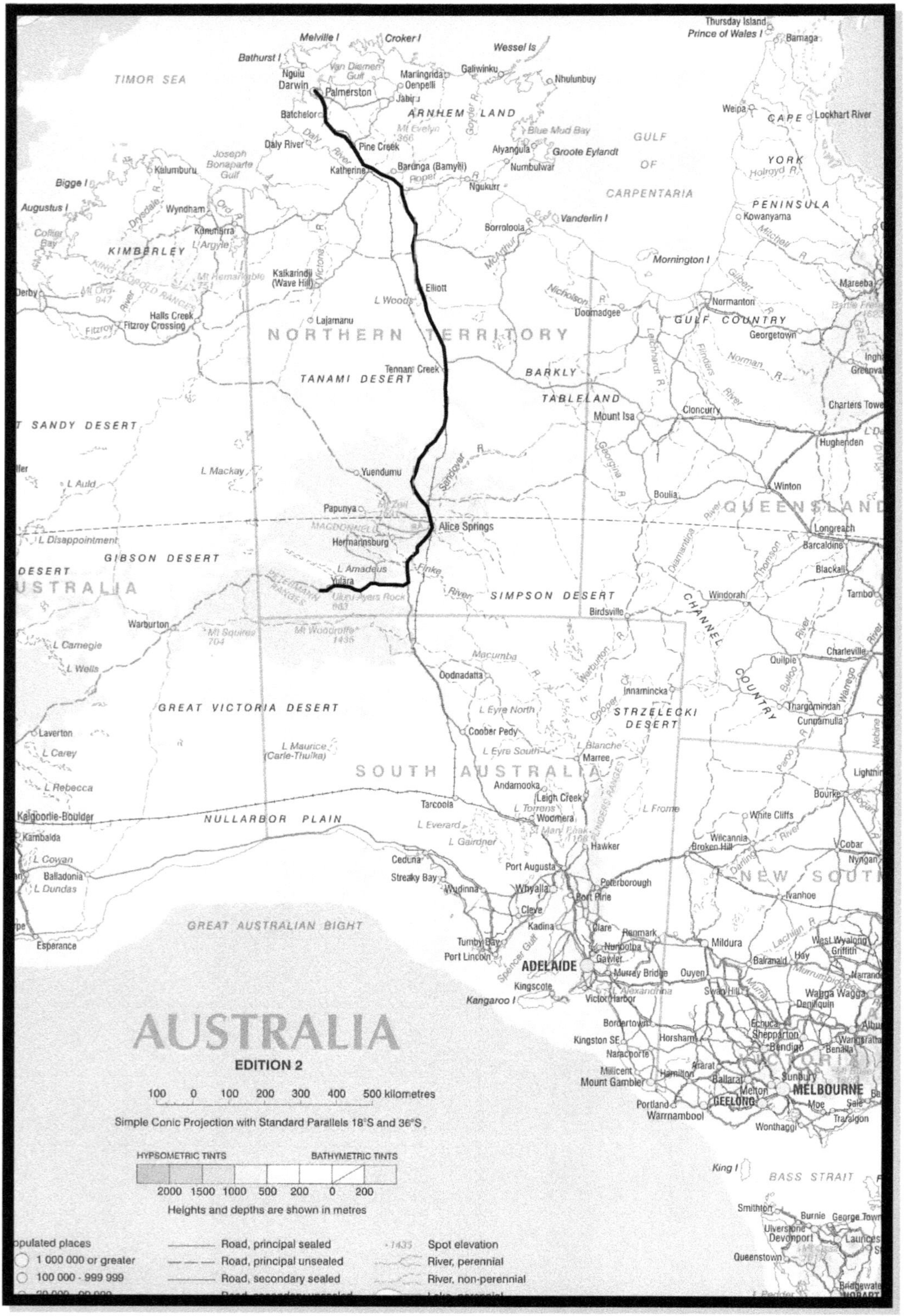
AUSTRALIA
EDITION 2
100 0 100 200 300 400 500 kilometres
Simple Conic Projection with Standard Parallels 18°S and 36°S
HYPSOMETRIC TINTS
BATHYMETRIC TINTS
2000 1500 1000 500 200 0 200
Heights and depths are shown in metres
opulated places
1 000 000 or greater
100 000 - 999 999
Road, principal sealed
Road, principal unsealed
Road, secondary sealed
Spot elevation
River, perennial
River, non-perennial
TIMOR SEA
Melville I
Croker I
Wessel Is
Bathurst I
Van Diemen Gulf
Nguiu
Darwin
Palmerston
Maningrida
Oenpelli
Galiwinku
Nhulunbuy
Jabiru
Batchelor
ARNHEM LAND
Blue Mud Bay
Daly River
Pine Creek
Alyangula
Groote Eylandt
Joseph Bonaparte Gulf
Kalumburu
Katherine
Barunga (Bamyili)
Numbulwar
Bigge I
Ngukurr
Augustus I
Wyndham
Borroloola
Vanderlin I
Kununurra
L Argyle
KIMBERLEY
Kalkarindji (Wave Hill)
Derby
Elliott
L Woods
Halls Creek
Fitzroy Crossing
Lajamanu
NORTHERN TERRITORY
Tennant Creek
TANAMI DESERT
BARKLY
TABLELAND
GULF OF CARPENTARIA
Mornington I
Doomadgee
Normanton
GULF COUNTRY
Georgetown
Thursday Island
Prince of Wales I
Bamaga
Weipa
CAPE
Lockhart River
YORK
PENINSULA
Kowanyama
Mareeba
Cloncurry
Mount Isa
Charters Towers
Hughenden
Winton
Boulia
QUEENSLAND
Longreach
Barcaldine
Blackall
Tambo
Windorah
Birdsville
CHANNEL COUNTRY
Quilpie
Charleville
Thargomindah
Cunnamulla
SANDY DESERT
L Mackay
Yuendumu
L Auld
Papunya
Alice Springs
L Disappointment
Hermannsburg
GIBSON DESERT
L Amadeus
Yulara
Uluru-Ayers Rock
SIMPSON DESERT
Warburton
Mt Woodroffe 1435
L Carnegie
L Wells
Macumba
Oodnadatta
Innamincka
GREAT VICTORIA DESERT
L Eyre North
STRZELECKI DESERT
Laverton
Coober Pedy
L Carey
L Eyre South
L Blanche
L Maurice (Carlie-Thulka)
Marree
SOUTH AUSTRALIA
L Rebecca
Andamooka
Leigh Creek
Tarcoola
L Torrens
L Frome
Kalgoorlie-Boulder
NULLARBOR PLAIN
Woomera
Kambalda
L Everard
L Gairdner
Hawker
White Cliffs
Bourke
Wilcannia
Broken Hill
Cobar
Nyngan
L Cowan
Ceduna
Balladonia
Port Augusta
L Dundas
Streaky Bay
Wudinna
Whyalla
Peterborough
Ivanhoe
Port Pirie
Cleve
GREAT AUSTRALIAN BIGHT
Kadina
Clare
Renmark
Esperance
Tumby Bay
Mildura
Port Lincoln
Spencer Gulf
ADELAIDE
Gawler
Murray Bridge
Ouyen
Balranald
Hay
Griffith
Kingscote
Swan Hill
Kangaroo I
Victor Harbor
Wagga Wagga
Deniliquin
Bordertown
Echuca
Shepparton
Kingston SE
Horsham
Bendigo
Benalla
Naracoorte
Ararat
Millicent
Hamilton
Ballarat
Mount Gambier
Sunbury
Melton
MELBOURNE
Portland
GEELONG
Moe
Sale
Warrnambool
Traralgon
Wonthaggi
King I
BASS STRAIT
Smithton
Burnie
Ulverstone
Devonport
Queenstown
Bridgewater

# CHAPTER SIX

# ULURU TO DARWIN

I am happy to let Facebook lead off once more —
*July 2nd 2018*
*Well I bring this to you from the relative warmth of my sleeping bag ... the smarter-than-me phone says it is 1° and whilst I can hear dawn out and about, with the bloody crows crowing and the grey nomads making their opening and shutting of door noises ... I am not budging till it is fully light and warm. I am already dressed so won't take long to get under way.*
*I am back at the Erldunda Roadhouse camp (centre of the continent) at the main road turnoff to Uluru. So we did it ... and yes it was wonderful. Of course we have all seen the photos and have an expectation ... but I was blown away by the shear presence of it. It is more than just the size. You stand back in wondrous awe, because this giant monolith does not look like it should be there in that almost flat desert landscape ... it really does look like a deity that you should be paying homage to etc. The aboriginal people have many dreamtime myths based on the formation of Uluru and hold it sacred. They ask you not to climb it, but until next year it is not illegal and many still do. I gently clashed with a mum here last night when she said they were specifically going there so the kids could climb it while still allowed. I declare I wouldn't disrespect the indigenous people by blatantly going against their wishes. An elderly Japanese tourist died on Uluru today and I can't help thinking there is a bit of karma going on.*

The ride to Uluru is about 270 km and was interesting in that it is not totally flat and there were also numerous abandoned cars littering the highway for me to look at. These are not tourists' cars that have been left while someone goes off for fuel etc. These are old bangers that have either been crashed or just run out of life. I am not dismissive or judgemental, as I've been there … and done that. I wonder how often they are collected and crushed.

Along the way I come across a van full of aboriginals, who flag me down. When I say 'full', I mean full as in the way we used to fill vans when we needed to. This bears no relationship to the numbers of seats or seatbelts. Again I am not judgemental, as I remember nine of my rugby club squeezing into my 1949 Morris Ten to get from practice at the gym, to practice at the pub. My interactions with Australia's indigenous people has been interesting but minimal to date. I'd seen some pretty anti-social behaviour by a small number of be-drunken women in Mt Isa, I'd briefly chatted in a pub in Coober Pedy to a guy with the softest, most-gentle hands I had ever shaken and seen their milling groups in shady settlements under bridges and the like. Normanton, back on the Gulf had a significant aboriginal population who were present in everyday life … but overall contact has been absent. I've been told that they can be aggressive among themselves but very rarely to others. I've never felt threatened by them and I always ensure I greet them cordially and appropriately.

I pull up and ask what is the problem. They are out of gas and needing to get to Uluru. I know there is fuel at Curtin Springs and that I will get there on my main tank, so I am happy to donate my fuel bladder's contents. We transfer this with quite a bit of banter and good humour. It is a multi-generational crew who wandered off in many directions while a good Samaritan was being sought. Tooting the horn seems to round up enough to push the van which then splutters into life and the pushers laughingly dive aboard through the side door. My addition should get them 50 km or so which will be more or less to Curtin Springs. Later I see them down the road, out of gas again, but there in nothing I can do so just pass by to their waves and laughs. Later at Curtin Springs I see them drive straight by. Maybe they had no money.

Finally, the iconic rock formations hove into view and it is an exciting last 30 minutes as Uluru grows larger and larger. There is a reasonably hefty entry fee to get you into the Uluru-Kata Tjuta National Park but it gives you three consecutive days' access. It was only in 1985 that the traditional owners were given freehold title deeds for the park. They in turn leased it back to the Australian Government for 99 years. 25% of the entry fee goes back to the Anangu people and there are work schemes which give neighbouring tribes the opportunity to have their young people work in the park and the visitor centre etc.

I ignore the luridly patterned hot air balloon and the helicopters and am pleased to be waved up to the front of the queue to be given priority entry over the line of camper-vans and car-loads of tourists. Closer in, I pull over for the obligatory photo opportunity and a couple of environmental scientists save me from ruining the record with an inept 'selfie'. I am surprisingly excited as I slowly cruise around the perimeter, taking in all the nuances that the monolith has to offer. Post cards don't do it justice. I find it quite a spiritual place. Its sheer presence is palpable. I stop and enjoy the Cultural Centre.

I met Harley-riding Brenton from Adelaide while checking in to the huge and expensive Ayers Rock Camp ($45 for a tent site!) which is outside the Park but close by, and we had a very collegial night in the hotel enjoying the cook-it-yourself BBQ. I had roo loin, and emu sausages. We hoped we would be joined by a round-the-world rider of a Triumph adventure-bike we'd met on our walk to the pub. He'd lost all his camping gear including his tent and sleeping bag. I offered to shout him a beer, because he was a little down in the mouth. He never found us and we didn't hear his outcome. He looked the real deal though ... a modern Dan Dare, all chiselled, clad in a blue and silver, prominently-armoured Cordura riding suit, big boots, far-off look in his eyes etc. Of course his bike had heavily-stickered aluminium boxes proclaiming where he had been and what he had done ... Canadian I think.

Next morning, I passed the comment to Brenton that he would look ridiculous in that get-up on his near-vintage Harley and Penelope would rise up in horror if I approached her clad so. Even anti-heroes are vain.

And did the Uncle Tobys' cardboard gasket cure Penelope? No! We have found though that if I only use no more than 1/3 throttle, we can purr along contentedly at about 80 kph. There is less than 2,000 km to go, so we'll stick with that heading north and I am ignoring my dip stick oil analysis and presuming my panic was caused by tiny bubbles. Of course I

**THE BIG SIT**

have no technical information to back that up ... but I trust Penelope to keep on keeping on ... she always has.

We've ticked off a couple of other Aussie icons recently. I got pretty close-up and personal with a dingo on the road (no Lindy Chamberlain jokes please) and had to give way to an impressive mob of emus. Google tells me that mob is the correct collective for emus, just like an unkindness of ravens, parliament of owls, clowder of cats, pox of Velocettes etc.

Back to Uluru ... the night was Central Australia cold. With not a lot between me and the densely frigid ground the night is predictably interminable with only a few robust, rumbling farts to warm me and provide a low-level of cheer. Once it was light and warm enough to emerge, I decided it must be coffee time. I told you a while back about the Kiwi Thermette. I'd always hankered over having the same but smaller ... and prior to this trip had indeed found just that. From Ireland is a similar device made of stainless steel, holding just one litre. This is ideal for motorcycling, whereas I always find the Thermette too big unless there is a group of us. Anyway, I do the whole deal with the Kelly Cooker and Aeropress, sharing a good, freshly-ground Rumble coffee with Brenton before he headed for home. It had been a very pleasant but fleeting interaction.

I do another loop of Uluru then reluctantly decide not to venture further away to take in Kata Tjuta (the Olgas). I know this will disappoint some of the family and friends who have been telling me it is a 'must see', but I have chanced my arm a bit with some of the back-country riding, and think that enough is enough. I go directly back to Erldunda, stopping along the way to photograph Mt Conner, another magnificent monolith. On the way in I had thought it was Uluru in the distance. I've since learnt that the locals call this 'Fooluru'. I get a good shot with Penelope in the foreground looking magnificent.

The night in Erldunda was interesting in that the roadhouse bar was busy and quite vibrant but the dusty, sprawling area for 'camping' is pretty faded and not especially good value, even at $11. I can smell sewage out on the boundary where I am sent. Maybe that is why there is a small area of green grass. The night was disturbed by outrageous fireworks going off close by and seemingly endlessly. I couldn't understand how no one was getting upset enough to put a stop to it. Only a couple of days later do I learn it had been the Northern Territory's anniversary day and fireworks are a tradition. The camp was also memorable for the snake warnings ...

freshly posted up in prominent places. As if I wasn't scared enough already. I wish I had found room for the device I saw for sale in Coober Pedy ... *The Raidar Snake Defence – Multi pulse solar snake deterrent and repellent*. I am not quite sure how it would work at night if it was solar, but that is why boffins are boffins ... I suppose it had batteries. I am also disturbed in the night by a neighbouring motor-home's heat pump intermittently coming on when the thermostat tells it that the master and mistress might need a bit more warmth. It is a shame that I can't fart to order when I feel cold.

Now that we are in the Northern Territory the speed limits are different and very contentious with locals. Traditionally, the between-towns roads had no speed limits. In 2007 this changed to 110 kph except for the four main highways, which allowed 130 kph. In 2012 the Stuart Highway which I am riding up, returned to being uncontrolled for the stretch between Alice Springs and Barrow Creek, a distance of 336 km. This changed again ... back to 130, in November 2016. This responsible move was done by the Territory's incoming Labor Government. They are not popular and most locals seem to predict a return to normality next time around. It is all a bit irrelevant for us ... it just means that the vehicles passing us are doing it quicker.

A bit south of Alice Springs I stop for a break at the *Cannonball Run Memorial* plaque. The Cannonball was a competitive speed run in 1994 for monied young blades. The event from Darwin to Alice Springs and back on non-speed-limited roads, attracted 118 competitors from around the world with exotic fast cars. The formal competitive side was limited to three 'Flying Miles' where the cars were individually timed for acceleration and scored accordingly. They were to enter the measured mile at 40mph and one mile later their speed was recorded by radar. Sadly, a Japanese Ferrari F40 mistook the entry point and crashed into it, bursting into flames, killing two officials and both driver and co-driver. Earlier he had been asked what it was like to drive at 185 mph on public roads. He'd said that "there were not the words to describe it". I wonder who got his remaining three Ferraris? Surprisingly the race was not cancelled and ran to its conclusion after a day's break. It's not a bad spot for a muesli bar, but no shade for a sit down and read.

I found Alice Springs a bit big and daunting. We've only done one town of any size since leaving Cairns and that was Mt Isa, nearly a month back. Alice is 25,000 big, spread-out and even has traffic lights. The timing is such that I decide I won't try to connect with George and his sister, there's more miles in the day yet … even if we're clicking off kilometres, at heart I am still an Imperial guy. A bit north of Alice … I feel I am on nodding terms, so can be a bit familiar in my name-dropping … I pass the turn-off to Boulia back in Queensland. This road cuts across the top of the Simpson Desert and I could have come that way instead of slogging down to South Australia and back. I've heard it is a tough ride and whistle by the sign post with a nod.

Less than two hours later a large hilltop figure draws me into the Aileron Roadhouse. It is so stunning and interesting-looking that I cannot ride by. It is only mid-afternoon but an early stop is usually a good stop. I've worked out that days over 500 km are hard and draining of man and machine. 400 km days are better than 500 … and 300 km is better still. This is a 334 km day, so pretty damn ideal. I set up camp and go off to explore and find my way up to the giant figure of the 'Anmatjere Man'. Erected in December 2005, at 17 metres tall and weighing 8 tonne, he strikes an impressive figure, as he overlooks the Aileron Station countryside. It is quite a climb with no clear path and I am pleased to finally get close-up and personal with such an enormous statue. Slender, almost naked, the tall figure holds a spear and is looking contemplatively out over the plains. I don't reach more than halfway up his shins. The sculptor was Mark Egan and it is positioned thus because his mate and sponsor owns the road house and they thought it would look good up there. Subsequently Mark has produced a woman and daughter to complete the family and these are close by the roadside, not necessitating the climb.

The camp is beginning to get a few campers in and I stop to talk to a youngish (the term is relative) couple relaxing in the late afternoon sun, sitting with their green and red parrots. I admire the parrots and also their camping trailer. It is like a 'transformer' toy … only bigger. It expands in various directions, it bends, folds, compartments slide out in surprising places and is an amazing piece of futuristic design. They say it wasn't cheap but they are thrilled with it. There's a really friendly Ocker groundsman who has readied the outdoor fire for later use, and was up for a chat. I was interested to find that an Indian family was running the roadhouse bar and café, and it was a bit incongruous to see the big hand-scrawled sign for the toilets was being held by a sandaled skeleton wearing a toweling sunhat. It boldly proclaimed 'Shithouse' with an arrow. Most of the folk in having a meal were road workers using the place as a base. Outside the Grey Nomads had settled in around the fire and an older woman was belting out tunes on an accordion. It was all very convivial and a little different from most camping experiences. Grey Nomads are universally friendly enough, but come dinner-time they go back to their aluminium capsules for the repast, and then settle in for a night of TV. Most of the older ones still conformed to this pattern, but two unconnected young couples with kids were back at the fire once the littlies were settled. Clearly, it was not often that they got the opportunity for adult conversations with anyone other than their spouse. Accordingly, a nice night unfolded and it was much later than usual before I hit the sack. Being north of Alice Springs, it was appreciably warmer and I was hopeful that the freezing nights were behind me.

Now I am in the Northern Territory, I am seeing the occasional quad-trailer road-train which can be over 50 m long and carry up to 200 tonne. In contrast, the longest combination permitted in NZ is 22 m and 46 tonne.

Needless to say, these behemoths are very impressive in action. They lack acceleration but once up to speed they are relentless and don't like to lose speed by being held up by a tiny irritant such as Penelope and me. A lot travel at night though, as I will observe later on.

We cross back into the tropics. It is the third time I have crossed the Tropic of Capricorn in Australia and I pause at the layby rest area commemorating this line delineating the temperate and tropical zones of the world. There is a bus-load of high school kids on an outing who take a myriad of different iterations of their group and the signage. I lose patience waiting to pose Penelope and ultimately don't bother recording the event. I take advantage of the mobile phone 'hot spot' to check emails and Face Book responses. These hot spots have a square-section steel post cut off about 1500mm from the ground with a sloped ledge for you to put your phone. Looming over you, umbrella-like, is what looks like an upturned satellite dish which is aimed at your phone. Somehow this gives your phone more oomph and you should get reception irrespective of which provider you are with.

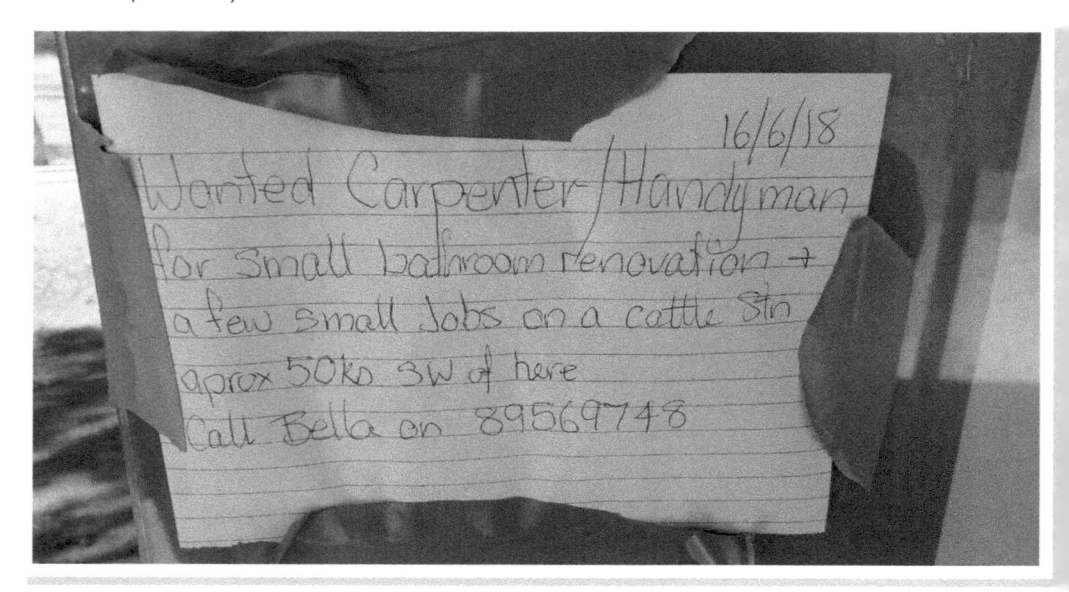

While I am waiting for another outside-world-contact-deprived person to do her thing, I spot a piece of paper taped to another post. It is dated two weeks earlier and is a request for a carpenter/handyman to do a small bathroom renovation and odd jobs on a cattle station 50 km away. I probably lack the skills, so don't ring Bella on 89569748. I hope someone does

Being that it is the only road up the middle of Australia, the road surface is good. There is not a lot happening, or things to see, as I sit patiently, fingers figuratively crossed, making our way snail-like across the map. Now that I can do it, I ride occasionally with my left hand operating the throttle. It is still a hard thing to get your brain to ignore the eyes signals and to work from known physics. If I want to 'adjust' to the right, I must counter-intuitively push the right bar away slightly … and if that is being done by the left hand … so be it! I know a lot of riders in my position have iPods but I haven't found speakers thin enough to fit in my helmet without hurting my ears. Of course, this means that I must entertain myself. I do a lot of reflecting, enjoyably recalling family times and events. I am amazed that it is now over 40 years since Steph and I battled the roads of Central and South America on Penelope. I wish Steph was here behind me sharing the ride. I know that she is always torn … "Go with Des for hot, cold, wet, dry, dusty adventure … or play with the grandkids in Melbourne?" So far Melbourne has been winning but she might still do one 'leg' with me, maybe in the West.

Dan, my Panther man in Darwin is giving me the interesting places to stop and linger at in the Territory. They're mainly pubs and I'd be unlikely to ride by anyway now that I am back in the hot part of the country. Accordingly, my lunch is at The Barrow Creek Hotel. I think Dan knows my style. This is not a salubrious place, it is Northern-Territory-rough, with the partly open-air bar adorned with hats, caps, bottles, bank notes, pennants and other memorabilia from all over the world. I quite like its in-your-face style, knowing that many of the potential passing-trade will be put off. There's no pretences here, and I think they are proud of that. I knock back an ale and nod my greetings to a milling crowd of aboriginals outside before kicking Penelope in the guts and riding on.

Inexorably we inch up the map towards Darwin. It's been a funny old time. I did a posting from Devils Marbles which went AWOL in the aether (again!) and be buggered if I was going to repeat it all. I thought it was a goodie too. I did laugh because the last few settlements have been Optus zones and I am Telstra … so no coverage … but the Northern Territory tourism people have an initiative where you answer a few questions via drop-down menus and you get a very short bit of free internet, and they get info about the demographics of the travellers … age, gender, nationality and reason for stay … simple stuff but NZ was not a nation included. Having the choice of New Caledonia or Nepal, I decided to be an elderly gent from the Himalayas. Maybe my posting went there???

… but that was then, and this is now, back in my subsequent life with a computer to write on and record for posterity the things I'd like you to read. Just like history is primarily written by the victors, usually to make them look good, I'm the one doing the writing, so you get my take on what I see and what I do. The Facebook stuff from the road was just immediate jottings on a cell phone.

I'd stopped during a 350km day for a lunch break of mandarins and muesli bars near a camp where already Grey Nomads were streaming in. I've been told that places in any camp are hard to get if you leave it until the late afternoon. Ringing ahead is also no use as the camps are not interested in reservations, due to a history of subsequent no-shows. I wonder why more don't free-camp as they are usually fully-kitted. It is interesting to see the change in 'type' of traveller on the main road, compared to those on the back-roads. Whilst stretching out, a large helicopter lands nearby. I wander over and find it is doing land-mapping with some pretty fancy recording equipment. They just fly grids and relocate every day. Their mate has arrived with the support truck. They lunch and we share a lot of laughs. They're a jolly crew. Ultimately they finish up and all three climb in for an afternoon session. The engine roars, dust flies, the whirry-bits whir … and nothing happens. It then settles down and the engine shuts down to an idle. The door opens, and land-guy drops to the ground. "They say I am a fat bastard, and too heavy for the chopper!" The engine starts to scream again and soon the helicopter rises from the ground, banks with a nose-down flourish and soon is just a dot in the distance. "Pricks! … now I've got to drive for two hours." Happy as a sandboy, he climbs up into his truck and is off with a cheery toot.

Devils Marbles turned out to be a good and interesting stop for me. The area for tents was immediately at the back of the hotel, and there were quite a few more tents than at my usual stops. I put up my tent at the same time as an attractive young couple from South Australia do. They have two enormous dogs and we converse congenially as we erect our night shelters. Later I join them at an outside table by the pool for drinks etc. Being that this is the only roadhouse for some distance and it is an area of scenic note, there's quite a number in for the night, necessitating sharing of the tables. This is good, as it brings all sorts into contact with each other. There are a couple of plumbers down from Tenant Creek who have tales of tradesman shortages – going 1,000 km to change a tap washer, helicopter flights to distant reserves and stations. They're from my construction world and I enjoy the interactions.

When it got dark my young neighbours slipped away, probably eager to do what the young have always done under the cloak of darkness. Into their spots slid two blokes, one possibly late 30s, the other mid-50s, maybe. The older one is wearing a faded Bell Helmet tee-shirt, so I pick him as probably a motorcyclist, as he doesn't look like a 'branded-clothing' poseur. I ask which way are they heading, and they indicate they are going home south. I ask where, and the older one says "Phillip Island".

"So you've been to some MotoGPs?" I ask, presuming an affirmative. I notice the younger guy smiles knowingly.

"Oh, all of them."

Slowly, I get the back-story. They've just been up to the Darwin round of the Australian Superbike Championship. It seems that the younger guy is a recent rider of note, now managing a team and the older guy is a track commentator. Over a few beers their background is unrolled a little. The rider has raced in NZ several times and the older guy seems to know every rider I mention. I tell them that I had watched the Dutch MotoGP on my cell phone in the middle of the night in my sleeping bag back at Erldunda, courtesy of still having my mate's sign-on password. I comment it was good to see Suzuki getting second as it was ages since they featured on the podium.

"Actually their results haven't been all that bad" the older guy responded and again I couldn't help but notice the knowing grin on the young guy.

I was then told every podium Suzuki had achieved over the last three years. The guy was like an encyclopaedia. Clearly he was a real fan. It soon came out that he was more than that, and had been an official television commentator employed by Dorna (The owners of MotoGP) for some years based in Spain, doing the complete MotoGP circuit every year ... every race. He knew all the riders on a personal basis right up to the current superstars. Man, I was in heaven. I was able to ask about riders and circuits and bikes. He'd even ridden one of the recent MotoGP race bikes. I asked him if any of the riders were 'real dicks', thinking he would name an Italian prima-donna from the early 2000s. Hesitantly he admitted that there were two Aussies he didn't really respect off the track. However, he thought that 'the biggest dick' was also the most talented rider he had ever seen, even better than Valentino Rossi. What a great night!

One last thing of interest about the Devils Marbles Hotel was the sign in the gents' toilets. *Please lift toilet bowl seat if not in use.* I photograph and reflect. I was brought up in a family of four males and it was normal for us to leave the seat up. Mum found it better that way, better than having one of us running in without time to lift the seat and splashing all over it. Steph's family had a preponderance of womenfolk and it was 'seat down' house. I've been retrained her way, and always leave down as a courtesy to the next user ... who might be a lady.

But from the 'Holy Shit' files ... remember our Kitty and her 'What if nothing happens?' ... south of Elliot we had a spectacular rear tyre blow-out.

BANG ... and I was instantly out of my late afternoon state of semi-torpor. Penelope began to wildly fishtail and I hung on and tried desperately to anticipate each violent zig-zagging slew. It may have been at her urging but I shouted out loud "FIGHT ... FIGHT!" ... and fight I did, all the while expecting to hit the seal in a shower of sparks and shredded flesh. We took up most of the road with our see-sawing antics before one last big sideways slide took us onto the left side verge and a shaky-legged halt.

A 4 x 4 had been about to pass us and the open-mouthed driver got out and came to us. "Got any fresh undies?" I greeted him with.

He was really good at just being there, as I slowly calmed down. For some time, I trembled and panted. I could not believe we had got away with it ... pure luck and instinct. Occasionally my new buddy would quietly mutter incredulously about what he had witnessed. We agreed it was a good outcome. We may be marooned again, but we were safe. Of course there was no cell phone coverage and the day was running away.

Interestingly, it took quite a while for me to recall that I had a spare tube, levers and $CO_2$ cartridges. Finally, I fare-welled my support person and set to getting us sorted before dark. Say it quickly and it never sounds too hard ... and yes I managed the tube replacement as dusk arrived ... never long in the tropics.

There was no option but to spend the night there. Apart from being very risky with all the roos and livestock wandering about … our headlight bulb assembly had shaken itself to death earlier. I decided against putting the tent up but moved Penelope over to the edge of the long grass and settled down with her. I covered the reflectors to make us less visible and told myself it was like a long-haul flight to Singapore, but with unlimited leg-room and no passengers to climb over when I wanted stretch my legs.

Actually, it wasn't too bad a night … the stars were fabulous, it wasn't cold, the flies went to sleep and the dingos and the guy from Wolf Creek never found us.

In true Des fashion, I had eaten the last of my cheese and salami that morning and Uncle Toby's finest muesli bars were gone too. I tell myself that in future I must remember not to eat all the emergency rations. I still had 3 mandarins and some tomatoes though.

All through the night, road-trains race through at full speed, all lights-a-blazing. They are the only vehicle that can risk the run. Even cattle beasts are no obstacle for a 140 tonne, 100 kph bull-bar-fronted truck running to a timetable. Every morning there's been a bloody testament to the previous night's carnage. Sometimes there'd be a group of big red kangaroos scattered across a 50 m 'killing field'. Interestingly, a Facebook posting from Jo and Russell in Cairns has the news that their recent short road-trip had them see only one kangaroo … but it had cost them $2,500 in repairs to their car,

So anyway … it is still onwards for us and I reckon I know what our stuttering is. Possibly a sticking exhaust valve. I've had all night to think about it.

After a long night I don't rush away at dawn. There is no way I am going to tempt fate with possible wild-life encounters. What if the omnipotent one isn't in a benevolent mood, what if my cuzzies have stopped putting in good words for me? An average breakfast is subsequently had in the

**THE BIG SIT**

pretty average town of Elliot (pop 330).

A short day follows because I have decided it would be foolish not to overnight at Daly Waters and enjoy the delights of this iconic outback watering hole. So it was that I pulled in the early afternoon, parked under the brilliant pink flowering myrtle tree which grows up through the pub's veranda, and spills over onto the roadway. A photo was taken, then I was dispatched off to the edges to put up my tent. The pub is everything it should be. It is a chaotic gathering place of everyone out and about. It has no glazed windows, it is dusty and everywhere you look there is something of intrigue, from the dead helicopter opposite, to the 'thong' tree with hundreds of rubber sandals nailed to it, to the thousands of business cards, to the hundreds of bras hanging from the ceiling in one room. It is not contrived … it is real, and you just know its history of brawls, murders and cattle stampedes are all true.

There is a duo playing live music. The lady singing is impressive, albeit probably a little too bawdy for the age of her audience early in the evening. The "hands up if you got it last night!" probably went over the heads of the kids running through the large open area, but brought a few laughs and a lot of raised arms. After dining and imbibing to a suitable level I wander through the camper-van area, going the long way back to my tent. To my delight I find the little family I interacted with back in Woomera. They've had a great time, although currently mum is struggling to get Rose, the eldest to complete her homework. A stand-off is underway and dad (why am I so crap at recording names?) and I are happy to sit a little away and yarn like old buddies. I tell him of my night under the stars and he says "Weren't you scared of the Eastern Browns?" He can understand why I didn't put the tent up but notes that he would have at least got inside the collapsed result. He felt I would have been like a nice warm attractant for the venomous brown snakes. I was a little sobered because this was an outdoorsy guy telling me I was naively foolhardy.

Ultimately I head for bed, noticing a slight stagger in my gait.

As before, day follows night and I face more challenges.

*So, possible dramas for the day ...*

- the 30°plus days are too hot for Penelope and her possible sticking valve. Can only be ridden for few hours a day?
- Penelope's petrol tank has started to drip?
- Des has BPV (Benign Positional Vertigo) attack?
- all of the above?

That was the opening of my next electronic missive over the aether to my followers. Of course it ended with:

*And those of you who picked*

- all of the above

... you know me too well.

I should explain a little about the BPV. In the early dawn, I sat up prior to attempting to assuage an old-man's bladder. I immediately fell over sideways in the tent, and quickly came to the realisation that my staggers earlier on had not been fully down to the Great Northern ales I had enthusiastically imbibed. I knew from the previous year's episode what this was, and I was more amused than worried. I crawled out the door of the tent and was a little dismayed to see that my closest aid to standing was a 44 gallon drum about 10 m away. A bit far to crawl, especially now dawn had enlightened the day. I manage to get to my feet and immediately am involuntarily sent off on a blind-drunk's zig-zag to the target drum. I cling to it for a while and try to compose myself. I hope that no one is watching. Finally, I feel ready to let go of my 'crutch' and walk. I tell myself to relax, be calm, look to the horizon ... look where I want to go. It partially works and I stagger off to the toilets, doing a mild-slalom. I hold on to a window cill while doing my business. I am a little lucky that I am over on the fringes of the main camp so I don't have a big audience. Rolling up my tent and getting to my feet again, is still a challenge, but the effects are diminishing.

**THE BIG SIT**

I know there are exercises to lessen the effects but I just can't remember them. I'll work on it. Ultimately I ride off with the challenge of taking it easy ringing in my ears. Meeting the main road and turning my head fully right, brings on the spinning head and I twist the throttle on strongly and trust Penelope to do the rest. I feel a long way from home and just a little vulnerable. I'll give myself a good talking to later on.

Dan has told me not to miss the 'Pink Panther' Larrimah Hotel, so I drop in mid-morning for a coffee. Larrimah is another legendary spot with a population of 11 mainly older characters. There is a campsite and lots of interesting tat scattered everywhere, inside and outside of the pub. Pretty much everything is painted pink and there is indeed a large pink panther seated outside. Penelope poses in the sunshine with her. I have a freshly-baked meat pastie and it was so good I get one to take away. I feel it was a good choice to go to the pub, not the alternative attraction, Fran's Teahouse, which also advertised pies and scones. Subsequently I read about the disappearance of the town's 12th resident a few months back. Paddy Morriarty and his dog have not been seen since leaving the hotel on 16th of Dec. His hat, glasses and part-eaten meal all were found in place in his small house. It seems he was the sworn enemy of Fran, who he lived opposite to. There are other suspects. Fran has a burly, bad-tempered gardener who had recently clashed with Paddy over the dog barking at Fran's customers. There is also an ex-barman from the pub who reputedly was drunk and nasty by lunchtime every day. He was the last to see Paddy. The last suspect is the pub's 'saltie', a crocodile named Sam. It is a mystery with no solution to date.

I press on, replete and reasonably happy ... a bit worn though.

There is an award-winning Irish Travel writer called Geoff Hill who many people like (read between the lines). A few years back he and a mate rode Aussie and wrote a book. In the book there is much angst over whether all the sponsors' stuff ... helmets, jackets, air tickets etc ... would come through in time for the start. More hyped-up concerns relate to whether Triumph would come through with kitted-out bikes, and was the publishing deal locked-in?

Of course, all these things came through otherwise there would be no book. So on brand-new machines they rode the fully-sealed 15,000 km that is Highway 1 around the perimeter of Aus, duly recording their days. I don't recall any concerns whether they would take a $10 camp in near zero temperatures ... or the $185 rooms. They just had a bit of banter ... and another day was done.

So NOTHING HAPPENED!

There are times when I envy those sorts of rides ... but not often, and usually I am back on song pretty quickly. For a brief period today though

I did feel a bit like James Aidie in Richard Thompson's song Vincent Black Lightning 1952 - '... *he was running out of road. He was running out of breath*'. But all is good now, the tent is up, beer and food not too far away.

I paused at Bitter Springs which is a lovely place, but sadly there were too many folk around for me to slip into the warm, sulphurous waters in my under-gruts. My modesty also means I don't have to trust the knowledge that 'freshies' (fresh water crocodile) ... even when eight feet long ($\approx$2.5 m), won't attack. We have adverts at home, which after an ambitious claim, finish with 'Yeah, right!' I also wonder what stops a 'saltie' breeding with a 'freshie'. It is not location, because they do overlap ... and if a 'freshie' is known to take a wallaby, how do I know it won't take a 'wannabee'? It was a pleasant walk around the springs watching the trusting lolloping around in the water with their floatation aids. Noodles anyone??

Nearby, there's a nice camp, with an extensive grassed area to put my tent up in. There's also a pretty good bar and eatery. I am contented and pretty confident. There should only be two more days to Darwin, even in our beleaguered state.

I enjoy some family time with Tom and Kat and their toddler. I'd spotted a 'Cactus' clothing sticker on their van so have to chat. Cactus is a New Zealand company in Christchurch who make rugged clothing from canvas. After years of never being able to afford any of their work pants ... they had a big sale, and now I am a member of the pretty exclusive club. I wear the *Trade-plus Super Trousers* as my every-day riding gear. Their branding is bold and distinctive, a stylised yellow cactus bush in a black circle. The stickers are displayed with pride on work vehicles all over New Zealand. Both Tom and Kat are industrial abseilers, and are in the process of relocating from Melbourne to Darwin for work. They found Cactus when doing a stint of work in NZ and have imported them into Australia as necessary ever since. "There is nothing to match them, mate!" I am told.

I had to laugh during the day's ride when an old guy told me how bad the road was (that we'd both been on) when you're towing a caravan. "The bumps were terrible, it is so hard, taking those hits, and always having to keep the van in the one lane … so much easier for you on a bike!" In their silver, air-conditioned capsules, the Grey Nomads never know if it is 3° or 30° … they never smell the road-kill, the diesel fumes or nature's gifts.

Actually, I am now pining for the dull hearth of home, companionably reading in silence with Steph, waiting for the "Do you fancy a cup of tea and cheese and crackers?"

We surge on with the end in sight, but possibly I am guilty of counting our chickens before they are hatched. Possibly that bloody voyeur upstairs has got sick of watching over us. Our day after Bitter Springs is rudely brought to a premature halt. Bugger … Ignominy! We snatch defeat from the jaws of victory.

The third section of the ride that I have come to call The Big Sit … ends without glory. There will be no cheesy photos on the Darwin waterfront. The Coober Pedy high-tensile screw 'will never fail' repair, fails. A recovery mission is got underway. Not the final end, but the end for this year. Wounds will be licked, plans will be made, modifications carried out … and yes we will be back.

The last few days in the heat have been hard, but I was sure we would make it. I'd pressed on through Katherine knowing we have to go back through there to get to West Australia. Adelaide River was to be my night camp on the recommendation of Dan Leather, my ever-helpful top end advisor. This would leave just a bit over 100 km for an easy Sunday morning canter to the finish line. Disaster struck 40 km short of Adelaide River … all drive was gone … again! Instantly I knew this was the end, and my next worry would be getting off the highway.

I stuck my thumb out at the first 4 x 4 I saw, and to my relief I saw the brake lights go on. Frank and Libby were returning from a short break away camping, and had a trailer on … but fully-filled with a Polaris four-wheeler.

Whilst I was pondering how we could strap Penelope to the trailer and let her run on her back wheel, Frank was muttering to Libby. I saw her hesitate ... then nod.

Frank unloaded the Polaris and we pushed Penelope up the ramp and tied her in. I then took Libby's place in the 4 x 4 and she took my place on the roadside in the 33° heat. She refused my offer of the emergency goodies and last I saw of her she was putting on a wide-brimmed hat and settling down with the water bag. Absolute bloody legends!

Frank is a motorcyclist and felt honour-bound to help the brotherhood. What a wonderful pair. I had been thinking there might be another roadside night ahead but this time fully-scared of Eastern Browns.

So an easy night in the Adelaide River camp followed. An effusively friendly Kiwi, Lucky Te Amo, made us welcome, proffering me a beer, then sorting out a tent site. Meanwhile, Dan was arranging for the final stage of our recovery, to get us to Darwin and Penelope into the QANTAS hanger, the headquarters of The Motor Vehicle Enthusiasts Club. Dan is off-shore with work, so not an easy chore. Amazingly, Dan works some magic from his far-away oil rig and a rescue is arranged.

And what of next year? What if an offer of a sponsored bike à la Geoff Hill came through?

"Aah Nellops, I've got something to say and it is not easy for me. I've been offered a BMW GS1250 for the next section of the ride. She's lovely ... frisky, fast, comfortable, reliable and rearing to go. So sorry old girl but this has to be the parting of the ways. Our day is done."

"What!"

"It's ok, you'll go to a nice home. You'll be cared for, repainted, polished .... you'll get a complete make-over and live in a warm shed under a soft cotton cover. You'll go to shows and rallies in a covered trailer ... no more thudding across barren wastelands. You'll love it."

"You bastard ... you'll give me 'death with dignity'. Now that it is easy, you'll go off with a Teutonic tart with big knockers sticking out the side ... I don't think so! Without me you are nothing ... just a non-entity with a beard. I've taken you to Machu Pichu, I got you across the Chaco Desert ... and The Gobi, the Karakorum. Would your fat German bint have done that? Answer me?? No she wouldn't have ... she'd have turned her nose up at the 72 octane petrol. I'm a working girl ... made in Yorkshire, born to do the hard stuff ... not some poncy princess show-pony. I love the feel of hot oil pulsing through me, I love the chipseal running under my tyres ... I even like the sensation of bugs and beetles splattering on my heaalight.

So get a grip! BMW ... hah ... way above your station. Fix what you have to fix ... and we'll do another chunk next year."

Well, maybe she is right. The London heat-wave 'summer of 76' brought me

**THE BIG SIT**

the dual delights of Steph and Penelope ... both will never be surpassed and cannot be replaced.

I'll let Facebook have the final word.

Probably the last of my missives for a while.

So sometimes you fall on your face ... and sometimes you fall on your feet. In both instances you need to be ready to accept the hand that is dealt you. I've had another winner!

My Darwin sojourn is all but ended. The wonderful Panther world, through Dan Leather, has housed me in sumptuous luxury. This means a bed indoors ... and actually a fridge full of refreshments and a fabulous 5th floor view over a golf course to the sea.

In the 1960s the Tremeloes sang "Even the bad times are good!" Penelope's demise brought this very result. My selected rescuer from Adelaide River has gone way beyond the call of duty. Richard Luxton picked up Penelope, and ultimately delivered her to the QANTAS Hanger in Darwin ... but on the way he showed me around the WW2 Airfield/base that is on what he calls The Farm. Fittingly our mode of transport was a period Willys Jeep. This was fascinating as were all his various 'projects'.

More can be found on http://outbackmag.com.au/runway-revival/

Coincidentally we shared a very similar career pathway as Quantity Surveyors morphing into education etc.

The QANTAS hanger is all I thought it would be ... but so much more. Think of a Men's Shed ... and times it by 50. It is open to the public so the vehicle and machinery collections can be appreciated, but MVEC club members also have work areas. Every type of machinery needed for resto work is there, including a car hoist.

Penelope will be happy there for the next year or so with Dan's three girls, June (met at 2016 SA Rally), Shirley and Helen ... all Panthers and all named

**THE BIG SIT**

*after Yorkshire relatives of his. There is also the makings of 'Marjorie' tucked away on a back shelf.*

*I've taken the cylinder head off to carry home for analysis etc … so my luggage will have a certain 'heft'.*

*Plans will be made for next year … health and wealth willing, so if you are happy for me to intrude again … I'll be back. Meanwhile I have been to the superb museum and art gallery and had my first ever iced long-black.*

*Oh, and I did a phone interview with the Northern Territory Times … or some such worthy publication.*

*Whilst I am pretty proud of our ride so far, and for us it has been just a little bit epic … it is still only an old duffer, sitting on his chuffer … it is not rowing the Tasman or walking the Pacific Crest Trail.*

*Des and Penelope signing off for 2018*

*And a final bit of serendipity. I open my emails and there is one from BRANZ. They are apologetic for the short notice, but could I do a 21-venue seminar series for them starting in 10 days?*

# THE BIG SIT

## CHAPTER SEVEN

# DARWIN

The aftermath of the 2018 leg up to Darwin had brought many emotions into play. Obviously it had been exciting and challenging, yet there was also a small feeling of failure. Yes, we'd done the Birdsville Track and been feted accordingly, but we'd sort of failed hadn't we. I left Penelope looking pretty forlorn in the QANTAS hanger. I sense that this whole Australian adventure has not sat totally well with her. We're 13,500 km in, but it has to be said she has not been the relentlessly reliable old girl that she once was. I've robbed the cylinder head and lug that home with me. Being cast iron, it is very heavy but I am pretty confident that my misfiring is resulting from one valve sticking when hot. Once home, it is left with Roly to research and rectify things. Dan will look at the leaking petrol tank and review its suitability for repair. The rear drive issue needs real thought. The wonderful Panther Owners Club do an exchange service. I am not too shocked by the price of £250 but the freight cost to and from the UK to Australia makes the eyes water. Interestingly their method is cunning and fool-proof. The original sprocket is turned off and a small shoulder left. A left-hand thread is then machined around the outside of the brake drum. Similarly, one is accurately done to the inside of the sprocket you are fitting and you wind it on with some Locktite and it cannot fail as the forward motion would only tighten the sprocket on the drum.

It is good to get home and straight into some meaningful work. For seven weeks I travel the length and breadth of New Zealand pontificating about timber. My co-presenter is again Greg, a well-known architectural designer from Auckland. We've done this sort of thing together before many times. We're chalk and cheese, and maybe that is why it works so well. He plays me as a yokel from hippiedom, whilst I do often reference his pointy-toed Italian shoes and car with the Olympic rings symbol on the front. The money replaces my selfish spend. I am not profligate when away, but I am using money that could be put against our mortgage. For the first couple of legs I was working full-time and in the background I let my freshly-earned old age pension money build up, so each time I was just emptying out my 'personal John Key money'. Since then I have stopped working as a direct-employee and we've had a change of government, so it is now Jacinda who funds these selfish sorties. The intermittent contract work from BRANZ is a bit of a Godsend and not only does the July and August series go well, but we're signed up for another round at the end of the financial year … which actually is locked in as mid-Feb 2019 through to the end of March.

Interestingly, Roly soon reports back that the valves are probably not nipping-up in the guides, but one in particular has very odd clearances and seems to have been installed with tapering insides to the guide which are too loose, rather than too tight. There are signs that the piston may have been 'kissing' the cylinder head. Without all of the engine in one place, a few things have to be guessed at. A full recondition of the head is undertaken. The opportunity is taken to source a few other goodies that we've never managed in the past, like a new cam and timing gear pinions. One of these was fairly worn before I embarked upon my Beijing to Arnhem ride in 2005, but new ones were not available then. Panthers were never made in large volumes and being a small struggling factory did mean it wasn't always trying to change or innovate to the whims of the fashionable young. Their designs often didn't change for a decade or two and many engine components remained the same from the 1930s to their final demise in 1966. Combining this with a strong and active owners' club has meant that most engine spares have now been remanufactured and are available to a level probably as good as many current models.

The period between 2018 and 2019's rides was notable for a slump in my normally buoyant optimism. In tandem my health seemed to take a bit of a dive and energy levels plummeted, a persistent cough couldn't be got on top of, and any cold conditions brought on chest pains when I breathed. My double vision was also markedly worse. Suddenly I felt vulnerable and the continuation of the ride became quite daunting. I had a dead bike in Darwin, I was suffering from age-related enfeeblement and my (brash?) confidence was low. I was having to face up to the fact that my physical capability was lessening. I really was becoming the 'old duffer' that I jokingly portrayed myself as. In contrast Steph remained the archetypal 'Energiser Bunny'. It was as if you wound her up each morning and she charged forth at full-speed until the late afternoon when the batteries slowly wound down and slumberous repose followed. Graciously she never made an issue of this imbalance of energy and consequent domestic productivity.

My cough has been around for four years or so, and various doctors have half-heartedly and unsuccessfully addressed the issue. To be fair to these medical professionals, my cough was never why I was in there. Usually it was just for a routine check-up at the time of pill re-assessment etc. Towards the end of 2018 we decided upon a specific doctor at our medical centre instead of getting whoever was available. Hannah impressed us with her determination to get to the bottom of my intermittent coughing for no real reason. Until 2010 I had a history of rude good health, a lifetime of rarely missing a day of work etc, presumptuously thinking this would go on forever. An unexpected heart attack was a road-bump which did rob me of a lot of oomph and a stent was installed to keep the blood flowing around in the correct volumes, a bit like the main jet in a carburettor is needed to not be blocked or constricted for the engine to run correctly.

Having cameras travel up and down your food's pathway to the sea

… so to speak, is not pleasant, but manageable … an amazing procedure when you think of it. Way back in 1966 there was a movie where they shrunk Raquel Welch to microscopic size and she travelled round some professor's body to fix something. Now-a-days we don't have Raquel, but a tiny camera instead. I just sought an assurance that they went down first, or at least cleaned the equipment thoroughly if they had to do things in the opposite order. The nurse duly smiled at my witticism with the look of one who has been nervously given that advice a hundred times. Of course it could also have been the resigned look of one who assists in shoving cameras up hairy bottoms day after day, dreaming of a job packing shelves in Pak 'n' Save.

The results show I am actually in great health although the blood tests show that my iron levels are way down again.

I've actually been daunted by the task of going back to Darwin and carrying on. I feel I need a wing-man, an oppo, a mate to share the load … and to be there should I need a push. I've had great mates along for some of my previous big rides but somehow I can't settle on a riding buddy for this ride. There is so much compatibility that needs to be factored in. Your off-sider really needs to match or compliment your attributes … and they need to actually like you. Similar levels of resilience are required. You can't have your mate sulking because Penelope is throwing a 'hissy fit' and being recalcitrant. You can't have them demanding food when you are out in the wops and sustenance is hours away, or not to their tastes. Fussy doesn't fit. Nor does cleanliness. This is not home. It is not going to go well if their budget is better than yours, and they want more luxury … or more food … more breaks, more fun. You also want people along that you can yarn to day after day when the riding is done. There has to be quite a bit of commonality. Readers are good … you can have companionable silences, yet also have book and author discussions.

Steph would be ideal and had indicated she would like to do a leg but it won't be this next one because work and family stuff preclude it. She'll see if she can fit in the last leg.

Meanwhile there are other local adventures to fit in. Life is pretty full with lots of things to plan and expedite. Fortunately the iron infusion seems to have brought back the needed vim and vigour. I'd promised my primary-schoolmate Andy that we would re-enact our first full South Island loop done 50 years ago. My 'London Crew' from 1972 were also having another get together. We'd had the first one at our place in 2012 and it had been such a success and so much fun that regular gatherings have followed. This one would be in New Zealand at Chris and Annette's olive grove just out of Akaroa. This would be in early Feb, so I could fit it in just before another stint of BRANZ work.

A busy Christmas period precludes Andy and I getting the timing exact for our ride. There would be no New Year's Eve stumbling around Nelson trying to kiss girls. Family comes first and Steph and I enjoy an extended visit from Kitty from Melbourne with Isaac and wee Nina who at seven months is a delightful blob, happy to grin at all and sundry but not crawl. January flies by and soon Anne from Canada is with us and we're off on a mini-adventure in our 1958 Goliath Combi, which is a little German station waggon. Anne is one of our London crew and we'd shared a huge ride on Ernie the ES2 (1957 500cc Norton) during 1973/1974. Last time she was in NZ I had taken her on my old 1965 BMW on a big back-country ride the length of the South Island. Our plan for this year's treat originally was going to be a sidecar jaunt on Dick's *Last Hurrah* Norton, but tight time-frames (and lack of preparation) count this out. The fall-back is Golly the Goliath and a wonderful few days on some obscure roads and tracks gets us across to the Banks Peninsular and the reunion in Akaroa. Just as huge men are often called 'Tiny', the German-made Goliath … isn't, and we struggled up hills with the three of us aboard, not quite making it up past the Otira Viaduct without boiling. Anne always engenders a sense of being ready for any adventure we can dream up. She and Steph often seem to gang up on me, but deep down there is a feeling we are a tightknit trio having a very special time. We all know it won't be our last exploit together.

With close to 20 of us remembering and reclaiming our youth, lots of inappropriate frivolity follows. Most of us had met (and some married) whilst sailing to the UK on the SS Australis in Jan 1972. We'd all stayed various lengths of time in London. In my case I lingered on until 1977 and along the way met and had been wooed by Steph. After three of the most wonderful days, it was time for Steph and I to leave others to continue the event with walks and bike rides … we both had work to return to. None of the others are currently troubled by being wage slaves anymore, and there seemed to be a few smug smiles as we waved the throng farewell. I fly straight from Christchurch to Hamilton, get a haircut, put on a good shirt and join Greg in telling our construction world about how to detail and construct junctions. At the end of the week I fly back to Christchurch, collect Golly and drive the seven hours home.

Seven weeks later the BRANZ work is done and the morning after, I ride off on the postponed adventure with Andy. I've known Andy since he arrived at St Annes Newtown, as a nine-year-old Pom with a foreign name. In addition to those handicaps, he then had to fight the other 11 boys to see how tough he was, race us all to see how fast he was, and pee against the toilet wall to see if he could threaten Robert Bouzaid's ability to project a stream of urine over into the Girls toilets. He proved to be pretty tough, fairly fast, and no challenge to Robert Bouzaid. We've been mates ever since, starting motorcycling together as fifteen-year-olds on an evenly matched Suzuki 120 and a Triumph Tigress scooter. For our 50-year anniversary ride Andy has imported a 1963 Triumph Tiger 90 from the UK. This is as close as he could get to the original Tiger 100 from the 1969 ride. I do my part by borrowing a 1966 Triumph TR6 from our good and generous friend Simon. It is the civilian version of the police bike I had back then. Andy even entered into the spirit of the ride by buying a tent and sleeping bag. Camping is alien territory for him, and I am impressed.

Our first day ended at the Tahunanui Beach Camp in Nelson and we re-enact a photo taken of us professionally at the time. Tim from the Nelson Evening Mail is along to do this and interview us. Our story is subsequently spread nationwide, via the newspaper portal *Stuff*. In 1969 we were made to feel like pariahs. The camp took our money but wouldn't let us bring our bikes in the gate. We had to camp outside and walk in to use the facilities. This time the camp was welcoming. Circumstances intervene, such that we can't do all of the real ride. A vital bridge has been washed away on the West Coast so we can't do the actual route down through the

Haast Pass. This is such a shame as a lot of the memories and disasters from the time resulted from that part of the ride.

Our week together is companionable and a lot of fun. It was good to discover that we weren't quite as inept as our youthful counterparts. After his one night in Nelson, Andy packs away his tent and always manages indoor nights thereafter. We chuckle often because we both suffer from age-related hearing loss. Andy's necessitates hearing aids, which he can't fit in his crash helmet so once 'hatted up' my only way of communicating is by shouting at the high-end of the decibel scale. We pledge to do a 60-year re-enactment if our bodies hold up. The only downside of our ride is the realisation that my double-vision is now becoming quite intrusive. If Andy rode in front early in the day I would see them as a pair riding side by side. By afternoon there would be one on each side of the road. I always followed the left one.

I've had my glasses adjusted for double-vision twice before over the last eight years, so it is a worry that my sight seems to be degenerating. Accordingly, I book an appointment with my Optometrist in Motueka. On the day, I find she has called in sick and I am referred on to another in a branch in Richmond. It is a lovely day for a ride so this is no inconvenience. My new man measures my double vision as an '11' and he hesitates to just get glasses done to match. He is concerned that there might be cranial reasons instigating these changes. His reticence is resolute and he books me a session with an ophthalmologist. Of course these sorts of things don't happen overnight and by the time I am checked and passed as sound, we're running out of time to get new lenses made before I head back to Australia. The specialist has measured me only as a '10' and says a 5 for each eye will work a treat. To help me out temporally, she cuts a piece of 3M clear-film into a suitable shape, runs it under the tap and sticks it to the right lens of my glasses, telling me it is a 10 and if I look after it, I might get several weeks use from it while I wait for my new glass lenses. It is like a miracle cure. Suddenly there is only one of everything in my vista. I face Australia a lot happier. My self-confidence also has bounced back, and I wonder what that was all about. Of course I don't want someone along with me. It is my ride ... my challenge. Deep down I knew I wouldn't conscript a wingman. There are too many compromises when it is not just your dream.

Meanwhile Roly has found a replacement tank and brake drum among bits and pieces in his magic shed. They belong to *Samantha*, the second Panther of our South American adventure in the 1970s. After a bit of work, they are pronounced sound. I find a big trundle-along suitcase that can take everything and plan the ride. I want to correspond with one of Dan's six-week home-visits so we can play in the hanger together. Despite tinkering with bikes for more than 50 years, I am still a bit of a klutz. I have reached a level of almost-adequacy, but am probably at my best when holding things and offering encouragement. Dan is a ship's engineer, so way more skilful and adept than I'll ever be ... and I'm in his realm so naturally defer to him.

Dan is one of life's natural leaders and he is single-handedly organising a fund-raising event in Darwin involving hot rods and classic bikes. The focus is on men's health and the beneficiary is the Prostate Cancer Foundation. Previously Dan was the main-man behind the *Distinguished Gentlemen's Ride* in the Northern Territory and whilst still a big fan of the event, he is aware that it just doesn't work for them at the time of year that is decreed. The DGR is a world-wide event featuring rides on the same day in over 850 cities, with the resulting funds going to similar charities. The date of the last Saturday in September works for both hemispheres … almost. For Darwin it has been found to be too hot and humid. Consequently, Dan has created a similar 'dress cool' event called *'Cruise for the Cause'.* This is set down for the 7th July 2019 and all going well, we'll have Penelope up and running for the event and I'll head away shortly after for Perth and maybe beyond. Dan hopes to ride with us on *June* for a day or so, then return to his off-shore rig for another stint.

Darwin's winter is delightful, with low humidity and temperatures in the low 30s … although it is quite a bit hotter working on Penelope in the historic 1934 QANTAS hangar. With Dan taking the lead we make steady progress. My myopic role is to hold things, drop things, lose things and forget what order the reassembly is. I had hoped for an end-of-June, mid-week fire-up and we only run a day late. We then do a loop of the route to be followed on the Sunday charity run. It is probably the first time that Darwin has seen two Panthers out together. Similar in many ways, yet clearly different, they look like a mother and daughter pairing.

Dan and I have enjoyed our time in the hanger, but for me it is also such a treat to have mid-winter warmth. Every day it is reliably 30 degrees with a blue sky, and the evenings are a sultry time of relaxation and reflection. There are beers to be drunk, tales to be told and books to be read. Dan's reading matter is of wide and varied interest. I love rooms with big bookcases. First-up I settle for a WW11 history of Darwin. Darwin still has the feel of a frontier town but back in the 1940s it really was an outpost of the still-burgeoning colony of Australia and in particular the empty wilderness of the Northern Territory. Early one evening while it is still light we amuse ourselves by throwing out-of-date lamb pieces off the apartment balcony for the wheeling kites. The kites are amazing, almost always catching the thrown morsels before they reach the ground five floors below. Their speed and quickness of eye, and speed of flight is astonishing. It is a delinquent win-win.

The mild evenings are great and we take in the beach-side night market on one occasion and enjoy the stunning sunset. It is a little too hazy for the elusive green flash. We also get to watch from on-high, out on Dan's outside balcony, the madness that is the night of Territory Day. This is the only place in Australia that still allows the purchase of fireworks. In the lead-up there is a buying frenzy with families often spending $1,000 on fireworks for the five-hour period they are permitted to let them off. The advertising is competitive and cut-throat. These are not the Tom Thumbs or Double Happies of my youth. These are serious fireworks being let off by a population that could be described as 'red-neck'. I also took in a night of speedway racing, something I hadn't seen for 45 years.

Facebook also records -

*Penelope now lives and wants to go out and play. It is a huge thanks to Dan Leather, because without his skills and relentless drive I would still be fumbling about. He even kept his cool when fitting the almost-unfittable pancake-air-filter. Choice expletives were expleted, but nothing thrown. Sea trials are underway. We've been photographed with a local hot rod for the local paper to promote Sunday's ride. Dolly-bird photographer loved the rod and ignored June and Penelope. Funds are steadily trickling in, which is great.*

It had been a busy week for both of us. Dan is relentless in juggling working on Penelope and finalising everything for the ride. I manage to fit in a haircut, which also reinforced my opinions of Darwin as a laid-back, frontier town. I was met at the Star Barbers by the proprietor who was a friend of Dan and his lady-friend Sascha. Joy was well-turned-out and bubbly. She welcomed me with "Would you like a beer … or a whisky?" A wee-bit gob-smacked, I chose a beer and supped appreciatively while I waited my turn for the scissors. I justified it by telling myself it I deserved one after walking two kilometres into town in the hot sun. Was I a special case? Not really, as others coming in behind got the same treatment. It made for a relaxed and convivial atmosphere.

There's a nice morning interlude when I get news from a good friend from our Wellington days. Steph and Judy had trained to be midwives together in the 1980s, subsequently worked together and became firm friends. With her two daughters now adults, Judy has been doing contract work in various spots around Australia for some years. She'd been in Katherine, but when I passed through last year, she'd already moved on to Rockhampton. She was now back in Katherine and I was looking forward to catching up for a couple of days when I pass through. Her text message tells me she is coming to Darwin for a tattoo and I am pressed into coffee duty. As a 'clean-skin', I've not ever actually been inside a tattoo parlour and find it quite intriguing. Judy gets *'Sage-femme'* inked on her upper arm.

**THE BIG SIT**

It is quite appropriate that the literal translation of *wise woman* is the French term for a midwife and Judy had been taken by the phrase when attending an International midwifery conference in Canada. It is great to see her again and as a bonus, we drop-in on another of Steph's old midwife friends, now in Darwin. There's not a lot better than catching up with old friends. I'll be seeing Judy and her tattoo again in a week or so.

There is one episode that doesn't particularly reflect well on either Dan or me. Whilst we've been enjoying a cooling amber ale each evening, there is no way that these are over-indulging 'sessions' ... after all, we are reasonably mature adults. Early in the week Dan had laid out a couple of local experiences for me. We'd go to the Deck-chair Cinema one night and he also wanted to take me to have a meal at a place which specialised in fine wines. These were to be on successive nights. On the night of the 'meal and wine', we'd just got up-town when Dan got a call reminding him of the movie, that night. Clearly, we had got things mixed up, but quickly made our way to the outdoor movie place. This outdoor experience had

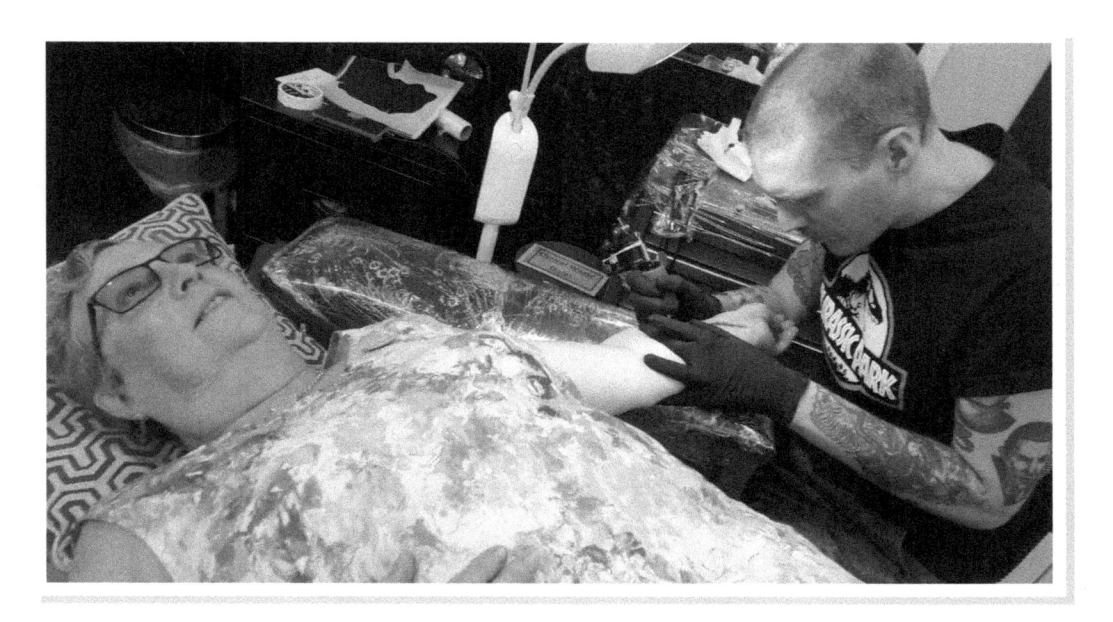

Indian food available and sold wine in the small 'airline' bottles. Both were enjoyed, and in the case of the wine bottles ... enjoyed again. The movie was delayed, so another wee bottle was quaffed while we waited. This went on for some time. The delays were passed off as technical issues that were being addressed. We filled in those delays by steadily chatting and sipping, sipping and chatting. Finally, the technical staff gave up on our evening and refunds were given. This has thrown our plans a bit, with half the night now gone. Dan chats up a Kiwi couple who seem to be heading back across town and they drop us off outside the fine-wine place. I would like to believe that we behaved appropriately, given the sophisticated nature of the place, but Dan's friend Sacha who later relocated us back to Dan's his apartment, later recalled that we were 'silly as chooks'. With our sensibility monitors now well-askew, back at home-base, Dan's finest whisky was brought out to enjoy. It has been a sadness of my adulthood, that I don't like whisky. I would love to be a connoisseur with a mature cellar of Scotland's finest ... but it is not so. However, on this evening of infamy, I join Dan (apparently) on his balcony, not willing to let the night go, and imbibe companionably and enthusiastically.

I awake slowly next morning in a very blurry state. I find Dan with a bandaged hand. It seems that at some stage during our night of immaturity, more ice was needed and during the process of breaking-free some for our glasses, he has stabbed the back of his hand. He is already on pain-killers and has cleaned-up what he describes as an abattoir-like scene. I have no recollection of any of this and am a little chastened by my actions. I am not a habitual big drinker, but know that on this occasion I was a very willing participant. I hope it is a lesson. A little subdued, we carry on with the week's work. I also take the opportunity to buy a new tent as my old one was suffering badly from jammed zips and general wear and tear. The old one was over 20 years' old and had given good service.

Dan and I do a big promo at the hot rod group's 'Chrome bumper' gathering down at the boat club wharf on the Fri night before the ride. This is a regular gathering of a disparate collection of cars in varying stages of modification. I am impressed as this is a real family gathering with several multi-generation cliques enjoyably scoffing fish and chips from the corner shop. I see more long, sleek 1950s Cadillacs than I thought would be in all of Australia. We give out flyers and info relating to the 'cruise'. We've also been putting flyers on motorbike seats through the town, so the word is spreading. Everywhere I go there is a poster. There are now TV adverts playing several times an hour and Dan is very hopeful of a good turn-out on the Sunday. His hand is giving him gyp but he is very resistant to going to get medical treatment.

What an exciting and rewarding day unfolds on the Sunday. The *Cruise for the Cause* brought out all sorts of exotica from the two-wheeled and the four-wheeled worlds. Fortunately, 'everyone's darlings' are different and there was something for everyone … from a WW1-era single-cylinder Triumph to a Chev V8-powered Boss Hoss. The cars ranged from standard Morris Minors to latest V8 convertible Mustangs. There were Trikes, a new three-wheel Morgan with 2 litre vee-twin power (subsequently I ask the mature owner what it is like – "Better than sex!" he tells me) and there were scooters etc. A veritable smorgasbord of sights and sounds. Lots of sharply dressed folk taking advantage of the 30-degree weather. It is one time when maybe it is ok to relax the "All the gear, all the time" motorcyclist's mantra.

At this point in time it looks like probably about $30,000 has been raised for providing a prostate cancer resource for the Northern Territory. The website will remain open to take donations for a few days

I post photos of the day so my Facebook followers can enjoy the sights of the event. It is a wonderful testament to the drive and initiative of Dan who almost single-handedly put this together. It has been a privilege to have been along for the ride. The after-match function was held at the 'Cav' hotel which had participated in the event. I win an award for a breakdown … bit of a jack-up. I'd stopped and replaced a sparkplug part way around. The wind-up is fun and low key with lots of prizes and give-aways handed out. The tropical setting makes this a casual wonderland with flimsy garb and tattoos being de rigueur for the young and beautiful. One barmaid is particularly beguiling. She is blonde and petite, wears office-secretary glasses and from the shoulders up, looks like the girl you'd take home to mum. Most of the rest of her is heavily inked and her torso is only partially covered by a white singlet. Clearly she has neglected to include any underthings in her selection of clothing for the day. As she confidently swoops in and out of the throng delivering drinks and collecting empties, she seems to be in a constant precarious state of being about to have a serious 'wardrobe malfunction'. The experience is captivating. I try not to gawp, but don't always succeed.

Now the event was over, Dan was convinced to let us look at his hand. He'd been toughing it out since mid-week on over-the-counter painkillers and the adrenalin of the moment. He had little confidence in the public hospital so had made an appointment with his own doctor for Tuesday. Sasha and Karyn the Cancer Society representative up from South Australia, urge him to get immediate help as the swelling is quite alarming. He is still resistant, saying he can endure it until Tuesday. A convivial evening meal is had with Karyn and the success of the day well and truly toasted. During the night the pain finally becomes too much for Dan, and in the middle of

**THE BIG SIT**

the night, early Monday morning he checks himself into the local hospital, leaving me a note advising me of his whereabouts.

Bureaucracy is always a big challenge on a ride like this. As noted earlier being as this was to be several years of rides, Penelope had become an Aussie. She happily had run on Victorian 'club plates' for the previous years of the adventure. Somewhere along the way, this year we failed to renew the VicRoads levy in the period while I was away home in NZ, living my other life. We did the club fees, but missed the vital one. No real problem … you just have to re-do the 'Road-safe'. The small issue being you need to be in Victoria to do this. So the only option was for Penelope to now become a Northern Territory resident. This meant she had to be 'sold' again this time from Joseph to Dan. A safety check was done but the NT 'club plate' regime is completely different from the Victorian one, and it doesn't allow interstate travel and the club, that I have joined so I could use the hanger, has a 5,000 km limit for the year – and you must go on 4 club runs. This meant that instead of 'club plates', the full bike registration had to be obtained. For six months this is more than two weeks of money from Jacinda – including her winter supplement. Reluctantly I paid over this money and resolved to live two weeks longer. My rationale being that if the joy of the ride gives me that fortnight extension, the rego has been free.

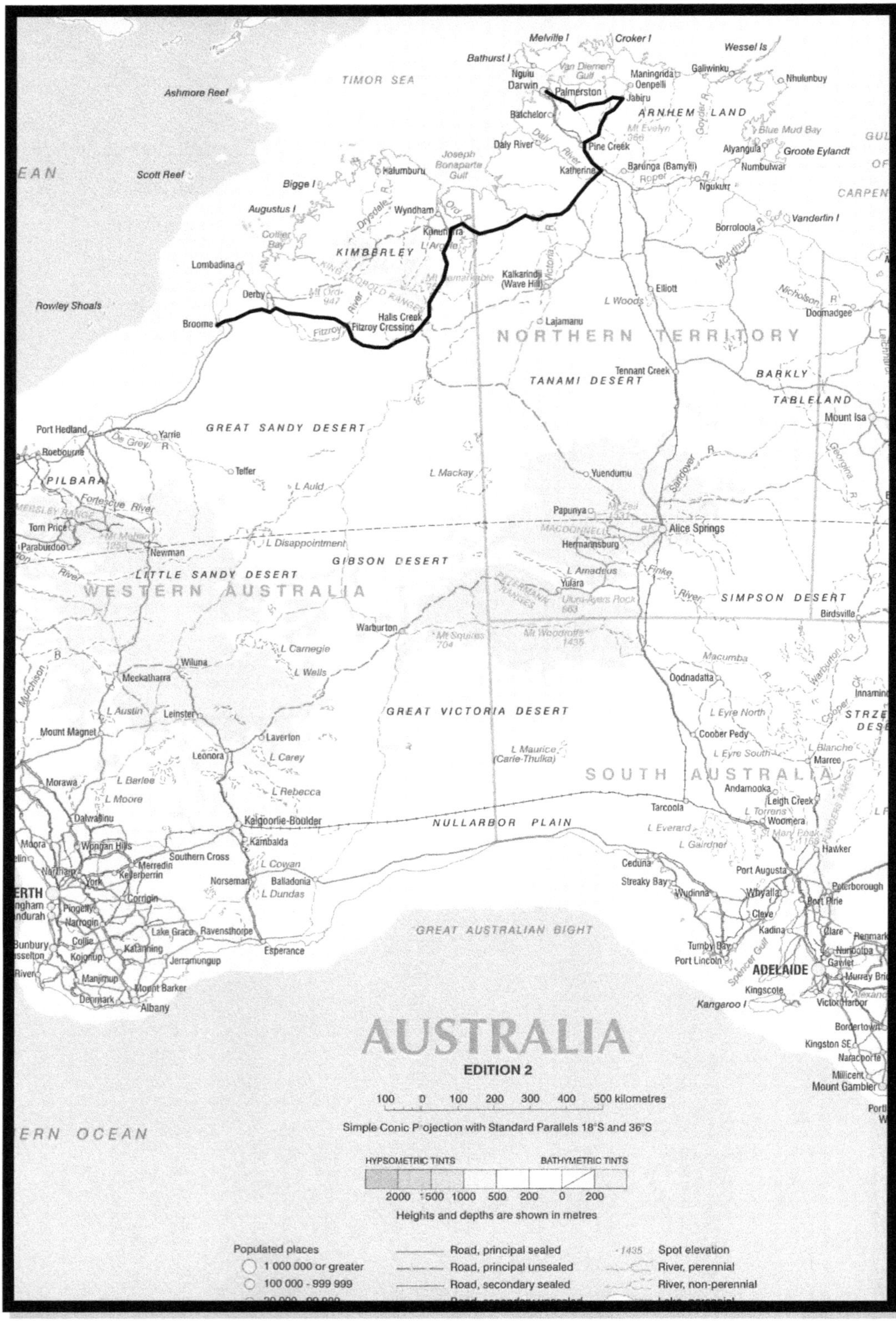

Melville I
Croker I
Wessel Is
Bathurst I
Nguiu
Darwin
Van Diemen Gulf
Maningrida
Galiwinku
Nhulunbuy
Palmerston
Oenpelli
Jabiru
TIMOR SEA
Ashmore Reef
ARNHEM LAND
Batchelor
Mt Evelyn 366
Blue Mud Bay
Daly River
Pine Creek
Alyangula
Groote Eylandt
Joseph Bonaparte Gulf
Katherine
Barunga (Bamyili)
Numbulwar
Scott Reef
Kalumburu
Roper
Ngukurr
Bigge I
Augustus I
Wyndham
Drysdale R.
Ord R.
Borroloola
Vanderlin I
Kununurra
Collier Bay
KIMBERLEY
Lombadina
Kalkarindji (Wave Hill)
Victoria
Elliott
Derby
Mt Ord 947
Rowley Shoals
Halls Creek
L Woods
Nicholson R.
Doomadgee
Broome
Fitzroy Crossing
Fitzroy
Lajamanu
NORTHERN TERRITORY
Tennant Creek
BARKLY
TANAMI DESERT
TABLELAND
Mount Isa
Port Hedland
Yarrie
GREAT SANDY DESERT
De Grey R.
Roebourne
Telfer
L Mackay
Yuendumu
PILBARA
L Auld
Fortescue River
Papunya
Tom Price
Alice Springs
Paraburdoo
Mt Meharry 1253
MACDONNELL RA
Newman
L Disappointment
Hermannsburg
LITTLE SANDY DESERT
GIBSON DESERT
L Amadeus
Finke
WESTERN AUSTRALIA
Yulara
River
SIMPSON DESERT
Uluru-Ayers Rock 863
Birdsville
Warburton
Mt Squires 704
Mt Woodroffe 1435
L Carnegie
Macumba
Wiluna
L Wells
Meekatharra
Murchison
Oodnadatta
L Austin
Leinster
GREAT VICTORIA DESERT
L Eyre North
Mount Magnet
Laverton
Coober Pedy
L Carey
L Maurice (Carie-Thulka)
L Eyre South
L Blanche
Leonora
Marree
SOUTH AUSTRALIA
Morawa
L Barlee
L Rebecca
Andamooka
L Moore
Leigh Creek
Dalwallinu
Tarcoola
L Torrens
Woomera
Kalgoorlie-Boulder
NULLARBOR PLAIN
L Everard
Moora
Kambalda
L Gairdner
Hawker
Wongan Hills
Southern Cross
L Cowan
Ceduna
Merredin
Kellerberrin
Port Augusta
Northam
York
Norseman
Balladonia
Streaky Bay
Wudinna
Whyalla
Peterborough
L Dundas
Corrigin
Port Pirie
Pingelly
Narrogin
Cleve
Lake Grace
Ravensthorpe
GREAT AUSTRALIAN BIGHT
Kadina
Clare
Renmark
Collie
Katanning
Esperance
Tumby Bay
Nuriootpa
Bunbury
Kojonup
Jerramungup
Port Lincoln
Spencer Gulf
Gawler
Manjimup
ADELAIDE
Mount Barker
Kingscote
Murray Bridge
Denmark
Albany
Kangaroo I
Victor Harbor
Bordertown
AUSTRALIA
EDITION 2
Kingston SE
Naracoorte
Millicent
Mount Gambier
100 0 100 200 300 400 500 kilometres
Simple Conic Projection with Standard Parallels 18°S and 36°S
HYPSOMETRIC TINTS
BATHYMETRIC TINTS
2000 1500 1000 500 200 0 200
Heights and depths are shown in metres
Populated places
1 000 000 or greater
100 000 - 999 999
Road, principal sealed
Road, principal unsealed
Road, secondary sealed
1435 Spot elevation
River, perennial
River, non-perennial

CHAPTER EIGHT

# DARWIN TO BROOME

Remembering to slather my snout with an unguent to protect from the scorching sun, finally it is time to go … for Penelope to stop being a show pony, and get back to her core role as a working girl, slogging her way around this huge continent. We said goodbye to the QANTAS Hanger where she has rested for a year. Then it was off to farewell Dan in the hospital. This was a bitter-sweet moment as we'd always thought Dan and *June* would ride 'a ways' with us … two Panthers gloriously thudding along in their inimitable way. His wound was serious and intervention was only just in time. He'd needed surgery and would be required to stay for a couple more days.

An interesting anecdote resulted from this time. Back in Wellington, Roly had Google switched on and I must have as well. He saw that I was at Darwin Hospital and urgently messaged me, asking if I was ok. Big Brother, truly is watching us, although in this case it is little brother too.

Just getting to Dan had seen a minor gear failure. Oddly, all the straps on my hydro pack had failed. They had just rotted and with a little stretching on the ride, they just broke. I was sent off to a camping store on my way to Kakadu … shouldn't be hard to find.

Only slightly geographically misplaced, I then suffered the moment all motorcyclists hate. The snapping of a clutch cable is never the highlight of your day. Nor is discovering you don't have a direct replacement. Several hours were spent modifying a brake cable sufficiently for it to work. It was of course extremely hot with no shade, and I could have done without the challenge. A small file, a brass abutment adjuster and uncharacteristic patience sees the job done successfully. I am quietly proud ... another small hurdle, hurdled.

Ultimately, we regain the highway with a new hydro pack wrapping around me like a Koala, but time has wreaked havoc with plans for the day. We do stop however for a late lunch at the Humptydoo Hotel. I kid you not ... that is the name of the settlement. I'd be honoured to live in such a place, just as son Joe wishes he lived in the Melbourne suburb of Batman. It is the little things that amuse.

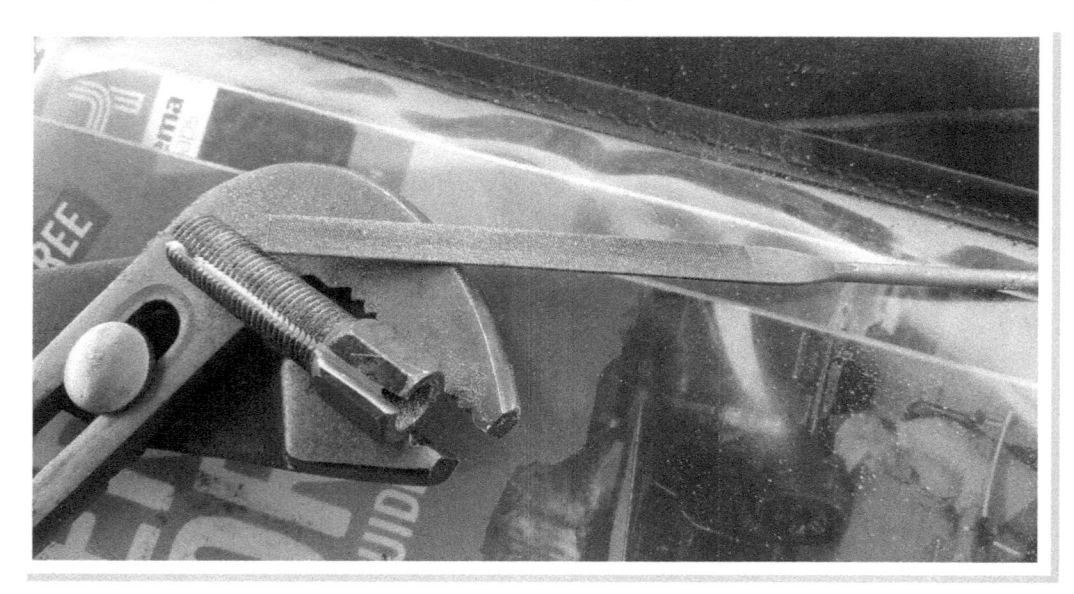

In the mid-afternoon we begin to suffer from last year's malaise. The bloody heat-induced stutter is back. The new carburettor and the reconditioned cylinder head have not cured it. Mind you, the temperature is uncomfortably in the 30s and there is no shade over the road. I am longing for some cooler riding. So with only 100 km beneath our wheels, I put up the new tent and called the day quits. Tomorrow we will aim for Cooinda, the gateway to the famous Kakadu National park. One small thing has been annoying me for most of the day. There seems to be no regulation or restriction on advertising hoardings. Overly large and intrusive signage is common, even in semi-remote areas. It is like being in the US with huge signs being 'right in your face'. This is not something that I have noticed elsewhere. I know that in NZ you are usually restricted to a 1 m2 sign at right-angles to the road … at your place of business. The visual pollution upset me as the ride had been quite charming otherwise – verdant and interesting.

A Facebook posting a couple of days later keeps my fans up to date.

*Just a short post tonight, with not very good coverage, so may not work at all. Another scorchio day, again with Penelope complaining after a couple of hours. The roads are straight and pretty dull. Maybe I should have stopped and photographed crocodile warning signs, but there'll be more of those. At a pause at Mary River, I met Bob and Sharon on their motos … taking 12 months to do their third circle of Oz. Bob rode a BMW 1600 which tows a camping trailer. Sharon a mid-weight Honda. Needless to say nothing was 'strapped on'. I envy them this resolve but have no desire to swap my life across to one of their behemoths.*

*I had a thought today that maybe Penelope's timing might be a bit advanced, so reasoned I would slip the relevant pinion around one tooth. Of course nothing is simple when you are a bit of a klutz. I eased out the middle timing pinion … and the magnets in the alternator immediately moved the magneto pinion … so now I have no real idea where things are timing-wise. We'll just have to try it and see how she goes. Then when stitching her up, I broke a through-stud. I sometimes wonder … " Have I always been this inept … or have I grown into it?"*

*Nice beer and pizza at Cooinda with hundreds of campers. I dunno how they get here because I have hardly seen any cars all day. Tomorrow is a dawn cruise through Kakadu. Will take photos!*

The through-stud passes from one side of the engine to the other but importantly it corresponds with an oilway. Without a replacement Penelope will almost certainly pulse oil to the outside. Go-to man Dan is instantly on-board. He's out of hospital and not quite yet away for another stint at sea. He'll rob June of the relevant piece and come to me forthwith. As I said before … he is a legend!

Later I send out to the Panther world a further request for assistance. *OK Panther folk, I am about to reset the timing. Penelope has an electronic BTH mag so no points. BTH suggest knocking back a few degrees due to their spark characteristics. But what figure do I use? I think the Nicholson figure of 5/8" has been discredited. I have a figure of 33 degrees in my memory. Does that sound right? Mag pinion has 50 teeth for the 360 degrees so a degree calculation is probably easier for me than a down-the-hole one. Meanwhile, I've just had stunning dawn cruise in Kakadu.*

Well, … and I think I have told you this before … my mum in her declining years had a mantra of *'every day above ground is a bonus'*. I was a bit disappointed in myself yesterday, turning a pretty simple task into a minor disaster. But instead of being maudlin and too reflective, I took the dawn trip at Yellow River in the Kakadu National Park. This was ab-fab, so to speak. As well as huge 'salties' we saw a large number of exotic birds in their habitat. Kakadu is half the size of Switzerland and the rangers don't interfere with the course of nature. I know so much more than I did yesterday, although I do suffer a bit from 'one in, one out' so possibly no longer know the way home. We saw sea eagles, whistling ducks, brolgas with 3m wingspan, blue-necked Kookaburras, all sorts of egrets and storks, kingfishers, darters, etc. What a day!

Of course there were also humans with camera lenses half a meter long. The first croc we saw, just slid away under the water and the guide said "We won't wait around … crocs can stay under for two to five hours." There was a dead cattle beast on the bank and a big croc had taken up

**THE BIG SIT**

MAG LOCKED AT FIRING POINT @ FULL ADVANCE

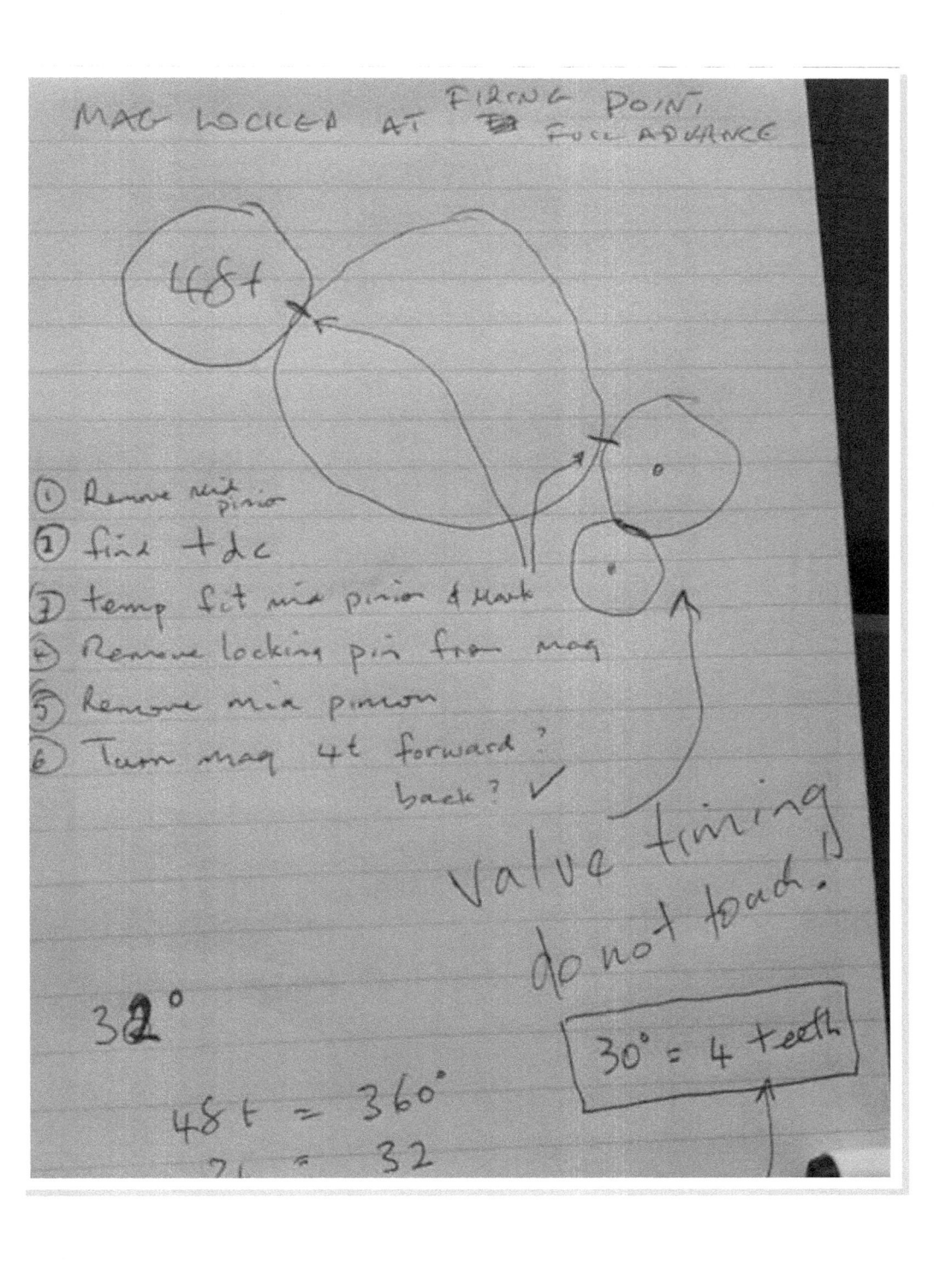

[Diagram of gears: large circle labeled "48t" meshing with larger gear, meshing with two small circles]

① Remove mid pinion
② find tdc
③ temp fit mid pinion & mark
④ Remove locking pin from mag
⑤ Remove mid pinion
⑥ Turn mag 4t forward?
        back? ✓

Valve timing
do not touch.

32°

48t = 360°
 1t = 32

30° = 4 teeth

guard, not looking to share. The only predators for crocodiles, are other crocodiles.

After an amazing time, we were brought back to a cooked breakfast. I briefly envy the owners of the monster cameras, knowing my pictures are cell phone standard. National Geographic, the internet and any number of other sources can let you know how stunning this UNESCO World Heritage park is. Just trust me, this is a world-class experience.

So back to Penelope. My heat-addled brain tried to work out how to set the timing just by moving pinions around. Those with technical expertise will soon spot the flaw in my logic. So I failed to re-time her. Meanwhile Dan Leather and Sasha were rushing to my rescue with a replacement for the broken through-stud. Being as they were in Dan's ute, it was decided that while they were out and about, they may as well get me the 150 km across to Katherine. This was enjoyably done with a stop for a welcome libation at the Lazy Lizard Tavern in Pine Creek. There was considerable jollity to the whole ride. Penelope and the Northern Territory did not seem to be gelling and I was increasingly looking like a world-class plonker. I resolved that once at Judy's place I would re-approach the task of setting the timing slowly and methodically ... yeah, right!

Dan reported to the Panther Facebook followers –

*Operation "Fetch D J Molloy, Northern Territory has beaten Penelope Rev2".... So a quick shoot out to Cooinda to fetch Desmond Joseph Molloy, now in Pine Creek at the pub. Gave him a part from June, will drop him into Katherine. Then we will drive back up to Darwin tonight as have to be at Airport at 4am tomorrow ... about a 700 km trip to keep the Penelope adventures alive ... I should really confiscate her, being her new owner and all ... technically ... technically.*

A few days later, I reflect. 'Well, never has so much time been spent by one man, to achieve so little. Setting the ignition timing on Penelope, should not really be all that hard. Yes, there are a few things that a doddery old duffer can get wrong ... but hey, an iterative process should ultimately get the right result. At least today I have had a shady spot on some paving at the back of the farmhouse our old friend Judy Hart shares while midwifing in Katherine.'

So after taking Judy to work in the pre-dawn cool, I sourced a nice coffee and toastie. No point working on an empty stomach.

Because there are no points in the electronic magneto, there is nothing to look at or check before stitching the engine up to test your handiwork. Well today I seemed to be chasing my tail, doing things over and over ... then getting not a peep from the old girl. This was severely challenging my patience and sanity. My calculations relating to pinion teeth and rotation (carefully drawn on a notebook page) seemed to also match the 'down-the-hole' measurement of 11mm. I was sure everthing was done right, but my efforts were rewarded by a resolute lack of response from Penelope.

It has often been said that the gender I currently represent, doesn't read instructions. I have a beard and just 'know things', so a quick perusal of the download from BTH was enough to ascertain that there is a hole under the generator which you put the supplied rod into, to find a corresponding locating hole in the spindle. This sets the 'advance'. Everything I did, seemed to match logic, yet the continued silence was deafening.

Late in the day, I read the instruction before the one telling me to put the rod in the aligning holes. That instruction told me to face the arrow on the end of the spindle downwards. Of course, this meant pulling the magneto fully out to find aforementioned arrow on the spindle-end. Sure enough, when I squinted … with my glasses off, I could determine an *upward* arrow. My efforts have been 180 degrees out – close but no cigar.

So now all is well, and some sort of normality resumed. Tomorrow will be a Katherine leisure day where I hope to catch up with one of Dan Leather's old-bike mates who actually accosted me this morning at the market when he spotted the Panther tee-shirt.'

**THE BIG SIT**

It is another nice early start to the day in Katherine (pop about 6,500). After dropping Judy at work, I again enjoyed a coffee and toastie from the Black Russian coffee cart before going for a walk down by the notorious Katherine River. I am always amazed that in Australia you really do encounter Kangaroos and Wallabies when you take a bush walk. It is like being in the National Geographic TV channel. Whilst down at the river I chatted with a Darwin couple (he was actually from Gisborne NZ, but you know what I mean) who were fishing for barramundi. We had a chuckle over the catch size rules. You can only take fish bigger than 550 mm and smaller than 900 mm. The reason for the cut-off at 900 mm is because that is about the size the males change sex and become female. Bigger females carry more eggs so are protected.

And 'notorious'? On Australia Day 1998 the river topped 20.3 m and inundated the town causing mass evacuations and huge destruction. In 2016 it went pretty close again.

I spent the rest of the morning in the fascinating museum, learning about the floods, Russian peanut farmers, the flying doctor that the flying doctor service wouldn't take ... because he could and did fly, the first European woman explorer, local indigenous mine workers going on strike ... for nine years! Sadly, I learnt in the NT paper that the existence if this gem is threatened because of funding shortfalls. I hope not, museums are important.

I then took Penelope for a gallop, and visited the newly-set-up Men's Shed. Here I met several Brians and Barrys but no Bruces. John Price, the fellow old-bike enthusiast friend of Dan's, hosted me and a good time was had. They have the makings of a great group with good equipment and enthusiasm.

Lastly, I joined Judy, and Nancy, whose farmlet I am camping on, and Nancy's friend Lynda from Freemantle, in a convivial meal at the local golf club. Tomorrow it is back on the road. No more luxuries ... it is time to walk the talk. I don't think it has ever been said that I am a quick learner … but more of that later.

It was delightfully cool in Katherine when I loaded up and hit the road. Penelope was positively frisky and needed a firm hand to stop her running away up over the 100 kph mark. A lot of the ride was Aussie-dull, scrubby trees as far as your eyesight allows … then we neared Victoria River after about 200 km and the surrounding landmass became interesting and visually stunning, even the road undulated and gently curved and swerved. A refreshing beer and a corned beef sandwich made me like the place even more.

You might think that with us not venturing over 100 kph and the NT speed limit being 130 kph, we would be a mobile road-block. Not so, even though it is SH1, sometimes our mirrors stayed empty for an hour at a time.

And today's lesson? In 2005 in the Gobi Desert of Mongolia, the flange on one of Penelope's exhaust pipes fractured. Wise old mechanic Dick Huurdeman, upon learning it was made of chromed stainless steel, gave me a right reaming out because I should have known it heat-hardened and became brittle. A discarded tin can was found and cut to shape to block the port. This happily worked for the next long while, as whilst there are two exhausts on Penelope, the gas comes out past only one valve before bifurcating. The performance seemed to be the same irrespective of whether you are running two exhausts or just the one.

Years later I sourced a replacement pipe from the same company who made the original *Last Hurrah* ones – an Aussie firm with reputation of nothing fitting first-up. I like the look of the twin front pipes sweeping away from the inclined cylinder. So this afternoon, about 14,000 km into my circumbulation of this big red continent … the ferking same thing happened. Now Dick has passed, but I still felt his ire, and amazement that I could be so stupid. I couldn't tell if he was looking down on me … or up via a periscope ... but he was there. I promise that when and if Penelope gets a make-over ... her pipes will be mild steel.

Of course, it was now hot and the flies found me after 15 seconds. I still have no idea what they do whilst waiting for soft, sweaty, white flesh to turn up. A discarded beer can was soon found and a similar operation to 14 years ago was carried out and the journey resumed. Just as I reached Timber Creek, I mused "I wonder how long an aluminium can lid will last in the fire of an exhaust port?" Instantly my question was answered with a flaming roar. 50 km was the answer.

So a non-aluminium can of peaches was sourced, the contents eaten and blanking discs inserted against the exhaust port, before winding up tight the screwed-on manifold nut. I have used both top and bottom of the can, so am pretty confident going forward. The wired-up non-used exhaust looks pretty odd, but the gases happily exhaust ok down the one pipe into the one silencer. Tomorrow we reach West Australia, so my mandarins have to be eaten. Bevan, a Panther owner in Kununarra, will be hosting me. I think we are both quite excited about this.

July 17 2019

    Victoria ... tick
    South Australia ... tick
    New South Wales ... tick
    Australian Capital Territories ... tick
    Queensland ... tick
    Northern Territory ... tick
    Western Australia ... tick

Woop, woop, we've made it to the big long state and have been given 1.5 hours back for doing so. My day started by eating my remaining mandarins as all fruit as well as honey can't cross into WA. It was good seeing people giving away stuff to people travelling East. Then getting my coffee from the hotel, I had another 'small world' encounter with Billie from the South Wairarapa, an area we lived in for 12 years. Of course we had mutual friends.

With only 250 km to travel, I gave myself a couple of reading breaks. At one, Frank and Grace from Wangaratta asked if I would like a ham, cheese, tomato and lettuce sandwich ... in fresh bread. Magic! They were both motorcyclists, with scars to prove it – also friends of the legendary Ken Lucas (owner of about 60 classic British race bikes, and still racing at 87). I enjoyed telling them that my old mate Dick had also been a buddy of Ken's and had earned undying gratitude when he'd sorted out tuning issues with Ken's racing Douglas.

I ducked in to an aboriginal community which advertised a general store but it wasn't open and the settlement was largely deserted. Under the shade shelter on the main road, I crack open a box of Arnold's Farm Snack bars – lovingly crafted since 1983 ... and am incensed to find the box to be 30% taller than the packaged bar ... then the unpackaged bar a good 25% smaller again. The actual bar is no more than half the height of the box. My calculations show that the box of six could actually contain 20 bars, given the size of them. No such false-advertising with the mandarin.

And late afternoon I found my man. The Panther family is wide spread and amazingly welcoming. Bevan and Bernice Spackman own the Kununarra IGA grocery store, in which a 1910 Douglas motorcycle hangs above the potatoes. Adding to the theme, in their tavern next door another four classics sit up high, behind the bar. Bevan's first bike was a mid-1950s Panther 350 and in later years he always wanted to find another. He looked in vain for a decade or so. Bernice was more successful and had a 'finder' locate one in NSW. Secretly, she had it restored and presented it to Bevan on his 70th birthday. What a woman!

We had a great night at their rural property with 1500 mango trees. It backs onto a river and a large wading bird visited at dusk. I was indoors in sumptuous luxury … didn't even unload anything. Bevan's back garage is the ubiquitous treasure trove of classics. In addition to the Panther, there is a 'modern' (from the late 1980s) Matchless G80 with less than 50 km on the clock. There is also a WW11 Jeep and a couple of vintage

Indian and Harley Davidsons with sidecars, a Chinese Chang Jiang, and a modern Harley, that they have ridden in the US. The front garage, houses the Cadillac that Bevan had bought Bernice and the big four by four that he drives.

What a change! Dawn in NT is about 7.00 am. Over the line in WA it is 5.30 am. Same sun ... it is only me who is confused. Smarter-than-me smart phone knew to change. After my luxurious night indoors, I had a simple brekky, farewelled Bernice and went back into Kununarra to fuel up and see Bevan, who had met contractors on site at 6.00 am.

Kununarra is a bit of a surprise in that it is a green oasis, and has some substance to it. It has a normal population of about 5,000, which does swell a bit in the winter, making it the biggest town between Broome and Katherine. The indeginous people make up nearly 25% of the population and 75% of the population were born in Australia. It is remote, being 3,000 km from Perth and the Spackmans' tales of stocking their businesses makes me appreciate the logistical demands that remoteness brings. Every Friday a truck and trailer with two drivers onboard sets off from Perth, driving

**THE BIG SIT**

non-stop northwards. They reach Kununarra on Sunday and rest that day and Monday while everything is unloaded. They then set off south on Tuesday, usually with no back-load … to start the process off again on Friday. It is understandable that everything has a premium on it in these areas and I appreciate more the reasons for the higher prices and non-availability of some items. The town is inland but on the Ord River that flows from Lake Argyle which was formed in 1971 by damming to enable irrigation to the surrounding countryside. A lake of 1,000 square kilometres resulted and the area began to flourish.

It was still reasonably early when I headed out of town aiming westwards and then southwards, hoping to make the holiday park at the turn-off to the Bungle Bungles. The day went well with a few rest stops, where quite interesting folk were interacted with. Penelope is such a conversation starter … even if she says nothing. One guy today asked if she was retro … or the real thing! One gas station was notable for having a 'live' cane toad disposal unit. Most people in Queensland and the Northern Territory are happy to inflict as much pain and suffering on this scourge as they can. Destroying them with the ride-on mower seems to be popular. This facility however promised to collect and humanely euthanise on Mondays and Fridays. Cane toads were introduced from the Hawaii in the 1930s to control a cane beetle. Of course, they were unsuccessful because the beetle tends to inhabit the sugar cane quite high up … and the toads are poor climbers and can't jump high enough to be effective. They have poisonous hides and have very few predators in Australia that worry them, unlike in the US where the caiman (small crocodile-like reptile) seem to love them and keep the numbers in check. There are now thought to be over 200,000,000 cane toads wreaking havoc on the eco-system of Australia's tropical areas, expanding their domain by about 50 km per year, seemingly unable to be checked. They'd reached Lake Argyle in the summer of 2009 and already are a huge problem.

The Bungle Bungles Caravan Park at Mabel Downs Station was barren. I had to choose between shade or grass. Shade won, so I take a site on a dusty red, stony patch with the other poor. Powered-site folk are a step up, possibly envied by some but not us.

The dirt road in to the Bungle Bungles is 57 km of corrugations. I had been advised against taking it and fleetingly considered taking a tour, till I was told it included two meals, two walks and cost $350. If I don't hook up with someone tonight we will just slowly make our way there … it can't be worse than the Roxby Downs road of last year … can it? The camp has also pissed me off as there is only one working washing machine, and a lot of laundry bags in front of me.

I suppose I can't have everything my own way. Just another day on the road of life. A day or so later I told my FB followers –

*Well the Bungle Bungles were almost a complete bungle on my part. Several folk had told me that the road was just too rough, too corrugated for us to take. Not always a good conversation-starter, as I hate others presuming our level of competence. Being as the only transport in was the $350 tour, I was in a quandary and in the absence of finding anyone taking their own vehicle in, I decided that I would gently have a go. After all it was only 57 km plus 15 km each way from the information centre to points of major interest … shiite …. that could mean 175 km or more.*

*Anyway I went off to sleep on it, disturbing a kangaroo on my way to the tent. He bounded off at high speed, not pausing at the barbed-wire fence and I last saw him racing past the helicopters. Amazing night time agility.*

*My boldness in the morning was short-lived. I laughingly told Adam and Laura, a nice couple going the long way round from Perth to Melbourne, that I might see them in half an hour. I soon found that the endless corrugations stretched full-width across the road and were constant. There was no letting up and the hammering of Penelope's steering-head bearings was too much to bear. There was no speed that I could find to smooth them out. Reluctantly,* defeated, I returned to camp. The nay-sayers were right. Don't you hate it when that happens!

Back in camp by the helicopters, I went off to try to get my laundry done and investigate a chopper flight. Initially it looked good as there was one flight looking for a third person. My initial joy was then tempered by basically being told I was too fat. You are weighed boots and all of course, and an accurate knowledge of the payload is vital.

Laundry was started and the kindle opened. Inspector Lynley and Havers still hadn't solved things, but things were unfolding. Whilst engrossed in this day of immobility. the office staff came over to say there was a seat at 11.00 and it would be $275.

So I didn't miss the Bungle Bungles after all. They were only brought into European consciousness in the late 1980s when they were discovered by a film crew. The area achieved World Heritage status in 2003. Sitting in the open front seat of a wee Robinson helicopter was wonderful. Less great was my phone being put in a plastic bag with a lanyard. This did mean it wasn't torn from my hands as we scooted along at 180 kph ... but the photos were not great.

There was one further irritation related to getting my washing done. Finally complete and 'hung out' over the fence beside my tent, I was subsequently and brusquely told to remove it all as it could be sucked up into a helicopter rotor possibly causing a catastrophic event. Of course they are right and I sullenly comply.

I know I should have bitten the bullet and taken the big 4 x 4 bus in and enjoyed the delights of the park, but I felt I needed to push on a bit, as days and days had been lost in Darwin and Katherine. I told myself that the aerial view would suffice … after all I'd got stunning views of the magnificent rock formations and the surrounding countryside.

The Bungle Bungles holiday park is a 'station camp' and whilst they provide a good two-course evening meal, there is no other food sold on site. The office does sell ice creams but that is all. So it was lucky I had my stock of mandarins and muesli bars. The station is over 750,000 acres in size and will shortly start their annual cattle muster. This will involve a team of helicopters, four-wheelers and horses.

A long, hot day followed. I foolishly dallied by the coffee machine with Inspector Lynley and Havers, and felt it was more important to be with them, as they sorted out a convoluted non-suicide, than it was to hit the road. This was a bit of a mistake. I've also met a few nice people and farewelling took a while.

Contrary to my cousin Pat's concerns about us getting stuck in the Halls Creek Hotel 100 km down the road, I dined and dashed from there safely. Leaving the Kimberley area meant leaving interesting long-range vistas. The horizons flattened and the ride again became interminably dull, and hotter than Hades. The air sitting above the tar was baking hot, and riding through it was like sitting in an oven.

Finally, Penelope started to protest, so we paused, even though time wasn't on our side. The late afternoon was a red-eyed squint into the setting sun. For a lot of the day my visor was up and my eyes had dried out.

I knew I was losing the race against the dropping red orb and almost called it quits as dusk appeared. Being this far north means there is no twilight. Suddenly, before you know it is 'roo time', not your time. With fingers' crossed, in the early evening murk I rode the last 20 km – and only saw two kangaroos hop across in front of me at the edge of Fitzroy Crossing, our destination for the night. Neither were especially close, although one was quite big.

I fuelled up and sought out the camp. On the way I was breath-tested, and the lead cop said "Did you get my message? … I texted earlier." Confused, I asked how he knew me. He took another look and decided I wasn't the local doctor … just his doppelganger.

Being as I was pretty spent, I asked about a cabin, but when comparing $18 against $185, I am under nylon again. I walked 2 km to the BP, to be told the kitchen was shut, but there might be a sandwich in the fridge. There was, and it was only slightly curled at the edges. You can't have everything your own way all the time, it seems

It is a Saturday and unlikely I would find a welder open, but I did leave Fitzroy Crossing hopeful of pushing on to Broome, a day of about 400 km. I knew Fitzroy was going to get another 34-degree-day but it looked like Broome might only be a nudge under 30. It had been a warm night so the day didn't stay cool long. There is not much to say about the day, except I bloused out halfway through it. The road was dull, and hot … more or less straight, nothing to see, nothing to do. By midday, I was done.

The tank bag seems a little fuller and precludes me swapping my hands over to see if I retain last year's hard-earned skills. Three days it had taken me to be able to ride with my left hand controlling the throttle. But that was then, this is now. Possibly not the cauldron of the day before … but close. I have noticed that when Penelope finally does start to hesitate and stutter, that if I roll off the throttle for a few seconds, she comes back smooth and strong for a bit. Maybe it is fuel flow?

Back in NZ, the 100 km ride from Nelson to home is a delight, here 100 km of baking-hot, straight road is akin to torture. I added a few bits to a short story I am pondering on, thought of family, wondered why I am so loyal to such an unlikely companion (Penelope, not Steph), and once again reflected on the UK's legendary 'summer of 76'. It was this time 43 years ago that Steph, Penelope and I became an 'item' in London. Good times, great memories … kept me going for a few miles. I've never been one for the latest fads, so we'll keep on, keeping on. I am looking forward to Broome but don't expect I'll take the camel rides, and if I do frolic down the legendary nude beach, there will be no photos.

I also reflected on something I learnt yesterday. Up here you don't leave your helmet on the ground. I had done so overnight and a fellow rider came over and told me of his mate's lesson. Setting off after a night's camping, and having done what I had just done … left his helmet outside his tent, within 10 minutes of riding he experienced ear pains … and ultimately was hospitalised because of termites in his aural canal. We checked my helmet and it seemed ok. 15 minutes into my ride, I got an itchy ear. The brain was playing games with me.

There are some times in life when the expression FFS (those who have lived under a rock for a couple of decades will have to have a guess at that one) is opportune and totally appropriate. We'll get to that soon.

With the temperature for the area ranging from night-time low of 17 to a daytime norm of 34, it is best to make tracks early, when it is in the sweet spot of early 20s. We were a happy crew thrumming along in a Goldilocks fashion. Everything was 'just right'. The 150 km or so to the Roebuck roadhouse, flew by. We stopped for coffee, being as it was still too early for beer. There were three dirt bikes there with pretty happy and soiled riders. They'd been out for a Sunday morning's play. Penelope drew them over and soon three others joined us. They were on two Harleys and a sports tourer. Also locals to Broome, they were chatty and soon we were all giving

**THE BIG SIT**

each other advice.

… and then the FFS moment. I had promised that this year's ride would be fuss-free and I would even stick to the tar. My reports were to be dull and repetitive. So what did we spot? A LEAKING PETROL TANK! I cannot believe this deja vu moment. That was last year! I have brought to Aus a different, *repaired* old tank. My panel man had repaired the front and declared it sound. Now it was leaking from the back!

Anyway, that is for me to overcome, just another bloody challenge. Broome is astonishing. It is a town of 15,000 which swells to 45,000 in the winter. The camp I am in has about 600 clearly defined sites … and every one is taken. I have been squeezed-in in a far corner, behind a seemingly-abandoned big work truck, next to an eccentric long-termer who repairs bicycles under his awning and sells them to any grey nomads who want them.

Tomorrow we will try to find a welder. Tonight, I may wander over to the beach and look for camels and clothes-free frolickers.

DONESIA
TIMOR SEA
INDIAN OCEAN
Ashmore Reef
Scott Reef
Rowley Shoals
Melville I
Croker I
Bathurst I
Nguiu
Darwin
Palmerston
Van Diemen Gulf
Maningrida
Oenpelli
Jabiru
ARNHEM
Batchelor
Daly River
Pine Creek
Katherine
Barunga (Bamyili)
Joseph Bonaparte Gulf
Kalumburu
Bigge I
Augustus I
Wyndham
Kununurra
L Argyle
KIMBERLEY
Collier Bay
KING LEOPOLD RANGES
Lombadina
Derby
Broome
Fitzroy Crossing
Halls Creek
Kalkarindji (Wave Hill)
Lajamanu
Elliott
L Woods
NORTHERN TER
Tennant Creek
TANAMI DESERT
GREAT SANDY DESERT
Port Hedland
Yarrie
De Grey
Karratha
Roebourne
Barrow I
PILBARA
Telfer
L Mackay
Yuendumu
Pannawonica
Onslow
Exmouth
HAMERSLEY RANGE
Fortescue River
Tom Price
Paraburdoo
Newman
L Auld
Papunya
Alice Sp
Hermannsburg
L Disappointment
GIBSON DESERT
LITTLE SANDY DESERT
WESTERN AUSTRALIA
Ashburton River
L Macleod
Gascoyne R
Carnarvon
Shark Bay
Dirk Hartog I
Denham
L Amadeus
Yulara
Uluru-Ayers Rock
Warburton
L Carnegie
Wiluna
Meekatharra
L Wells
Murchison R
L Austin
Leinster
GREAT VICTORIA DESERT
Mount Magnet
Laverton
Leonora
L Carey
L Maurice (Carle-Thulka)
SOUTH A
Northampton
Geraldton
Dongara
Morawa
L Barlee
L Moore
L Rebecca
Dalwallinu
Kalgoorlie-Boulder
NULLARBOR PLAIN
Tarcoola
L Everard
Moora
Wongan Hills
Kambalda
Lancelin
Northam
Southern Cross
Merredin
Kellerberrin
York
L Cowan
Ceduna
Streaky Bay
IAN OCEAN
PERTH
Norseman
Baliadonia
L Dundas
Corrigin
Rockingham
Mandurah
Pingelly
Narrogin
Lake Grace
Ravensthorpe
GREAT AUSTRALIAN BIGHT
Bunbury
Busselton
Collie
Kojonup
Katanning
Esperance
Jerramungup
Margaret River
Manjimup
Mount Barker
Denmark
Albany
AUSTRALIA
EDITION 2
100 0 100 200 300 400 500 kilometres
Simple Conic Projection with Standard Parallels 18°S and 36°S
SOUTHERN OCEAN
HYPSOMETRIC TINTS
BATHYMETRIC TINTS
2000 1500 1000 500 200 0 200
Heights and depths are shown in metres
Government
Australia
Populated places
1 000 000 or greater
100 000 - 999 999
Road, principal sealed
Road, principal unsealed
Road, secondary sealed

## CHAPTER NINE

# BROOME TO TOODYAY

22 July 2019

So there has been no movement today … well no Penelope movement. I am personally blessed with metronomic regularity. I was at the welder at just after 7.00 am and Jolly, the owner of *Ali Worx* took it upon himself to see to our ails. I whipped off the exhaust and tank. The tank was seen to drip ominously, but Jolly was confident that he and his team would soon fix that.

The exhaust ring was TIG welded back on, and the exhaust hanger re-attached to the frame. Things were going well. Their young lad sluiced out the tank a dozen times or more, often with degreaser. Finally, it was adjudged that there was no petrol smell and the repair could be commenced. The affected areas were wire-brushed clean, a gas bottle (oxygen?) was attached to a fuel tap, the cap closed and vent blocked, tank flipped, soapy water applied … and guess what? No leak could be found! No matter what was tried, we could get no tell-tale bubbles.

Ultimately, we decided as there was nothing he could weld, we would slobber an epoxy over the outside where we thought the leak would have been. The tank is left to cure, and my sojourn in Broome extended slightly. This is not unpleasant. The beach and cafés are just a pleasant walk away and the sunsets of course stunning, the evenings warm and sultry. I see camels but still no clothes-free frolickers.

The Broome Museum is suitably interesting. I find the pearling history in the region fascinating because of the ethnic diversity it brought to the area. The war-time raid when nine Japanese Zeros flew in and sank 15 flying boats is a sobering display as over 80 people died, many being Dutch civilians fleeing from their Asian colonies. A US Liberator repatriating war-wounded was also shot down with 30 on board. There is an intriguing account of diamonds being stolen from a DC3 aircraft after it was shot down by a Zero returning to base. This was about 50 km north of Broome. The equivalent of over $20,000,000 of diamonds was being transferred from Indonesia to the safety of Australia. One of the plane's engines caught fire during the attack and the pilot managed to crash-land at the beach edge and as he did so, splashing water put out the fire and the plane remained intact. Several people, including a baby were killed by subsequent strafing of the plane by the Zero. The survivors were rescued after six days and yet another Japanese attack. Jack Palmer, a local mariner turned up a couple of days after the rescue and later handed in a small quantity of diamonds. He and two associates were charged with stealing the diamonds but they were acquitted and the balance of the diamonds never found.

> Palmer, Mulgrue and Robinson were charged with stealing and in May 1943 were committed for trial in the Supreme Court in Perth. The charges were dismissed, probably assisted by Jack appearing in his army uniform at the trial. Jack was known as "Diamond Jack" after the trial and remained in Broome, buying a house and a blue Chevrolet. He always had cash on hand and once even paid the wages of a dozen wharfies when their pay was late. Jack died in Broome in 1958, aged 63.
>
> *Missing Diamonds*
>
> What happened to the rest of the diamonds? In a small town such as Broome rumours abound.

Known as Diamond Jack thence forth, supposedly be bought a house and a new Chevrolet car shortly afterwards and never was short of money.

Broome has been a funny old town. It has an interesting history, but now mainly seems to be a destination for comfortably-off, older folk who wish to shelter from the southern winter cold. The most popular vehicle in the camp is the Toyota Landcruiser V8. They are usually white and are needed to tow the big caravans. Neither of which are cheap. These long-term Grey Nomad campers have quite sophisticated set-ups, always including pegged-out astroturf lawns so sand doesn't enter their demesne. It is obvious that little communities have sprung up all over the camp. As an itinerant, I am not bothered with. I do get to interact with other 'passers-through' though.

Downtown, I experienced true love. In the heat of the day I retreated into the famous Matso Bar and brewery, and had their specialty Mango Beer. This is based on a wheat beer with added mango for sweetness and zing. Out of 10, I give it a 12.5.

I also gave the camp pool a go, as I figured that it could double as a shower/wash. Even though with my white furry pelt and ursine shape, I probably looked like a geographically-misplaced Polar Bear, there were no shrieks of terror, nor mass fleeing from the area. Possibly a lot of the elderly really do need to go to Specsavers. I then finished the day with a reasonably posh meal of dukkah-encrusted kangaroo loin with veggies in a red wine jus. The de rigueur, stunning sunset confirmed that every day above ground … ain't bad.

I recover Penelope and she is now back to being a twin-port single again and no longer is incontinent. I plan for an early departure heading south-west. I like 300 km days as that leaves plenty of time for learning stuff and seeing Aus. A 600 km day can be endured but it leaves us spent even though we've done nothing but sit and look at endless blacktop, which is usually grey. We may be riding around the perimeter of the continent but sights of the sea are now rare.

So the Big Sit continues with more hot rides on dull, straight roads. OK, the land did occasionally open out and display tussock right out to the horizon with not a scrubby little tree in sight. Didn't last long ... soon the scrubby trees were back. I note that I see two cyclists during one day, one going each way, and just one sole motorbike. I got to use my fuel bladder as well, as we didn't quite do the distance between roadhouses. I hadn't filled right to the top in Broome, as when it is hot, fuel expands and spills out over the tank if you are not Instantly riding down the road. Going in to pay is often enough. But anyway, that is why I carry the five litre bladder.

The 10 km road into 80 Mile Beach was mostly good red dirt with small corrugations allowing top gear travel. Of course, to keep me focused, there were a couple of scary soft bits to give the sphincter-clench a work out. It has been a 377 km day according to the tracking app I sometimes use. Riser also records that Penelope had run away to 102 kph at some stage in the day and we'd been on the move for 5 hrs and one minute. I note it as a good day and am soon tucked up in a camp next to two Tasmanian couples. The lads know Pete Willoughby who was part of the Plastic Expedition, our foils on the legendary New Orleans to Buenos Aires ride of

1976/77. I am sure Pete will be pleased to hear that Penelope is still thumping along 43 years later.

The camp has quail and butcher birds (like a small magpie) wandering about. Quite a few Grey Nomads too. Their habitat is widely spread and varied. Usually seen nesting in huge white caravans though. I get to experience them close-up as the camp has a 'fry-up-special' night and it seems pretty much everyone in the camp takes the opportunity to let someone else do the cooking. I do as well. It was ok, but not so memorable that I can remember the fare. It was pretty good sitting though, on the bank in the early evening warmth, looking out over the Indian Ocean.

There was quite a bit of mirth shared the following morning, because when camping in this climate – where there won't be rain for another couple of months and where there is no dew, we all tend to leave stuff out. Well, at 2.30 am there was the patter of raindrops, followed by the zzzzzing of zips all around as the tenters emerged to 'put away'. It was time to pee anyway, so I joined in … and I was surprised to find all I had to cover was my helmet, hanging from the bars like a bowl begging to be filled. Of course it didn't actually rain, although while I dined in the Pardoo roadhouse, a traveller passing the other way said it had rained in Karratha, about 350 km further south.

Actually, the day I left 80 Mile Beach started with a couple of minor disasters. Firstly, a neighbouring caravaner asked if I would like coffee. I regretted it in an instant … it was of course, instant. Lazy me has not always been breaking out the beans and grinding them because the priority is to get on the road while it is cool. Second disaster involved the corrugated road back to the highway. Even though on the scale of outback roads, it wouldn't even register as being the slightest bit memorable … it was still rough enough to shake my oil container from its spot. Of course it dragged along the ground and was holed … so giving some of itself back to Mother Gaia. I've had it balanced upside down all day since.

And the rest of the day's ride? Hot and dull, relieved only by running into the Tassie crew twice. I had to like them because they reckoned the Cable Beach Camp was 'too posh' for them. I hadn't wanted to articulate the same feeling. Down-to-earth folk with no pretences. Not everyone on the road is humble or nice. I've never aspired to or admired affluence and that is something that many of the Grey Nomads often seem to wear as a badge of honour. The size of their toys seem to matter to them a lot. Don't you love an opinionated generalisation!

… and I learn that a woman got bitten by a snake at Pardoo and rushed off to Broome. Aussie can be unforgiving sometimes.

Port Hedland hadn't wanted me in 2013 when I was recruited by Keller Ground Engineering to be part of a year-long project. I spent $1.2M on their behalf, on mobilisation … only to have BHP axe the job just as we moved to site. Now they don't want me either, as the caravan park wouldn't even squeeze me into a corner. So anyway I move on to another grassless camp at South Hedland, and that polar bear makes another appearance in a camp pool.

"OK folks … nothing to see here! But there is a lot of it." That could be the theme of many of my days.

I tell my followers –

*Well two out of two ain't bad. Yesterday I got my guesses about day and date both wrong. Ok, so I know it is now Friday the 27th and I am camped in the red dirt behind the Fortescue Roadhouse next to Kev and Ken who have been providing me with shade and interactions.*

*The day initially delivered a disappointment when the Whim Creek Hotel was found to no longer be trading. Later, serendipitous timing delivered me Louise … who might have actually been called Julie, for an early lunch. I passed her pedalling along just before Roebourne. I was delighted when she pulled in at the cafe I had stopped at. She was most surprised when I insisted on paying for her lunch in exchange for her company.*

**THE BIG SIT**

She had left Adelaide something like eight months earlier and had been doing amazing side roads to keep off the main dull and scary ones. Her equipment was all high-end that worked for her. Her tyres were special 2" Swalbe ones she'd imported; her tent was a little bigger than most cyclists endure. She has a vestibule where she can sit in her special Swedish fold-out chair. Her bags were all Ortlieb and trailer Topeak, her drive-hub Rolhoff 14 speed of course. No bunny, she'd just come off the 650 km Gibb River Road, along which she'd carried 30 litres of water. She's also done the Birdsville and Oodnadatta Tracks. Of course, she's also ridden Salta to Ushaia in South America, as well as Italy and Greece. We had lots of fun comparing gear and dissing the Grey Nomads and their "Where are you from … and where have you been?" This opening often leads to their life story. I tell her that fellow cyclist Lilo is behind and judging on claimed daily mileages, he might catch her in a few days. Our time together was very enjoyable and one of the trip highlights.

She also added to the legend that is the French girl on the foot-powered scooter. I'd heard tales of this girl scooting along with few possessions and little money, such that she was known to scour the rubbish bins. Julia/Louise saw her wheel and footprints in the Gibb River Road, bewildered by the one foot-mark. Later she learned it was a scooterist.

What did I learn today? The Pilbara area we are passing through is almost all iron ore and there are four ports. The trains from the mines are usually 260 wagons long and in the Karratha region are driverless. The BHP ones back in Port Hedland have drivers. I think each train load is about 280,000 tonne.

And Penelope's petrol tank is leaking again!!!!

Oh and the other thing I learned yesterday from the jungle drums is that the iconic Birdsville Bakery is no longer open.

It was a warm start to the day as I left South Hedland, threatened to become yet another sweltering slog … but after an hour or so we rode into an umbrella of thin cloud. This took away my lovely shadow, but was central to a 'Goldilocks' day … not too hot, not too cold, not too long, not too short … just right. In a tee-shirt under my light cotton jacket with its armpits open, we were perfectly adorned. I pick the temperature was about 28. As we head south, I will progressively introduce the long-sleeve shirt, the three merino tops and the alpaca jersey. If that isn't enough I will go to an opp shop. No bikes or treadlies in the day's ride, but a 'wide load' of stacked swimming pools gave me a chuckle. We're also passed a few huge loads of mining equipment going the opposite way. A pilot vehicle up front waves the traffic off the road so these behemoths can go slowly by. Research tells me that the big dump trucks weigh over 200 tonne and can carry 400 tonne of ore … so you can imagine the size of the low-loader that is required to carry one of those. The wheels project out over the sides of the deck and the result is something a lot wider than one lane of highway. I've heard that many of these giant 'Tonka Toys' also don't have drivers.

Penelope and I cross the Tropic of Capricorn again, and it is the fifth time we've done it together. Possibly that is the first time that an ex-Berhampore boy of Irish extraction, now living in Golden Bay, riding a 1965 Panther M120, has done this … but you can't be sure. I won't bother the Guinness Records' people or trumpet it from the roof-tops.

Ray Checketts from home keeps me informed about the All Blacks rugby game while I tinkered with Penelope in the evening. I am hopeful the tank leak has been from around the tap and I have fitted a small 'O' ring and used some magic thread unguent the old duffer parked up next to me had. Fingers' crossed.

A week after leaving Broome I finally get relief from the relentless heat and it comes upon us quite quickly. For some time, I have been asking northbound travellers when it first got warm for them. I am a bit over being baked. Again I share on Facebook –

*Be careful with what you wish for. Last night the temperature dropped to 13 degrees, which meant a fully zipped-up sleeping bag was needed. Morning dawned chilly and for the first time this trip there was dew on the tent. That was a minor irritation as the tent gets rolled away with the sleeping bag.*

Based on how well we would go in the forecast 26-degree day, it was a leisurely start after a reasonable coffee. Soon we were humming along, wearing my long-sleeved shirt, more or less at our ideal percolation speed in the high nineties. Nearing Carnarvon, the landscape dramatically changed with roadside fruit and veg stalls appearing in front of productive plantations of bananas etc. The red wilderness was over ... for now. There was also a ramp-up in vehicle numbers. Suddenly I wasn't just riding along in my own lonely little bubble.

I snacked on my staple of a mandarin and muesli bar on Carnarvon's waterfront and chatted to a couple from the Busselton old bike group down past Perth. He was a Norton buff, but they were nice, unlike some of the boorish dullards I have struck lately. Two days in a row old duffers have wanted to tell me all about their Matchless motorbikes they had in their youth. Ironically one, who kept harping on how he would love it now, had earned a 1927 Panther for chopping 10 cord of firewood as a 14 year-old in Tasmania. I suppose I just need more patience and to develop better

**THE BIG SIT**

'duffer' tolerance. It is possible I may even become one.

I'd also stopped because Penelope was oozing oil out from somewhere 'up top' and I now had an oily gear lever, boot, trouser bottom and even my lower leg is showing discoloration. There are times when my loyalty is tested. I decided to cut short the day and try to effect a cure. As I pulled into the dusty little roadhouse and camp at Wooramel, I decided I wanted an indoors night – if it was under $75. To my surprise, the salt-of-the-earth Ocker matron said I could have a donga for $40 … so indoors it is. What's more, later she gave me some spare body wash as the shop was out of shampoo. Another nice couple have just given me two bottles of water … also great.

Meanwhile, I found the source of the leak to be a dropping pushrod tunnel. Whether the damaged 'O' ring will keep oil in, and whether the two-piece pushrod tunnel will stay 'stretched', only time will tell. I grind the coffee for the morning, and line up the Aeropress, then I shower and settle down with Anne Cleeves on the kindle. I relish not having to use the torch for illumination. All in all, life's good. I almost purr with contentment. A Five Star room in the Ritz wouldn't be any better than this.

Funny old day! I think it is a Monday, but it doesn't really matter. My day sort of started last night when I learned that Clive Cooper (and others it turns out) was embarking upon a Panther adventure from the UK, heading off into Europe for thousands of kilometres. How great is that! As Penelope and I settle in the evenings, we'll send our thoughts across the aether. "Morning Clive, time to hit the road! There are countries to conquer, damsels to woo!" So two Panthers … with combined bike and rider ages of 260 years are thudding along the highways bringing joy and surprise to many along the way.

My next day started WA blue-sky normal but with a chilly wind, necessitating the first of my merinos. Only an hour into the ride, Penelope suddenly tightened … and so did my clenchy bits. We'd got through the hot, hot stuff and now she'd 'nipped-up' on a lovely cool morning. What gives with that? Compression down of course, but after a rest she fired up and we proceeded slowly for a while. Contrary old thing … if I wasn't such a loyal bugger, I really would give her the flick.

We took a break, and positioned ourselves a little away from the throng at a roadhouse. I took sustenance and cogitated. That didn't do much good, but another serendipitous meeting lifted my spirits and brought forth yet another frisson of excitement. A large man of uncertain age, with his Chinese wife, wandered over for a chat. He was interested in Penelope and told me he knew Lawrie and Suzanne Goddes, the Aussie Panther stalwarts who I had met in 2016 and 2017 at the rallies. Then he said "Hey, aren't you the guy who rode through Pakistan etc?" Admitting I was, he told me they had our DVD and we chatted congenially … and then without fanfare he showed me a photo of the bike he is known for. Well, you could have knocked me down with a feather. This was Bob Dibble whose tales of riding around the world on a CT110 Honda Postie bike and sidecar called *'The Little Runt'*, I had followed in awe and with huge admiration. Here he was, in the flesh. How great was that! His exploits over the years make mine look pretty pale and puny, but we weren't point-scoring, nor big-noting. It was just a memorable meeting with a fellow adventurer.

Even with an ailing Penelope, we still put 375 km under our intermittently spinning wheels and go indoors again. This time I have a TV to be annoyed by. I've just passed by Geraldton, a town of substance … and at least seven sets of traffic lights. Big Red also isn't red out there now either … there are green paddocks with sheep in them. I am now only a big day from Bruce Sharman in Toodyay, although that is quite a stretch and depends whether I find Ian Boyd at Jurien Bay with the world's largest collection of Vincent motorcycles. Supposedly he has one of every model made except one.

"Be still oh beating heart!" The old ticker got a severe workout when I had an unexpected encounter with an emu in the early morning. For

**THE BIG SIT**

a while there, I thought the day was going to involve the demise of one, if not both of us. This was the first Emu I had seen this leg and I don't need to see another close-up, thanks. The ride now followed the Indian Ocean Highway for a bit and was a delight, apart from that meeting with a ground bird taller than Penelope. Emus stand 1.5 m tall and can weigh close to 50 kg … not something you want to hit at 90 kph.

Penelope had been quite recalcitrant and reluctant to start, presumably as a result of the previous day's small seizure. Once running, she resumed the first kick hot or cold normality. The BTH electronic magneto has always meant reliable, easy starting. It will be interesting to see if she repeats the reluctance tomorrow. If so, we may have to go inside and look at the state of the rings.

But back to the ride. What a delight it was to be riding through greenery, on undulating roads, with views of the sea and the salt-white sand dunes. I paused at Jurien Bay to see the motorcycle collection of Ian Boyd. He was welcoming and an affable host. He has about 60 exotic bikes including approximately 40 Vincent's and other products from that Stevenage firm, including a WW2 drone engine, a moped and the 3 cylinder two-stroke engine intended to be used in marine rescue. All Vincent's are expensive and recently the rare race-model Black Lightning (22 of the 35 produced are thought to survive) of Australian champion Jack Ehret sold for $1.3M. In Ian's collection is the Black Lightning purportedly raced by Prince Bira of Siam. Put a figure on that one!

An interesting side jaunt took me to The Pinnacles and my second wildlife encounter of the day. Whilst trickling around the road through these unusual stone structures, a kangaroo and I surprised each other and he/she more or less jumped over Penelope's front mudguard. This was not especially dangerous … just impressive.

The day was long and the speeds are down, till we do a diagnosis. This meant getting to Toodyay later than desired or prudent. Dusk fell before I got there and fortunately the only kangaroo spotted was 30 m ahead, nonchalantly crossing the road as if it was his habitat. I did wonder about 'third time lucky' and resolve not to do any more dusk riding.

Bruce Sharman fetched me from the Toodyay Hotel and a convivial evening with him and Linda followed a roast meal and good Aussie red wine. The Panther family is such a welcoming bunch. I settle down in sumptuous luxury, gently amused that Penelope is also indoors, down in the shed, snuggled up to another of Cleckheaton's finest. It's been a good day to have been alive.

Bruce and Linda are as wonderful as I had hoped they would be. Vibrant and colourful, they live on a lifestyle block about 10 km out of Toodyay and Bruce restores vehicles for a living from a large purpose-built shed on site. This is not a 'fill it with bog and give it a spray' operation. Bruce revels in being a perfectionist and a metal worker par excellence.

He tells me that he originally served his time as a butcher back in the UK but over the decades he taught himself the skills and obtained all the tools and equipment needed to offer this artisan service. He has a second, compatible business producing cloth-covered wiring looms for the older vehicles which had them as an original fitting. The equipment used to weave the braiding over the wires consists of more than 20 large spools of cotton arranged around a central core where the action takes place. When switched on, the spools all dance and swivel around the cluster of wires in the middle. With mostly black spools and only a small number of contrasting colours like white, green, yellow etc when the dance ends there can be seen flecks of colour in the woven covering. Very few of these machines are still in use around the world as this stopped being the way of doing it more than sixty years ago. Bruce and Linda's daughter also helps with this business. I was surprised to see that every loom produced is drawn out full size on its own sheet of plywood as a durable pattern for future use.

Linda complements the dapper figure that 'out of the shed' Bruce cleans up to be. They were youthful sweethearts and clearly they still are. Linda is a social worker and an avid reader and sometime writer. Of course I warm to her. Steph is now also a social worker and I know they would have much in in common. Their house is a wonderful eclectic mix of the old and the new. Toodyay (pop 1,400) is an hour north east of Perth and is part of the area known as the Wheatbelt. It is quaint with a centre featuring the old hotel, a small number of cafes and a museum in the historic gaol. I like it a lot as it has a river and an undulating countryside surrounding it.

Bruce manages to find and fix the leak in the petrol tank. It is another example of poor design on Phelan and Moore's part. The back fixings of the tank get squeezed towards each other as the frame through-bolt tightens against the rubber buffers. Over-tightening stresses the fixing lugs and tank base meeting point, ultimately causing failure. A little Roly voice comes back to me ... "Don't tighten the tank too much at the back." Why hadn't I listened? It is interesting that when the tension was released upon taking the tank off, the leak point closed up and no evidence of petrol escaping could be found.

Bruce's early 1950s 600 cc Model 100 is way more pretty than Penelope, being svelte and nimble ... possibly as good as Panthers ever got. We look good together though, and enjoy a day out, exploring a little and taking in a market and a bit of wine tasting.

*Ok, so we're ready to go again. My time here is done! I have been resting and recreating (No ... that is procreating!) in Toodyay with the Sharmans. About 4,500 km are behind us this trip, possibly 4,000 to go before we pause.*

*Bruce Sharman has led the servicing of Penelope and I reckon we are in a better state than we have been for some time. Cables have been tweaked, the carb fiddled with, rider replenished etc.*

*I had lovely day off on Fri in Perth and Fremantle, wandering not-as-lonely-as-a-cloud etc. Today we went to the International Food fair in Toodyay as well as visiting a local winery selling intriguing fortified wines.*

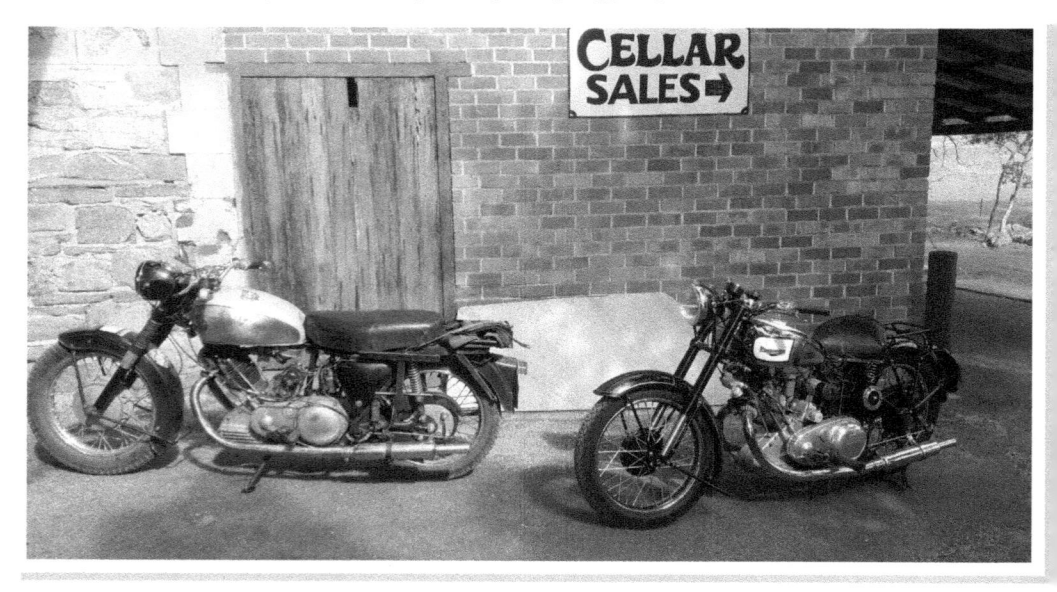

**THE BIG SIT**

*My plan is to ride around the bottom corner via Margaret River, Albany and Esperance before hitting the famed Nullabor. It is now pretty cool, leaning towards cold. I have moved south out of the heat and tomorrow will have on most of my merinos ... and the alpaca jersey. With a bit of luck and determination 8-10 days should see me in South Australia to the next Panther Service Centre.*

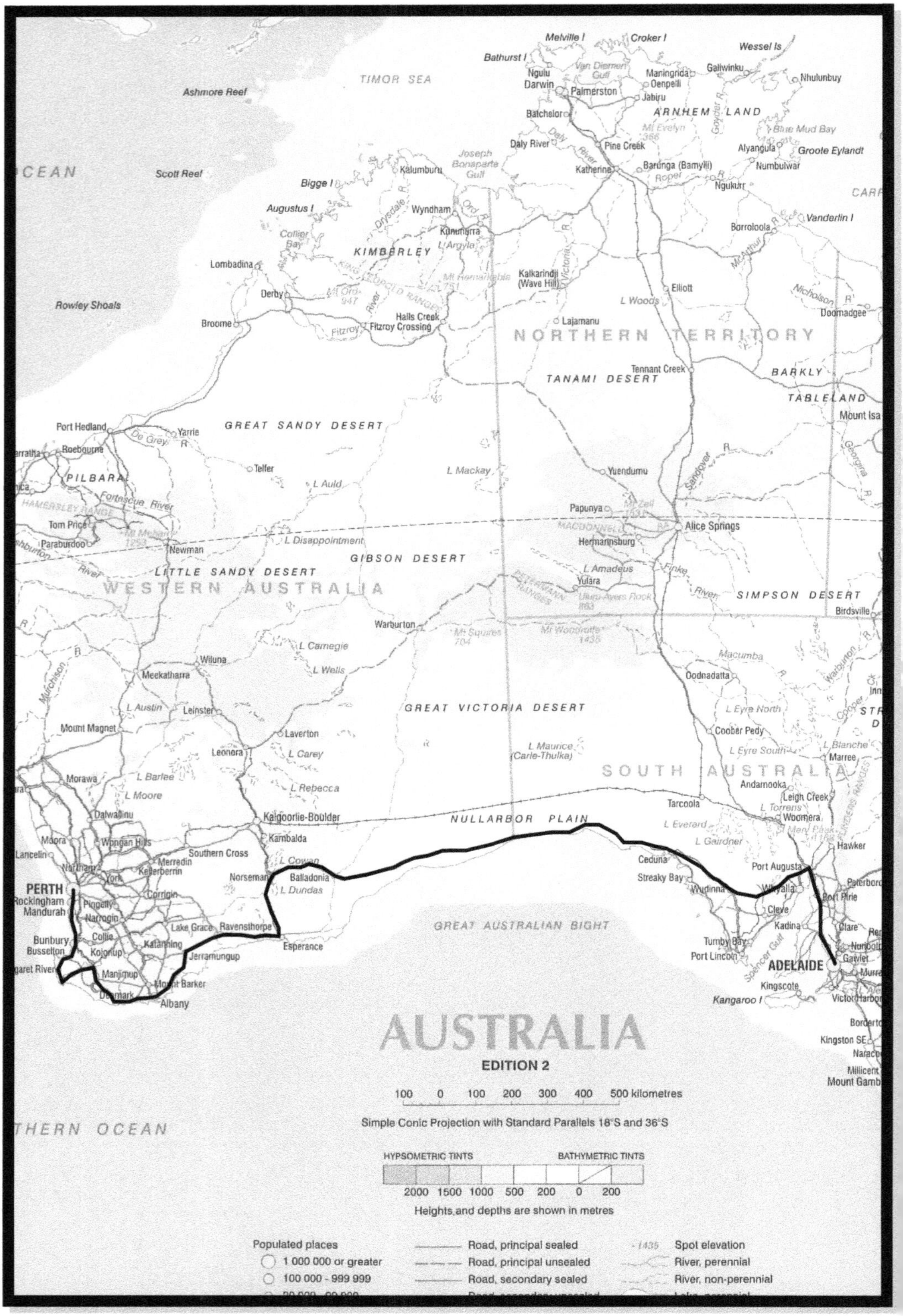

Melville I
Croker I
Wessel Is
Bathurst I
TIMOR SEA
Ashmore Reef
Ngulu
Van Diemen Gulf
Maningrida
Galiwinku
Nhulunbuy
Darwin
Palmerston
Oenpelli
Jabiru
ARNHEM LAND
Batchelor
Mt Evelyn 366
Blue Mud Bay
Daly River
Pine Creek
Alyangula
Groote Eylandt
OCEAN
Scott Reef
Joseph Bonaparte Gulf
Kalumburu
Katherine
Barunga (Bamyili)
Numbulwar
Roper
Ngukurr
Bigge I
Augustus I
Wyndham
Kununurra
Vanderlin I
Borroloola
Collier Bay
KIMBERLEY
L Argyle
Lombadina
Kalkarindji (Wave Hill)
Elliott
Derby
Mt Ord 947
Halls Creek
L Woods
Nicholson R
Doomadgee
Rowley Shoals
Broome
Fitzroy
Fitzroy Crossing
Lajamanu
NORTHERN TERRITORY
Tennant Creek
BARKLY
TANAMI DESERT
TABLELAND
Mount Isa
Port Hedland
GREAT SANDY DESERT
Yarrie
De Grey R
Roebourne
PILBARA
Telfer
L Auld
L Mackay
Yuendumu
Sandover R
Georgina R
Fortescue River
HAMERSLEY RANGE
Papunya
Tom Price
MACDONNELL RA
Alice Springs
Paraburdoo
L Disappointment
Hermannsburg
Newman
GIBSON DESERT
LITTLE SANDY DESERT
L Amadeus
Yulara
Finke
WESTERN AUSTRALIA
PETERMANN RANGES
Uluru-Ayers Rock 863
River
SIMPSON DESERT
Birdsville
Warburton
Mt Woodroffe 1435
L Carnegie
Macumba
Wiluna
L Wells
Meekatharra
Oodnadatta
Murchison R
L Austin
Leinster
GREAT VICTORIA DESERT
L Eyre North
Mount Magnet
Laverton
Coober Pedy
L Maurice (Carle-Thulka)
Leonora
L Carey
L Eyre South
L Blanche
Marree
Morawa
L Barlee
SOUTH AUSTRALIA
L Rebecca
Andamooka
L Moore
Leigh Creek
FLINDERS RANGES
Dalwallinu
Tarcoola
Kalgoorlie-Boulder
NULLARBOR PLAIN
L Torrens
Woomera
Moora
Wongan Hills
Kambalda
L Everard
Hawker
Southern Cross
L Gairdner
Lancelin
L Cowan
Ceduna
Merredin
Port Augusta
Northam
Kellerberrin
Norseman
Streaky Bay
York
Balladonia
PERTH
Corrigin
L Dundas
Wudinna
Whyalla
Peterborough
Rockingham
Pingelly
Port Pirie
Mandurah
Narrogin
Cleve
Collie
Lake Grace
Ravensthorpe
GREAT AUSTRALIAN BIGHT
Kadina
Clare
Bunbury
Kojonup
Katanning
Tumby Bay
Busselton
Esperance
Spencer Gulf
Gawler
Jerramungup
Port Lincoln
ADELAIDE
Margaret River
Manjimup
Mount Barker
Kingscote
Denmark
Albany
Kangaroo I
AUSTRALIA
EDITION 2
100 0 100 200 300 400 500 kilometres
Simple Conic Projection with Standard Parallels 18°S and 36°S
Kingston SE
Millicent
THERN OCEAN
HYPSOMETRIC TINTS
BATHYMETRIC TINTS
2000 1500 1000 500 200 0 200
Heights and depths are shown in metres
Populated places
1 000 000 or greater
100 000 - 999 999
Road, principal sealed
Road, principal unsealed
Road, secondary sealed
1435 Spot elevation
River, perennial
River, non-perennial

CHAPTER TEN

# TOODYAY TO MCLAREN FLAT

I know it will look like I complain when it is hot ... and I complain when it is not. Up north a cool morning was 25-28 and it didn't stay like that for long ... well now, a cool morning is 15 and it stays just above that all day. We actually started with a fog at Bruce and Linda's. Bruce led me away and then tag-teamed his mate Jeff who escorted me down to Armadale and got me on the old road south. Navigating around Aus isn't really that hard because you just have to keep the sea on your right ... if you are going anti-clockwise.

I have kept my waterproofs on the outside of my bed roll under the superb 'piggy-back' 50mm wide elastics for all the ride ... for easy access. For the 15,000 km since we left southern NSW, we have not needed them. Today, skirting Perth, a bit of precipitation was encountered. Did I stop ... or did I ineffectively race the rain? I think you can guess my action or rather non-action. And following the path of cause-and-affect, I sought hot comfort-food at my petrol stop, to fuel and cheer the dampened soul. Of course, it was dire and repeated on me for a couple of hours. I pledge once more to never indulge in fried food from the warmer.

The countryside has been green and lush, interesting and varied ... so unlike my last few weeks. I don't pause for photos today, the effort seemingly too much for me. At the end of a steady ride of about 370 km I hole up in the touristy town of Margaret River. For the geographically-challenged … this is the bottom left-hand corner.

I report in a day later –

*Not a lot to say tonight as our wheels never turned today. It poured in the night and the rain continued through quite a bit of today. The forecast was for all-day lightning ... which never quite eventuated. It was a good opportunity to catch up with a bit of home-related work and pretend I wasn't blousing-out.*

*Three bright green parrots kept me entertained for a bit. One was happy to go in my cabin, then couldn't get out. Several attempts were made to fly through the closed window, before I ushered it to the door. They were the Australian Ringneck, also known as Twenty Eights because of their distinctive calls which sound like someone calling 28. Very tame and happy to have a quick stop on my knee, looking for my crumbs.*

*Some of you will have spotted that I am now carrying a spare tyre. This is last year's front tyre which had a good amount of tread on it, so I had it forwarded to Bruce Sharman. My ride in 2017 on Dunlop K70s had seen premature wear on the back tyre (less than 5,000 km to bald) so I had changed to an Avon SM2. This worked well in 2018 so was replaced with the same in Darwin. The front is a Mitas and also wore well. A new one was also fitted in Darwin even though wear was minimal. Too good to abandon, it was sent ahead. The 4,500 km from Darwin has not worn out the back tyre and rather than send the spare ahead ... I'll carry it.*

*And why all the palaver? Suitable 19" tyres are not 'stocked' along the way. They must be ordered from specialists.*

It is great to know that there are now several Panthers on long distance rides in Europe all aiming for the club International rally in Finland. What a great testament to the club ethos and the adventurous nature of the members. Clive Cooper, Chris and Jennie Strawford, Tom Norman and others are all arrowing along, overcoming the vagaries of machines all more than 50 years old and bodies often considerably older again. I am loving their posts and photos. What a thrill ... to be riding through Poland, Lithuania, Estonia etc.

"Yeah mate ... you go down to Augusta and turn left." So said an old speedway rider as we chatted in Margaret River after I had filled up. My map had got wet and shredded itself as I got it out, and Google Maps couldn't be reached because Telstra hadn't activated my account. He was nearly right. When I got to Augusta I found the sea ... on my left, next stop would have been Dan Leather back in Darwin.

We adjusted, photographed a sign to Molloy, and after yet another emu encounter, passed through wonderfully diverse terrain. There were paddocks with horses ... ditto cows, ditto sheep. There were vineyards and tree-lined avenues with sun-dappled shading to delight and amuse. All the while the road undulated and even twisted and turned. If it had been 10 degrees warmer the ride would have rated as memorable. For a period, we passed through the karri forests the area is known for. The karri is one of the tallest hardwoods in the world and some were quite magnificent. And to add to your knowledge of trivia. Hardwood is a genetic grouping that does not mean the wood is actually hard. Balsa wood, that soft light stuff modellers use … is a hard wood.

I paused at Denmark for a photo opportunity, musing that some of the other Panther adventurers speeding towards Finland, could also be in Denmark. I think most are traversing the Baltic states … but I couldn't find a Latvia or Estonia here in Western Australia. It was fortunate I stopped because my gear lever was trying to escape, damn nearly got away too! That could have been interesting. A piece of aluminum can, has now been added as a shim on the spline and the through-bolt tightened. The addition of two cable ties make me feel a bit more secure.

Late in the day after 460 km, we reached Albany which to our surprise turned to be very substantial with a population of over 35,000. Another cabin was found and $50 cash was handed over to the guy 'minding' the camp while the owner was away. Chilled to the bone and when I couldn't find a heater, I warmed the place using the hot plates of the stove. Interestingly the oven and grill wouldn't work when the top plates were on.

Thurs Aug 7th … birthday of our third-born Kitty Molloy. I never made it to Melbourne in time for the celebrations, but as it was to be a surprise, I am forgiven already. So the day dawned raining. Some days and rides are seen as character-building. Well, I have long since moved on from wanting more character. Even if I had more grit and resolve, an early start was not an option, as I needed to front Telstra in person and sort out my non-serving mobile phone service. Albany, being the big town it is, had a Telstra shop and ultimately we were sorted. It has only taken 6 days.

Even if it had not been cold and wet, the day's ride would never have equalled yesterday's. The road no longer undulated or twisted. On a sunny day I might have enjoyed the contrasting yellows that have appeared in the landscape. There have been magnificent acacia trees and huge areas of rape seed, but the cold and the rain kept spirits low.

TOODYAY TO MCLAREN FLAT

There was an instance when I knelt at Penelope's side carrying out a minor adjustment in the pouring rain, hands trembling from the cold … and I wondered for a moment if there was somewhere else I would like to be. Maybe there is another 'hobby' I could pursue, I thought. Then my terminal optimism returned, I laughed at the thought and we carried on.

The cold and another bit of serendipity took me to the highlight of the day. I pulled into Ongerup looking for petrol and hot food. The roadhouse was closed due to illness but a card-activated pump supplied the juice. On the way in to the town I had spotted a bird sanctuary advertising a café, and so it was I became a fan and advocate of the malleefowl. I went in for coffee and a toastie but when the rain kept up, I was reluctant to leave my warm haven, so invested in the $8 entry fee to the displays etc. I was blown away by the wonder of nature.

Look it up. This amazing ground bird spends most of a year making an enormous mound for a nest (up to 1.5m high, 3m dia.) where the eggs are incubated at a strict temperature of between 32 and 34 degrees. The male adds or removes the nest material to keep the exact warmth within those parameters. When finally hatched, the wee new-born may take up to 15 hours to get to the surface … where the parents ignore it. Amazing!

The ride didn't get me across to Esperance but did get me to Ravensthorpe. I spied The Palace Hotel, a big old pub and stopped. Sadly, my accommodation was not upstairs in the old girl, but in a motel unit adjoining. It did have its own facilities though, and I indulged in a full-body hygiene make-over.

I was hoping that the 'Low' that had been following me would pass over and get ahead. The temperature topped out at something like 12 today. I have already learned that L on the weather map doesn't mean 'lovely'. We may get to Norseman tomorrow … the beginning of the Nullabor Plain. Fingers' crossed.

So yesterday I got the day wrong again, well that is because they all just roll along with no discernible difference to them. Today, the 8th Aug, is a month since Penelope and I set off from Darwin. We've confirmed that Australia is a big country and in the north it is hot even in winter, but in the south it is not. The Met Service have been shouting out the phrase 'Polar Blast' on the TV, and I have to say they probably are not wrong. It was a day of two halves, each 200 km long, each cold as charity. The first half had sunshine so spirits were high. 40 km short of Esperance, where we were to turn away from the coast, I stopped to add fuel from the bladder (no, not mine!) and felt the icy wind. It had been behind us. It then rained, to make this part of the ride miserable. The fuel stop had no seating, so I stood around with a hot coffee and a surprisingly good chicken pie from a cellophane bag.

Esperance was a sprawling town of 15,000 with lots of small industry, car yards, boat places etc. I never saw the centre and my opinion was moulded by the bitter inclemency. For the afternoon, we endured the wind across our bows so to speak. This was not pleasant, especially when the road was wet.

Two chunks were all we could face and Norseman was reached mid-afternoon. This is the turn-off to the Nullabor. We have reached the main road again. Norseman is smaller than expected and the woman in the i-Site tells me the population is 450 and falling. A walk downtown showed a town centre largely empty of shops that were open and trading. There was evidence of three cafes, now all closed up. I had a solitary pint in the pub, the only customer. Such a contrast to last night where the pub was full of miners ... who awakened me at 5.30 this morning as they headed off to work.

*And one last thing about yesterday's malleefowl. The main area they are thriving in, was saved because when the owner of the time went to clear it, his bulldozer broke down. It was fenced then to keep the sheep and cattle out because of a tree there with berries which naturally contain the same toxins as the 1080 poison used for pest killing. It happens that the malleefowl love the berries and are not harmed by them. A win all round because when they share an area with sheep, the ground cover gets cleared, and the foxes, eagles etc can more easily predate on the almost flightless malleefowl. It is nice that there are folk looking after their wellbeing.*

*Tomorrow begins several days of the Nullabor. Straight and dull. Let's hope Penelope is up to it. She has been a reluctant starter on these cold mornings. Her compression isn't great and she is again drinking oil like a dipsomaniac. Oh, sunrise is 7.00 am and sunset 5.45 pm, so the days are not long once you factor in avoiding those times because of kangaroo activity ... and the cold.*

Friday ... I think.

Supposedly there is no plural to nemesis. But if there was/were for us life-long motorcyclists they would be ... wet, cold and straight. Oh yeah baby, this being a motorcycling pin-up for the elderly and infirm, is not all fun and laughter, beer and skittles etc. Today we got all of the above in spades and endured Australia's longest straight road, which didn't really end with a corner or anything dramatic like that, it just paused being absolutely straight.

So it rained, and it stopped raining ... and it rained ... and it paused etc, etc. I watched a tiny rainbow attached to a cloud for a while and I thought about a few of you ... and I watched the converging white lines ahead of me a lot, and I watched the converging white lines behind me in my mirrors a lot ... one at a time. And then I did what I had promised I wouldn't do. I shut my eyes and counted. Remember I told you that when young and on similar roads I could get to 10, then as I matured, I found I could get to six steadily then would rush the seven, eight, nine and ten. Today I got to FOUR! Is this a sign of real maturity or just a marker that I am becoming a wuss?

At my lunch petrol stop I saw the Repco Reliability Trial cars pulling in one after the other. Some very cool cars were participating but as a group I thought they were a bit up themselves. Later I saw three cars on recovery trailers. I didn't snigger because it can happen to any of us.

My singing isn't improving and I can't believe that at home I can sing along with Leonard Cohen to his *Live in London* double album, every word … yet here on the road I don't know why we are taking Manhattan before Berlin, Marianne doesn't stay long … and surely Suzanne doesn't take her knickers down, at a place by the river … and what's the bit about oranges from China? I think tomorrow it might be back to 'Busted flat in Baton Rouge'. Or some Van the Man.

Through the marvels of modern technology, today I receive a photo from last year's ride … when I'd passed through Mt Isa an encountee had taken a few snaps and now had sent one through. I include it in my posting to the 'fans' … just because there is nothing much for me to photograph on this dull plain. This contrasts with the wonderful shots being provided by our Northern Hemisphere Panther riders heading to Finland. Their photos of Estonia etc make me very envious. I hole up in the Cocklebiddy Roadhouse, and monitor the weather.

Déjà vu, Déjà vu, Déjà vu … Déjà vu, Déjà vu, Déjà vu! That was the next morning's chant. I couldn't bring up any Van Morrison, so mindless chanting it was. So much the same. Same cold, same straight dull roads with initially nothing of note to interest the mind.

The day had started with a bit of a reminder about not driving when the marsupials are about. As I took back my key and TV remote to reception, I intercepted a couple of motorcycle riders who had already done the 80 km from the next staging post. They had pulled in to arrange help for a guy who had hit a kangaroo the night before. His airbag had gone off injuring him a little and he had stayed in his car all night. They were kindly sorting things out.

I'd not rushed my departure, despite the need to put in a solid day. It was interesting that we were temporarily in another time zone, one that my smart phone didn't recognise. It is just a little one and we can only wonder why.

About 1.30 in the afternoon I passed another solo woman cyclist.

**THE BIG SIT**

It was raining and I didn't spot her standing with bike and trailer until too late, and then I castigated myself for not making the effort to offer encouragement etc. She was looking at the 60 km sign which was probably telling her it was too far for the afternoon. She was already more than a normal cycling day beyond the last roadhouse, so I reckon she would have had at least two nights of side-of-the-road camping in the rain … rolling up her wet tent with all the clinging red mud sticking to it in the mornings. I admired her resilience and presumed resolve, as I thudded by, aiming for another night indoors. The cold temperatures mean that my hydrapac is just a dead weight that I carry along for the day. In the hotter climes it has been a vital piece of equipment as all day I would intermittently slug away, keeping myself hydrated. Often I would need to refill a couple of times a day. Now it is cold, the desire to take on water while I am riding is completely absent.

Once again I betrayed my promise not to go soft if it cost more than $75. The night at the Nullabor Roadhouse hit a new low/high … $139. The Des of old would have put his tent up and worn all his clothes to bed.

I suppose it is a sign of the times, standards slipping, moral foundations crumbling, the strong becoming weak. I know they are a remote spot with lots of extra costs ... but it still pisses me off.

It had been nice riding along the coast seeing the Great Ocean Bight for a while. The sun shone for most of the afternoon beyond Eucla. I was breathalysed when entering South Australia and my licence scrutinised. They were happy with the NZ licence ... the cop said it was Victorians they were after.

Another Panther connection was encountered. A Victorian couple with a VW Combi are friends with the Sergeants of the Aussie Panther clan. Just another example of the small world we live in. Yesterday a 79-year-old ex-Kiwi told me he did his motorcycle mechanic's apprenticeship in the 1950s at a Matchless and Ariel dealership in Auckland, and in the spares department for the whole time he worked there ... was a pair of Panther forks!

**THE BIG SIT**

... and a less than joyous end to the day, the All Blacks fell far short of beating the Wallabies, but tomorrow is another day.

Well, I paid back the rip-off Nullabor Roadhouse by spending nothing with them, other than for the petrol and $139 room. I had a two-day-old ham salad bread bun, and I drank water while watching the rugby. My morning coffee was my own beans and I did without brekky ... so that will have taught them a lesson. You don't mess with Mr Pissed-off. My Kiwi neighbours in the cell next door were also not impressed as it was an extra $20 to have the wife indoors.

At 4.00 am I'd got up for my old man's pit stop and flicked on the heat pump. Snuggling back down to the drone of the wobbly fan, I thought of the young woman cyclist who I knew would be foetally-curled-up in her tent, toughing out another cold, wet night at the side of the road. Another First World problem was that I awoke with chapped lips – so luxury and warmth comes with consequences. Pawpaw cream to the rescue.

Anyway, the Nullabor is now done, just a tick on the calendar of life. The countryside now has more trees and Ceduna (pop 2,200) has people, shops, a wharf, a supermarket and a flash pub. It also has three caravan parks. I entered the first one and it had a good vibe, friendly folk interacted with me even before I was off Penelope ... and in a prime spot was a split-screen VW Combi just like the one my mates and I had toured Europe in all those years ago. A grin came across my face as I realised just how small these old girls are ... and we slept five in the back for months on end. The young office-wallah was affable. I was naturally buoyant ... till he said $120. "I don't need facilities, just a basic donga". I really couldn't let myself down two nights in a row. Gently, he told me to go down the road to A1 Cabins. "They'll have something for you."

And they did have, for half that price, complete with an ensuite and tiny shower. To top it off I found my way to the seaside hotel for specials' night. It was humming and I congenially shared my table with a local couple and their friend who lives back at the WA border at the ocean's edge by the Eucla roadhouse and historic radio repeater building ... you know, the one they couldn't stop the sands from taking over ... they taught you at school all about it.

And I posted to the immediacy of Facebook –

*Anyway my time with you is coming to an end ... for now. All going well and if the cold doesn't stop me achieving two 400+ km days, I should pause this ride Tuesday evening and you can go back to your lives without my daily updates.*

*Oh, and I did my laundry, so will be fit to meet people again.*

So I cracked the first 400 km chunk. One more to go and this leg will be done. It wasn't a bad old day. There are nice things to see, as South Australia shows itself. Still no swervery, but there are undulations to interest me. We pass by huge cropping paddocks and every tiny settlement has enormous grain silos as big as I remember on the prairies of the USA. And we followed a pipeline!

It has been relentlessly cold and my comfort has not been helped by leaving my alpaca jersey in the cabin back in Norseman. An ex-Kiwi returning to WA mentioned this morning as I togged-up, that he expected to see me shoving a *NZ Herald* down my front for warmth. An hour later a *Weekend Australian* was sourced and this old trick made the day bearable.

It was a day of huddled-up reflection. It's been a good leg. My eyes and other senses have taken in a lot and I feel we have given a lift to many people's days. Sometimes it may even be mutual envy, other times mutual pity. We've been a little bedraggled this last week, not quite cutting the dashing figures we envisage is our normal front.

Sometimes I've sensed sniffy opinions of the oily old man with no companion except his down-at-mouth old motorcycle. Penelope is my ears and eyes, always reporting back.

"Oh Harold, you're so lucky I saved you from a life like that!" an elegant matron in well-cut casual clothes, whispered to her male consort as they sauntered back to their gun-metal grey Audi A8. Flicking her cashmere pashmina over her shoulder, she opened the car door and slid in … all the while delicately holding two pieces of French nougat in a tissue. "I think a little Vivaldi" was the last of the one-way conversation that Penelope heard as the Bose sound system gently overpowered his deferential nodded response.

Interestingly, I'd caught his eye momentarily and for a second I reckoned it'd gone a bit rheumy … probably recalling his University days and the metal-flake purple Norton Commando that filled his life with joy at the time.

Oh well, we couldn't resist staying at Iron Knob and wondered how Harold was faring. We posed for some photos, hoping to invoke some ribald commentary from our fans. The hotel had four patrons but two left early. The remaining two old Brits both had Panther connections. One, who was a youthful 84 told me he ran away from home at 70. He just couldn't face any more joyless years. I am not sure if he is to be held up as a figure of inspiration or not. Being as 'voices' told him to go to Iron Knob, I think not. Iron Knob is a failed mining town. It was Australia's first iron ore mine and BHP ran it for 99 years. It now has a population of about 140. It is amazing to think that it is the last day of the ride tomorrow … for now. I battle in the night with a sole mosquito.

Over top lads … this is it.

The day dawned … as they do. I took the opportunity to go for a stroll around Iron Knob in the cool three degree sunshine and took a few photos. It is the sort of ghost town that you walk down the middle of the road so as not to favour either side. Already there was a woman gluing the C back on to her 'Coffee' sign outside the Christian Book Shop … the only

THE BIG SIT

shop. I decided that 8.00 am was a bit early for Christianity, so exchanged pleasantries but didn't partake of her coffee. Iron Knob had been a good stop. It is a funny little non-town, enjoyed because of the characters I met.

With no sense of occasion, the ride was just 'another day, another dollar' chore for Penelope ... although I thought I sensed her unease as we approached a 'Cash for scrap!' sign. I whispered a few reassuring words and we whistled past. Lots of the ride now looked like NZ, green and lush with rolling hillsides etc. A couple of wind farms were passed, one lot spinning, one lot not.

Google Maps and others said I had to go through Adelaide. What a nightmare! Worst traffic since the Melbourne rush-hour four years ago. Red light after red light drove us crazy. I had to keep reassuring Penelope that we'd survived other big cities. She didn't seem to think that me saying "You've done Mexico City, you've done Beijing, you've done Ulaan Bator" was much encouragement. The little minx then tried to throw away her gear lever again ... twice. If we weren't on our way to stay with nice people, I really could have got very irate and actually done the Basil Fawlty on her that I have previously threatened.

Ultimately, we reached the South Australian service centre for Cleckheaton's finest. Mick and Jane make us both welcome and Penelope is penned with some mates ... and I am suitably cosseted.

I reflected on Facebook –

*In 2016 the Australian Panther Rally was held here in McLaren Flat and we rode down from Melbourne to begin this Aussie adventure. Tonight the circle was completed. They call it 'doing a lap'. If you go up the middle via Alice Springs etc then go either way at the top ... it is 'half a lap'. We've done up the East coast, across to The Gulf then down the Birdsville and Oodnadatta Tracks to South Australia then back up the middle to the top and around the west ... and south-west and finally across the bottom, so really can claim 'a lap with extras'.*

Google works it out to be about 22,000 km.

We're pretty proud. When people look for my support team and express surprise that there doesn't seem to be one, I tell them that the whole Panther family is supporting me. It is quite reassuring having almost immediate interactions and responses with our friends, family and followers. On our first adventure together in 1976/1977 I would write a monthly account of how it was going and send it off to the editor of Sloper, the club's magazine. He would decipher the scribblings best he could, type it out and publish. We had no feed-back for the 10 months it took us to ride from New Orleans to Buenos Aires … now it can be within minutes of posting.

The ride is to pause here in McLaren Flat. I've got commitments back at home so I book a ticket on the train from Adelaide to Melbourne for the Friday morning. It is however not the end of the rainbow … there is another leg to do in October. Penelope may be ailing, but she still has an important appointment to make.

**THE BIG SIT**

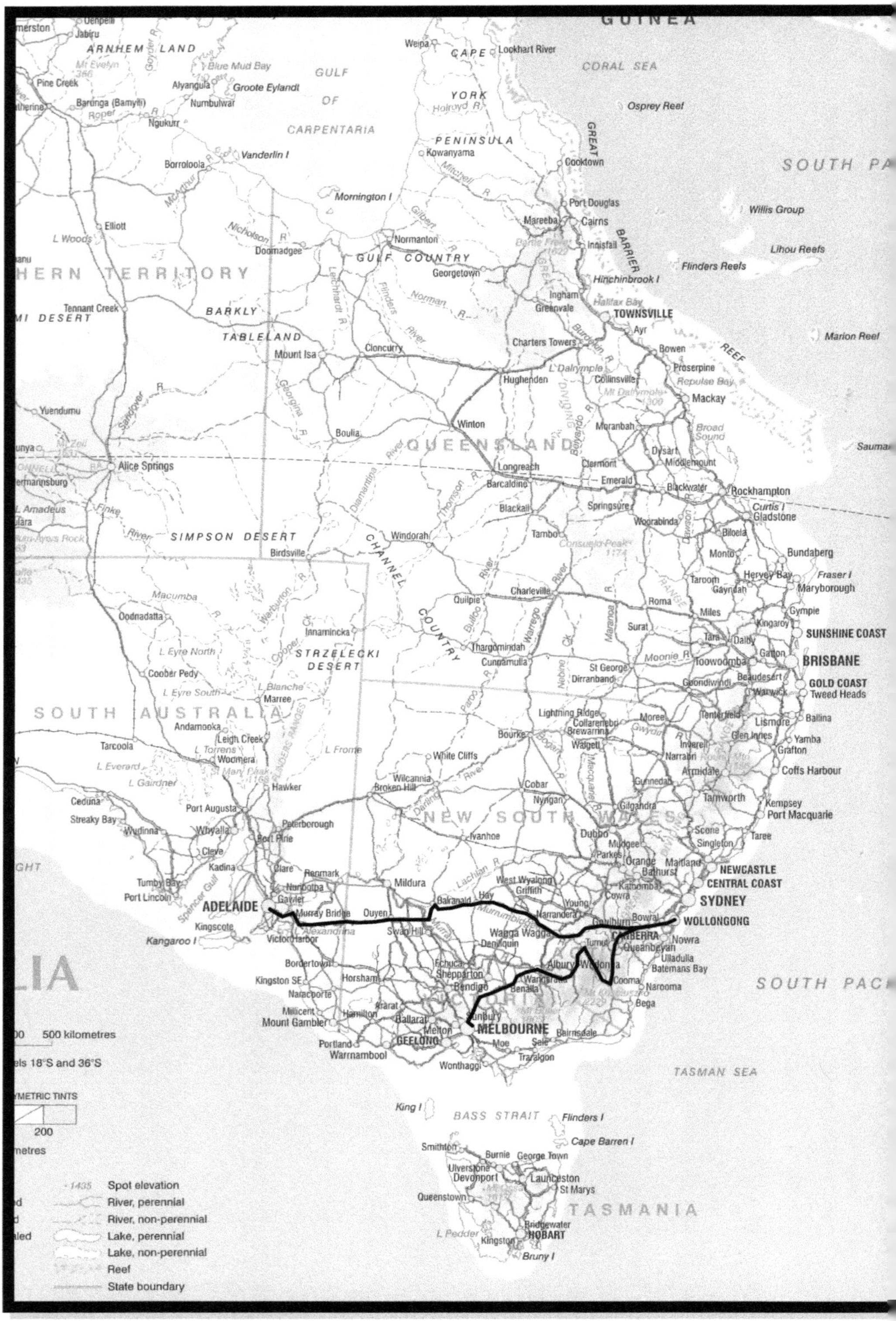
GUINEA
Oenpelli
Jabiru
ARNHEM LAND
Mt Evelyn 386
Goyder R
Blue Mud Bay
Pine Creek
Alyangula
Groote Eylandt
GULF
OF
CARPENTARIA
Barunga (Bamyili)
Numbulwar
Roper R
Ngukurr
Borroloola
McArthur R
Vanderlin I
Mornington I
Elliott
L Woods
Nicholson R
Doomadgee
Tennant Creek
BARKLY
TABLELAND
Mount Isa
Cloncurry
Leichhardt R
Flinders R
Georgina R
Sandover R
Yuendumu
Alice Springs
Hermannsburg
L Amadeus
Finke R
SIMPSON DESERT
Boulia
Birdsville
Diamantina River
CHANNEL
COUNTRY
Macumba
Oodnadatta
Warburton R
Cooper Ck
Innamincka
L Eyre North
STRZELECKI
DESERT
Coober Pedy
L Eyre South
L Blanche
Marree
SOUTH AUSTRALIA
Andamooka
Leigh Creek
FLINDERS RANGES
L Frome
Tarcoola
L Torrens
Woomera
L Everard
L Gairdner
Hawker
Ceduna
Streaky Bay
Wudinna
Port Augusta
Whyalla
Peterborough
Port Pirie
Cleve
Kadina
Clare
Renmark
Tumby Bay
Port Lincoln
Spencer Gulf
ADELAIDE
Gawler
Nuriootpa
Murray Bridge
Kingscote
Kangaroo I
Victor Harbor
L Alexandrina
Bordertown
Kingston SE
Naracoorte
Millicent
Mount Gambier
Weipa
CAPE
YORK
PENINSULA
Lockhart River
Holroyd R
Kowanyama
Mitchell R
Gilbert R
Normanton
GULF COUNTRY
Georgetown
Norman R
Cooktown
Port Douglas
Mareeba
Cairns
Innisfail
Hinchinbrook I
Ingham
Greenvale
TOWNSVILLE
Ayr
Charters Towers
Burdekin R
Bowen
Proserpine
Repulse Bay
Hughenden
Collinsville
L Dalrymple
Mackay
Winton
Moranbah
QUEENSLAND
Belyando R
Broad Sound
Dysart
Middlemount
Longreach
Clermont
Barcaldine
Emerald
Blackwater
Rockhampton
Curtis I
Gladstone
Thomson R
Blackall
Springsure
Woorabinda
Dawson R
Biloela
Windorah
Tambo
Consuelo Peak 1174
Monto
Bundaberg
Charleville
Hervey Bay
Fraser I
Maryborough
Taroom
Gayndah
Quilpie
Roma
Miles
Gympie
Bulloo R
Warrego R
Maranoa R
Surat
Kingaroy
SUNSHINE COAST
Thargomindah
Tara
Dalby
Gatton
Moonie R
Toowoomba
BRISBANE
Cunnamulla
St George
Dirranbandi
Goondiwindi
Beaudesert
GOLD COAST
Tweed Heads
Warwick
Paroo R
Nebine Ck
Lightning Ridge
Collarenebri
Brewarrina
Moree
Tenterfield
Lismore
Ballina
Bourke
Walgett
Gwydir R
Inverell
Glen Innes
Yamba
Grafton
White Cliffs
Narrabri
Armidale
Coffs Harbour
Wilcannia
Broken Hill
Darling R
Cobar
Nyngan
Gunnedah
Tamworth
Kempsey
Port Macquarie
NEW SOUTH WALES
Gilgandra
Ivanhoe
Dubbo
Scone
Singleton
Taree
Mudgee
Parkes
Orange
Bathurst
Maitland
NEWCASTLE
CENTRAL COAST
Mildura
Lachlan R
West Wyalong
Griffith
Katoomba
Cowra
Young
SYDNEY
Ouyen
Balranald
Hay
Murrumbidgee R
Narrandera
Goulburn
Bowral
WOLLONGONG
Swan Hill
Wagga Wagga
CANBERRA
Queanbeyan
Nowra
Tumut
Deniliquin
Ulladulla
Batemans Bay
Echuca
Albury
Wodonga
Shepparton
Cooma
Narooma
Horsham
Bendigo
Wangaratta
Benalla
VICTORIA
Bega
Ararat
Hamilton
Ballarat
Sunbury
Melton
MELBOURNE
Bairnsdale
Portland
Warrnambool
GEELONG
Moe
Sale
Traralgon
Wonthaggi
CORAL SEA
Osprey Reef
GREAT
BARRIER
REEF
Willis Group
Lihou Reefs
Flinders Reefs
Marion Reef
SOUTH PACIFIC
SOUTH PACIFIC
TASMAN SEA
King I
BASS STRAIT
Flinders I
Cape Barren I
Smithton
Burnie
George Town
Ulverstone
Devonport
Launceston
St Marys
Queenstown
TASMANIA
L Pedder
Bridgewater
Kingston
HOBART
Bruny I
LIA
500 kilometres
els 18°S and 36°S
YMETRIC TINTS
200
metres
1435 Spot elevation
River, perennial
River, non-perennial
Lake, perennial
Lake, non-perennial
Reef
State boundary

CHAPTER ELEVEN

# THE FINAL SURGE

Now that I am officially an old duffer, people often asked if I am retired. My response is usually "I am not sure." I thought I might have been, but BRANZ keeps coming to me and contracting me to do educational roadshows. This is a very good gig, as it gives me a concentrated infusion of money to balance my semi-profligate, indulgent spending on these adventures with Penelope. They want me again for seven weeks in October and November 2019. This takes some negotiation and compromise. I have committed Penelope and I to be at the Australian Panther Register's annual gathering, which is scheduled to commence on Friday 18th of Oct. BRANZ are pretty good about this and split the schedule so I do two weeks of being a 'talking head', have ten days as an adventurer, then come back to five more weeks helping with the educational needs of New Zealand's building industry.

The gathering in Orangeville, New South Wales was also to be the occasion of the launch of my book *No One Said It Would Be Easy* which chronicles the first big adventure involving Penelope – from New Orleans to Buenos Aires in 1976 -1977. Due to a variety of reasons and let-downs, I had decided to self-publish through a Melbourne 'enabler'. This in itself had been a big adventure and was nearing the end. The Panther 'rally' would just be a small launch, but a very suitable one. Tablo Publishing arranged for a box of books to be printed in Australia and forwarded to the Dickies who were organising the event and hosting us. It has been a busy old time getting this far. My seminar series starts well and on the Friday of the second week after the presentation, I fly from Dunedin to Christchurch. Here I meet with Steph who has flown in from Nelson. Finally, we are to do a leg of the big red continent together. There are quite a few things that we don't do well together – like shifting furniture – but we do gel when travelling. She's the best possible pillion and has wonderful resilience. After more than 40 years, we still enjoy the same things and an adventure together is something to savour.

We fly through the night and have an enjoyable family day in Melbourne before flying to Adelaide in the late afternoon. We've booked a room through Airbnb on the outskirts of the city. It is not the cutesy old place that the website showed, but it did the job for an overnight stay. We venture downtown and somehow end up in what seems to be the red-light area with barkers calling out over the strident music emanating from each gaudily-labelled venue. Often scantily-clad young women are in evidence, seemingly to entice punters in. None of it looks or sounds very inviting. We are also slightly bemused by the sight of several groups of young women dressed as Bavarians. Initially we thought it was a 'hen's night' group, but the large numbers and no cohesive direction, seemed to dispel that. Days later we found it was the aftermath of a big beerfest event.

Nothing in the leery, neon-lit strip has any appeal to us and we are beginning to despair of finding a suitable place to take victuals and suitably imbibe. We are not fussy, but we don't want bright lights or loud noise. Finally, we spot a discretely adorned old-fashioned shop-front. Initially, we were not totally sure that *Apothecary* is even a bar or an eatery. It has a frosted-glass front window and upon entering we see no diners, only chemists' memorabilia from the past. We are taken down stairs into the brick-walled cellar area. Ultimately we experience fine dining at its best.

Everything is discrete and tasteful, including the fare.

Mick and Jane are away visiting family until Sunday afternoon, so I take the opportunity to show Steph the Fleurieu Peninsular that I had enjoyed so much in 2016. We've got a small minor-brand Asian rental car which unusually is not an automatic. Of course, this doesn't concern us as all our cars and utes have been manuals. Being modern it has all sorts of confusing digital displays, which we ignore with the superiority of the elderly. After about an hour of driving on the Sunday, I notice that one display is sometimes showing a number which seems to be one different to the gear I am driving in. I find this fascinating as it doesn't always get it right, sometimes telling me to change up when I am about to change down. I am confused though by sometimes seeing 4 when I am in 5th, cruising along in the open road … but sometimes there is a 6. Yes, it took quite some time for me to learn that the car had six gears. Who would have thought?

There have been so many times during my big peregrination that I form the words "Steph would love this!" in my head, sometimes even saying it out loud. This time I am able to show her things I saw and enjoyed when Penelope and I were being led all over this wonderful part of the world by Mick and his mates back in 2016. I can't quite find the spot where we had morning tea on the Saturday, but we explore a little of the southern side of the peninsular, before heading for Victor Harbor where I was sure we had lunched and displayed the bikes. The spelling of Harbor is unusual for us as in NZ we always include the 'u' – as in harbour. It seems the Aussies usually do, but not in this case. Victor Harbor is nice … but not as I had remembered it. There wasn't a paddle steamer at the wharf or a steam train. This threw me a bit as I had been promising Steph lunch, and you guessed it … time was fugitting it. Google quickly worked it out that maybe we wanted Goolwa which was the other end of the steam train line … and did have a paddle steamer!

Our short time at Goolwa was relaxing and enjoyable. It was just as I had left it. The dockside bar could only do toasted sandwiches, which we adjudged perfect for our needs on a Sunday afternoon. A middle-aged troubadour pulled up a seat next to us, letting on that he'd been mowing the lawn when he got the urgent call to replace the scheduled singer for the afternoon. He was pleasant and his songs matched his acoustic guitar and gravelly voice. We would have liked to have stayed longer but we had a call to make before we finally hit Jane and Mick's for the evening meal. I'd met Karyn Forster up in Darwin at Dan's *Cruise for the Cause*. She was the Prostate Cancer Foundation's State Manager for South Australia and the Northern Territory. We'd gelled over a couple of days last year and upon learning of the several strings she had to her bow, including editing books, I'd brought the proof-copy of *No One Said It Would Be Easy* for her thoughts etc. I'd also sensed that she and Steph would hit it off. It was a bonus that she had a place in the country at McLaren Vale up on the hill above Jane and Mick's. She was recovering from a serious leg operation but had kindly invited us to visit.

**THE BIG SIT**

Karyn's place was enchanting with stunning views over the McLaren Flat vineyards. To say it was eclectic, only tells a tenth of the story. From the gate in, there were remnants of colonial history appearing to be gently and slowly returning to Mother Earth. None of it looks posed or unnatural. Her house continues the theme. Everywhere we looked, there were curiosities. Mostly they were from the 'outside working-man's' world with also numerous items from the building and draughting past I am familiar with. None of it was 'displayed' … it just was there for you to look at, touch … or even ignore. Steph was in heaven. She loves the old, she loves the ramshackle. She hates the 'arranged' or faux. There was nothing twee about Karyn's demesne. I'd describe it as 'honest'. She was still wheelchair-bound but there was plenty of room for her to scoot around. Her man was down the hill a bit playing with some fencing so after watching him through the window for a while, we settled in to afternoon tea, wine and a chat. Of course Steph and Karyn did immediately hit it off. Karyn's our vintage and well-worn – I mean that as a compliment. It was a lovely time that we all feel is a shame to truncate, but we have a pretty relentless schedule to stick to. We exit through the back door and note the cactus zone which Karyn informs us is a wild-fire barrier.

We slowly idled down the hill enjoying in the sights. We pass by the house dug into the hill that Karyn had told us of. The construction site had been dug into the hillside and when the house was finished, it was covered over again, leaving the glazed frontage facing the view as the only visible sight of it. This results in a very thermally effective solution, as heat loss is minimal except for through the front. They do have to be built well, with particular attention paid to waterproofing the whole envelope of the building. Sadly, this one started leaking some months after construction and had to be dug up to carry out remedial work.

Jane and Mick welcomed us warmly and sincerely. Mick had the BBQ going with two chickens on board …you can't get much better than that. A lovely meal with their son and girlfriend followed. It is a minor disappointment to learn that Jane and Mick will not be able to join us for the rally at the Dickies. The original plan had them leaving a day after us with their bikes on a trailer. Being as Penelope is ailing and I'd decided that there was not really enough time to investigate, determine her needs, source them and repair … it seemed ideal to have them following along somewhere behind. Mick is low on annual leave and can't really spare another three to four days, when he is also desperately busy. This news takes nothing away from the enjoyment of the short stay, which was sublime. It was a wonderful bonus that they are coffee people and each day would start with Jane making a 'proper' coffee. In many ways I see her as a younger version of Steph, trim and full of vim and vigour. They are both like wind-up 'Energiser Bunnies' with easy smiles. Mick was always off pre-dawn to the environs of Adelaide to project manage large-scale housing construction. With shared backgrounds in construction … and motorbikes, we always had something to talk about in the evenings. Mick had built a smart cottage on the property since I first visited in 2016 and it was now run as an Airbnb rental which now kept Jane busy on site. They are both competent, quiet high achievers who have done many things in their lives and had many moto adventures, often on bikes as outrageously unsuitable as Penelope. Although Jane's main ride is now a Honda 400/4 from the 1970s, she has had many fun times on her little 1950s 125cc BSA Bantam. Mick and his mates have similarly adventured all over on 250cc side-valve BSA C10s, even riding once all the way to Queensland for a BSA rally … and not getting the 'furthest travelled' because someone had *flown* from the UK.

I am always chastened when I enter my peers' tidy sheds and garages. Honestly, I want to be like that, but something inherently precludes it. I am somehow genetically untidy and sloppy. Mick's sheds contain an eclectic mix of motos with obviously a love for Panthers, but also Moto Guzzis. He has splendid examples of both. He even has a pre-Panther P & M. I am very envious and smile a lot. He has great tools, memorabilia and even a sign proclaiming one shed for Panthers with an appropriate sign.

Penelope has managed about 4,500 km since nipping up and whilst she is drinking oil like she wants to single-handedly keep the Saudi Arabian economy afloat, she still starts ok and is doing her best to get us to the pot at the bottom of the rainbow … wherever that is. I'd already decided that we'd just change her rear tyre and fettle her best as we could in the few days available. Being as we were now back in the more populated part of Australia I'd decided we would be able to 'hotel-it-all-the-way', and abandon the camping gear. In fact, I'd decided to go with a complete change of luggage, dumping the tent, sleeping bag, bedroll, camp stool, Kelly Cooker, Aeropress, coffee grinder etc. The big leather saddlebags (made in the 1980s and gifted to brother Roly to use on an International Vincent Rally in Europe) sat a little too far forward on the seat for Steph to have comfortable access to the pillion foot pegs. They'd have to go! My new layout had a set of canvas throw-over saddle bags which went on the petrol tank. I'd made these prior to our *Last Hurrah* ride in 2005, so I knew they fitted. The rest of the gear would fit in a rubberised army kit bag on the carrier and be restrained by the wonderful 'piggy-back' stretchies. That would still enable us to have our waterproofs on the outside within easy reach. We'd travel light. I am always appreciative that Steph doesn't require a hair dryer or a full luggage-side of beauty products when we travel. A big plastic bin was sourced and most of the surplus gear and detritus went in it and was stacked away for later repatriation.

The few days fly by. I tinker, Steph and Jane do a local walk and also some of the local second-hand clothing shops. Steph and I also independently explore the McLaren Vale village, managing to muck up the meeting arrangement and both wait, irritated and hot … and apart. On the Tuesday we take the rental car back, stopping along the way to purchase new riding trousers for Steph. We'd decided back at home that her gear was pretty well past it, and this would be the opportunity to come into the world of armoured knees, reflective bits, zip-out linings etc. A nice young woman, fiddling about in one of the many aisles of bewildering clothing options, initially seemed reticent to help us. She went to deflect us back to the counter staff, who had already spotted our age and demeanour, dismissed us as tyre-kickers, and gone back to gazing at computer screens. However, she asked what we were after and then took us through all the options, being very attendant to Steph with suitable motorbike chat etc. She was a rider and imparted good advice. Finally, Steph chose a pair of textile riding trousers that would be waterproof and tough. "Any old-duffer discount for poor Kiwis?" I hit her with. She laughed and said she would give it … if she worked there … but we'd have to ask the shop guys. It seems she was a rep, checking on her stock levels. We put in a good word about her at the counter, and the guys did give us $20 off.

We have a lovely last night, and then it is time to hit the road Jack. The morning is cool and drizzling, so we tog up in less-than-elegant waterproofs. The ride across to Strathalbyn was delightful, even in the light rain. The road undulates through vineyards and green pastures. We're heading for 'Strath', as the locals call it, for breakfast. It is always nice to get some early miles under your belt. It is some years since Steph has been behind me on Penelope. Apart from the fact that she's been in Aus for four years, back in NZ *nellops* often took a back seat to others in the garage for our longer rides, so it was pretty special to be a team again. It was a bit like getting 'The Blues Brothers' back together. The synchronicity was almost instant, the enjoyment palpable. There is something special about an adventure with a loved one … and in this case it is with two loved ones.

We're more or less repeating my ride of 2016 for our first day, heading what I think of as north. Because Adelaide is in South Australia, I think of it as being south of Melbourne which is in Victoria. A look at a map would dispel this notion ... but I can't help it. Today however, we're heading more or less due East, so diverging away from the road to Melbourne. Strathalbyn is a superb stop. It is quirky, quaint ... bohemian and arty with lots of cafes all fired-up and in action, even though it is Wednesday morning. You can sense that this would be a hub, a gathering-up spot for special-interest groups on the weekend, be they car clubs, moto riders, families, retiree conventions etc.

For me it has one more special attraction, one that is more than just a memorial to the town's most famous son. Kenny Blake was possibly Australia's most winning motorcycle racer of the 1970s. Part of what made the gritty Aussie a legend, was that on February 8 1976, he beat 15 times World Champion and absolute Super-hero Giacomo Agostini in the Australian TT held at the Laverton Air Force base near Melbourne, Victoria. Ago was the reigning 500cc Grand Prix Champion and had won 121 Grand Prix races from 1966 onwards, mainly on the screaming four-stroke Italian MV Augusta machines. He had also shown he could ride the two-strokes of the era by winning on Yamaha in 1975. For the Australian race he brought the MV on which, later in the year, he would win the German Grand Prix, the last ever by a four-stroke in the 500cc class. In a real *'Boys' Own'* tale, Kenny took delivery of a new four cylinder RG500 Suzuki only days before the race ... and went on to beat the world's greatest rider. It is thought that as many as 50,000 spectators had flocked in to see the event, but as the security company managing the event was sacked and replaced by volunteers at the last minute, only 13,500 paid and subsequently the promoter did a bunk and none of the overseas riders got paid their appearance fees and their bikes were initially impounded.

With his winnings Kenny Blake went off to race on the world stage. He had intermittent good results, often popping back for the Australian season, but sadly lost his life at the cruel Isle of Man TT in 1981. Such was his standing with fans, there is a Ken Blake Memorial lunch held every year in a Melbourne hotel. This has been held every year since his death and attracts guest speakers who knew and competed against him. There is on the main street of Strathalbyn a most innovative art installation by renowned Goolwa artist James Stewart. It is made out of mechanical parts (mainly motorcycle) and tools of all shapes and sizes, welded together to form the shape of Kenny racing at his hardest. A Coopers' beer bottle cap on his helmet "claims him back to South Australia". The half-tonne sculpture is stunning and I line Penelope up close, so she can appreciate the speedy lines. The portrayal of Kenny Blake at speed, all leaned over is evocative and poignant. He was a rider I had read about in my youth.

With the sun now out and a good hearty breakfast behind us, it is time to bank some miles. We continue on the B45 heading for Wellington. I like the connection, being that I am from New Zealand's Wellington, which is of course our capital city and home of the government. This Wellington is a hamlet of possibly a couple of hundred people. Both named after the same Duke of course. This little Wellington is near the end of the mighty 2,500 km long Murray River and due to the physical similarity to New

Orleans, the early Aussie settlers thought it to be an ideal spot for a major town. A ferry across the river was established, the name approved by the Duke himself, the location surveyed and sections sold on both sides of the river. It became the original crossing of the River Murray for people, livestock, and goods travelling overland between Adelaide and Melbourne, and remained so until a bridge was built about 30 km upstream in 1879. Sadly, the town never flourished. A free government cable-drawn car ferry still operates today and this is our first stop. The countryside has become less entertaining but still gently undulates. The road is quite narrow but two-laned, with little traffic.

It is nice to pause and await the ferry. We've enjoyed the first hundred km of the day and it gives us a sort of respite, to compare notes and agree upon how much fun we are having. The river is maybe 750 m wide at the crossing point and the 30 m ferry carries about six to eight vehicles at a time, taking about ten minutes to be winched across. The service is slick and well-organised. Upon disembarking we follow the road up the other side of the river to Tailem Bend where we need to get ourselves sorted with the right road. Last time I stopped at Tailem Bend and visited their pioneer village which, apart from the new motorsport facility, is the principal attraction of the area. This time through, we only have time to get geographically misplaced for a short period, before we find the B12 and scoot on. From here on in the day is straight, and back to what a lot of Aussie is, namely less than interesting. This is Steph's first experience of straight, featureless roads arrowing away to the horizon. The Murray River has delineated the landscape. The lush greenery and rolling countryside filled with vineyards is no more. The land is now featureless, decidedly pastural, the highway lined with spindly eucalypts. Occasionally we spot the railway running parallel. We learn later that it is one of the few remaining oddities from the past when each region seemed to select their rail gauge without consideration of the bigger picture. The line out from

Tailem Bend has been converted from broad gauge to standard gauge as far as Pinnaroo which is the small town closest to the South Australia to Victoria border. The track that continues on to the traditional rail-hub of Ouyen still remains broad gauge which limits its use to very local grain trains as they cannot get through to Adelaide etc.

The long afternoon ticks off quaintly-named spots Sherlock, Geranium, Lameroo, Pinnaroo, Cowangie, Boinka, Underbool, Walpeup before we finally hit the burg of Ouyen. This is a proper town of about 1,000 people, so has a few shops to look in the window of. We're a bit too late to see anyone on the streets. It has been a determined 400 km. We're happy with the day and Steph is thrilled with the Victoria Hotel as I knew she would be. If you had to find a cheap-and-cheerful example of the Australian small town, two-storey old hotel ... this would be it. It has the requisite presence, the obligatory Victorian filigree decoration, the wide veranda at the first floor, the amazingly long corridors, shared bathrooms, the extensive use of coloured lead-light glazing etc. We often chuckle at recalling the first time we stayed a one of this genre of pub. When they gave us the price ... and we decided to stay ... we didn't know it the price quoted was per person, or for the room.

We pose Penelope out front before stashing her away in the big shed behind. The Victoria is everything we desire – we're two-star folk. We sup in the bar, take a walk, imbibe again then go through to the dining room where I'd had such an enjoyable evening with the Dickies four years earlier. Everything about the stay is just what you would expect. This is not four or five star. A breakfast is included in the night's tariff and is a basic help-yourself to cereal or toast from the corner room upstairs. We're up quite early and this humble offering is taken outside onto the wide deck and enjoyed in the morning sun. A quick start is not on the cards today as we need oil. Penelope seems to be drinking at least one litre every 100 km, so a full pack of oil is needed each day. I've long since been unable to get the good-stuff formulated particularly for her needs. The 'high zinc, low detergent' oil for old vehicles is not often found now, and I quietly rebuke her for being such a fussy tart. I get a five litre pack and we set off in the direction that dear old Google advises. We are now diverging away from the route I took back to Melbourne. We won't be going down to Echuca to see all the waddling paddle-steamers, nor Lake Boga with the sea plane museum. In fact, there doesn't really look to be much to entertain us on the way ahead.

The day starts a bit late due the oil shop not opening until 9.00 am. This gave Steph some extra time with a book out on the veranda. Getting on to the right road is not hard and soon we are humming along, only to discover that I had been a little too casual with my stowing of the oil under the wide elastics. Steph has noticed that the oil pack is not there ... nor my crocs! A slow return to Ouyen finds the oil but not the crocs. That's not too bad, and the container has not burst. The day is not long, but the next couple will need to be for us to get to Orangeville on Friday night before it gets dark. After about 120 km we leave the B12 at the tiny dot of Kyalite and travel along an even smaller road which doesn't seem to have a number, but we've been told to follow the Kyalite Road … so we do. We're now back in New South Wales. After nearly another hour, we pull off the into the little settlement of Moulamein. It is wind-swept and fairly bleak. The sun is watery without much heat and we've maybe gone a bit far without fuelling the bodies. There is an old-fashioned tea rooms with pretty average fare. Sitting outside, pondering if it was too windy and cold, we were approached by a fortyish bloke who was enthused about meeting us. He was out, scouting back-country motorbike roads and routes. He was slightly embarrassed that he was in the ubiquitous pleased-and-proud family station-wagon. We can't remember if he was doing this for a publication or as a tour-leader for a guiding group. It was an affable and pleasant interaction and his knowledge and maps gave us some good guidance about the way ahead and the choices we needed to make to get to the Dickies effectively.

Bidding our new mate farewell, we whack out another 90 km or so before I decide there is only so much barren, featureless countryside to be tolerated at any one time, so we go indoors for a deserved libation at Pretty Pine. This is a pretty insignificant spot … but has a tavern. The publican oozes bonhomie and local anecdotes, but we can't tarry too long as there are still some serious km to do. There are about 700 km left to get us to the Dickies, and we don't want too big a day for our last. We refuel in neighbouring Deniliquin which is our first town with a population numbered in thousands rather than hundreds that we've encountered since Adelaide. Wikipedia tells me it has close to 7,000 residents. Being as there are not many other towns of note along the way and a lonely straight road ahead, we tough out another 200 which leaves us pretty sore and spent … and in Lockhart (pop 818). Ideally we would have liked to get to Wagga Wagga, but the extra 65 km is just too far on the day. We roll into town pretty pleased that the afternoon is more or less over. The Commercial

Hotel looks like our kind of place. It is the archetypal two-storey old beauty that we love. An enquiry for a room rocks us. They wanted well over $100 which set us agin them. We went off to the holiday park, and it was full, and so was another hotel. It was looking grim, so it was back to the pub again … to eat some humble pie and take a room … please! It seems that even though it is only Thursday evening, the early arrivals for the weekend's annual *Spirit of the Land* festival have taken all the cheap spots in town. A Moto Guzzi rider joins us for a beer. He is from Sydney and heading for the Spaghetti Rally which is being organised by the Victorian Moto Guzzi Club. He knows John Ferguson well and doubts that Ferg will be with us, as he is organising this camping event in the hills near Wangaratta. He has a tent and is unwilling to pay the premium that the Commercial is asking for. After a convivial pint, he leaves us to find a spot to camp. The bar is very popular and the kitchen is doing a roaring trade with pretty earnest pub meals … nothing fancy, just what you would expect a small-town pub to serve.

**THE FINAL SURGE**

The publicans are interesting and quirky. He has a long, long beard which has been bunched-in a few inches down, then plaited and be-ribboned etc. She has a long back-plait that reaches down to her bum. They are young grandparents, ex-bikies and seem to be popular hosts. They are pretty attendant to us, now we've decided on a room … which whilst small, does have a huge new-looking bed and a TV in the room on the wall. We will be in compressed luxury. Penelope meanwhile has to overnight on the main road outside. We do have a substantial cable lock, but the hotel folk are fully confident that no one will nick her. The night unfolds quite well over a few glasses of wine. It then takes a turn for us. Neither of us are fans of karaoke, in fact Steph loathes it with a passion, even though our exposure to it has been minimal. Our host however, not only is a big fan but she sees it as the night's entertainment. To that end she starts the proceedings by belting out a typical karaoke ballad … then drags one of her mate's up, and so it goes on. Of course she urges Steph … as her new best mate … to have a go too. Steph is a musician and plays the piano competently. She also has been known to say that she would have liked to have been a backing singer in a band … however this is not her time, nor her forum. We politely sit through a small selection of pretty dire performances before sliding away to our plush cell.

The last day heading north is a struggle, but having Steph along makes it so much easier. The morning was OK but a lot of the afternoon's ride ends up on a main highway. We're too slow and we struggle on some of the long uphill gradients. We pass signposts to Bundanoon bringing back fond memories from 2017 for me and a 'placing the scene' for Steph. At a layby we interacted with a moto rider on a Honda. There was a time, back in the day when Penelope was in her prime, that Hondas were little bikes. This was a Honda that absolutely shattered that stereotype. This bike was a six-cylinder 1800 cc leviathan. It had weather protection almost to the level of being a two-wheeled car. There were even ducts to carry hot air from the engine to the riders legs, when needed. It had a tall whip aerial hinting at the sound and communications system on board. There was 150 litre of covered carrying capacity, a tow bar of course, and reverse gear. We oohed and aahed suitably to the rider who was a pleasant young man. It is an interesting reflection that we were both doing the same ride, yet having such different rides. I know that an outside lap on that beast would be effortless, yet clearly they'd never make it down the Birdsville Track. We admire but don't envy or covet. For me it is a bit like a fantasy world encounter with Pamela Anderson. I would admire breathlessly … but not covet. It is horses for courses. We know our place … and that place is on Penelope through thick and thin, good and not-so-good.

Orangeville is an area rather than a place and right on dusk, after some difficulty, we find the Dickie's place. Their block is semi-rural with room for camper vans. It is to be a small gang this year, some staying on site and others nearby. We have been chosen to have the luxury of a room in the house. I am pleased to see that David's mum is still hanging on in there for her 100th birthday and message from the Queen.

Having Steph along for this last leg has already been wonderful. It is 1977 all over again. Although she had to endure the dull, straight roads heading East from Tailem Bend in South Australia to New South Wales, she's also had some good times and good rides, especially the wonderful back-country roads our Panther Rally hosts had selected for us in the green hills inland from Sydney. As was to be expected, playing with the other Panthers was great. Penelope was the newest, and Ian from Brisbane cavorted on the oldest … a 1927 500cc. This was a very pretty bike, which boomed out a lovely baritone utterance via 'fish-tail' mufflers. This year's gathering was not a big one, but as we all know, often quality is much more satisfying than quantity. As I remarked to Steph "All the people here, are ones I like a lot!" In addition to the Dickies, Jordan and Carol from the 'Muster' of 2017, David and Robyn Lewis from Sydney and the Watts (Glenys, Graeme And Riley) are all there and enjoyed as previously. Steph fits right in and immediately is 'tight' with the womenfolk. A few laughs were at Penelope's expense. Although still quite frisky and wanting to play near the front of the line of bikes … no one wanted to follow her because her smoky exhaust was not only visually off-putting, it had an acrid smell. All the other riders dashed past every time we got going after a break.

The rally was always to be the soft-launch of my book of our first ride together. I have a few colourful banners showing evocative images from the ride and these were spread out on some outside tables. A couple of piles of books then made for a good photo opportunity. The launch was done to the popping of a bubbly cork (I can't spell Champagne?) … thanks Dickies! Signings were done, my ego stroked once more. On the Saturday night David Lewis and I watched rugby from the World Cup in Japan … both of us are 'rugby tragics', and proud to be.

*All too soon we had to leave the Panther fold and head for Melbourne and grandparent duties. We left the others after specialty pies in Thirlmere and zig-zagged our way across to the village of Cooma at the northern end of the*

Snowy River region. To get there we spent some time on The Monaro Highway. We were surprised to learn that the road wasn't named after the Holden Muscle car ... the car was named after the mountainous region. A night was spent in the art-deco Alpine Hotel. 'nellops' was ensconced in the garage with a passel of Moto Guzzis returning from Ferg's Spaghetti Rally. The subsequent ride through the Kosciuszko National Park past Thredbo was a stunner. Snow was not far above us, but the day was sunny and not cold. We were thrilled to come across wild brumbies in the flesh. The day was a little spoilt by us breaking a clutch cable. This however brought meaningful interactions with a couple of guys at the Corryong Honda shop. Finally, we have fetched up in the historic village of Yackandandah, and are tucked up in a motel unit. Steph is now responding to most social interactions with a "No worries" almost worthy of an Ocker. She'll need to retrain at home next week. We should make big-city Melbourne tomorrow in time for a pizza and ice cream party for five-year-old Arthur. A good ending to a damn good ride. Naturally we have seen kookaburras, kites, galahs, cockatoos and the occasional wedge-tail eagle, only one live kangaroo however, but we've smelt and seen dozens as road-kill. Aussie, Aussie, Aussie ... oy, oy, oy!

**THE FINAL SURGE**

Yacandanda was as interesting and quirky as I remembered it, however we struck it on a day when so much of the town was closed. A local identity, the co-proprietor of the bric-a-brac shop which mainly sold Buddhas, had died and our arrival corresponded with his funeral. We'd been directed to the Buddha shop by our friend Janet who had enjoyed a week's painting workshop in Yacandandah. Her recommendations for eateries had us salivating but her first two choices were not open. We had a nice reflective night sitting at a table outside the old Star Hotel though. This was a little bit twee but it still had a nice ambience and some of its 150-year history was evident. Our time adventuring like young'uns was coming to an end. It may have just been one week of our more than 40 years together … but it was a good one, and I hope for more of this ilk. Quality time to reminisce, reflect, seed future dreams and just enjoy being 'in the moment'.

The final day's ride was both good and awful. The roads coming south from Yackandandah were interesting and the day was pleasant. A lot of this was a reverse of the first day John Ferg and I had traversed four years earlier. It was good to treat Steph to some of the same stops and sights I had enjoyed. The Whitfield to Mansfield section was as good as I remembered it and certainly right at the apex of motorcycling enjoyment. However Penelope was clearly nearing the end of her usefulness. She really was just limping along on her last legs. We were tipping oil in and she was spewing it out as partially burnt blue smoke. We were leaving a toxic trail behind us. This wasn't too bad until we started to reach the peripherals of outer Melbourne. The day hadn't quite unfolded as quickly as we had hoped and we were also not arrow-straight in our navigation to Preston. It was now the late afternoon rush hour of congested roads. The stop-start urban riding was an embarrassment to all. People yelled at us. Clearly they weren't happy with us belching such awfulness into their realm. We also weren't happy, Penelope certainly was not happy. We got lost, we got hot and bothered to match our oily mate, and we were late for the party.

This was not a triumphant end to the circumambulation of this big red continent.

Ultimately with the help of Google we got to familiar landmarks and finally 8 Brown St. Of course the welcome was warm and the pizza and ice cream had been kept for us. Photos were taken, hugs given and Penelope put away for another day, not in shame … not in the naughty corner … just put away. We both know that given a bit of time and the right medication, she will rise again and once more prance and purr along the highways to the encouragement of her adoring fans. There is still Tasmania to be conquered.

I can't leave Tassie off the map. During my time in the UK in the 1970s there had been a girl known universally as Tassie and her mission in life seemed to be to add Tasmania to the Australian maps she encountered that were missing such. Amazingly she found many, including a museum with a Tasmania-less portrayal of Australia. Usually it was just the often inept paintings on the sides of VW Kombi vans that she had to improve.

Tasmania also spawned an image that even fifty years on I chuckle at. Back in those London days of my youthful OE … when Brazilians were the population of Brazil and womenfolk had no thoughts of below-the-belt topiary, the more crass of my Aussie acquaintances referred to the female nether region as their 'Map of Tasmania'. This mysterious zone was something we all aspired to view and explore.

"What's there not to like about Tasmania?"

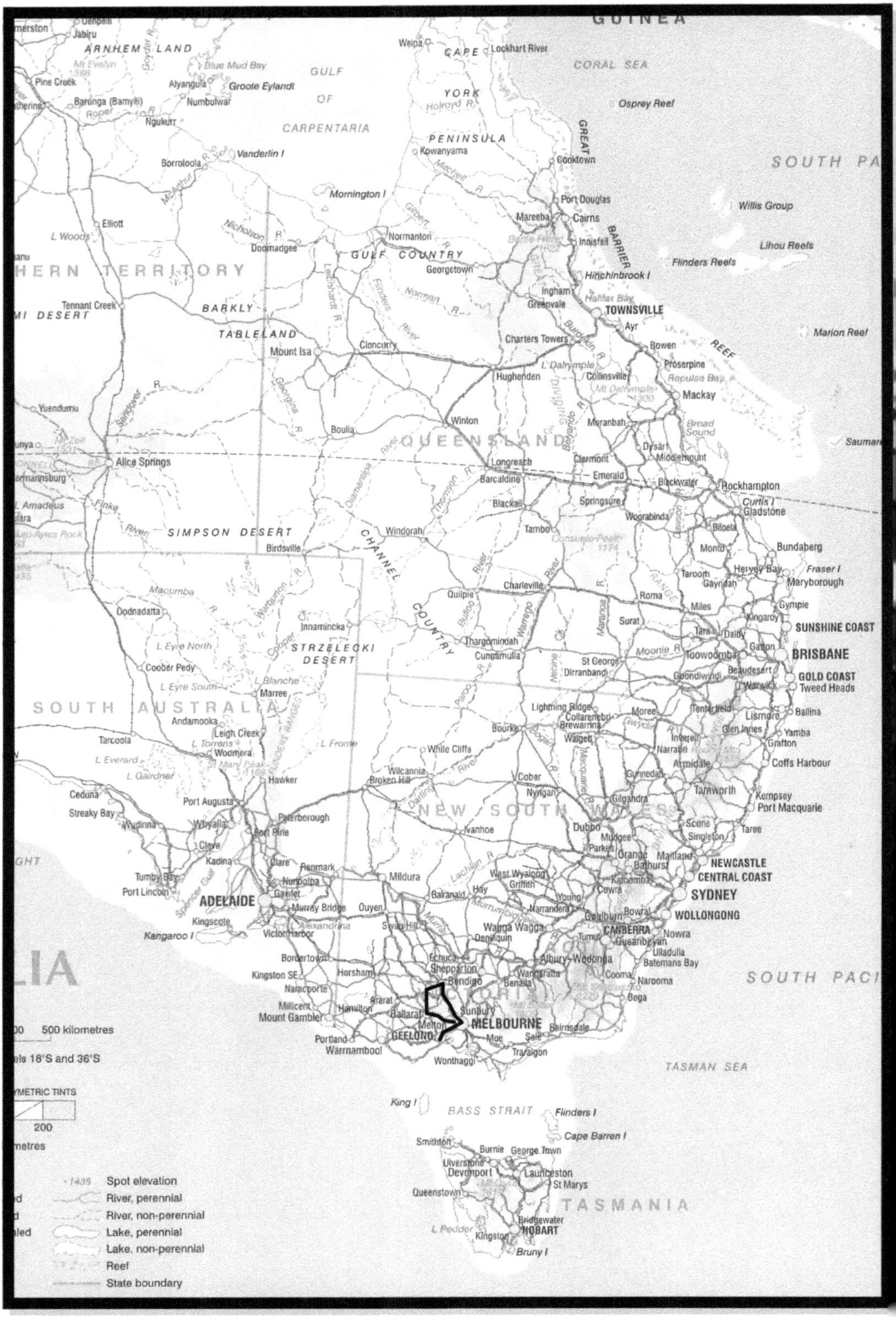

GUINEA
ARNHEM LAND
Jabiru
Pine Creek
Alyangula
Groote Eylandt
Numbulwar
Ngukurr
Borroloola
Vanderlin I
GULF OF CARPENTARIA
Weipa
CAPE YORK PENINSULA
Lockhart River
CORAL SEA
Osprey Reef
Kowanyama
Cooktown
Port Douglas
Cairns
Mareeba
Innisfail
Mornington I
Elliott
Normanton
Doomadgee
GULF COUNTRY
Georgetown
Hinchinbrook I
Ingham
Greenvale
Willis Group
Lihou Reefs
Flinders Reefs
GREAT BARRIER REEF
SOUTH PA
NORTHERN TERRITORY
Tennant Creek
BARKLY TABLELAND
TOWNSVILLE
Ayr
Bowen
Marion Reef
Mount Isa
Cloncurry
Charters Towers
Hughenden
Proserpine
Mackay
Collinsville
Moranbah
Winton
Boulia
QUEENSLAND
Yuendumu
Alice Springs
Longreach
Barcaldine
Clermont
Emerald
Dysart
Middlemount
Blackwater
Rockhampton
Gladstone
Saumarez
Blackall
Springsure
Woorabinda
SIMPSON DESERT
Windorah
Tambo
Biloela
Birdsville
CHANNEL COUNTRY
Monto
Bundaberg
Hervey Bay
Fraser I
Maryborough
Charleville
Taroom
Roma
Miles
Gympie
Quilpie
Oodnadatta
Innamincka
Surat
Kingaroy
SUNSHINE COAST
STRZELECKI DESERT
Thargomindah
Cunnamulla
St George
Dirranbandi
Dalby
Toowoomba
Gatton
BRISBANE
Coober Pedy
Marree
Goondiwindi
Beaudesert
Warwick
GOLD COAST
Tweed Heads
SOUTH AUSTRALIA
Andamooka
Leigh Creek
Lightning Ridge
Collarenebri
Brewarrina
Moree
Tenterfield
Lismore
Ballina
Tarcoola
Woomera
White Cliffs
Bourke
Walgett
Glen Innes
Inverell
Narrabri
Yamba
Grafton
Coffs Harbour
Armidale
Hawker
Wilcannia
Broken Hill
Cobar
Nyngan
Gunnedah
Tamworth
Ceduna
Streaky Bay
Port Augusta
Whyalla
Peterborough
Port Pirie
NEW SOUTH WALES
Ivanhoe
Dubbo
Gilgandra
Kempsey
Port Macquarie
Taree
Scone
Singleton
Mudgee
Parkes
Orange
Bathurst
Maitland
NEWCASTLE
CENTRAL COAST
Tumby Bay
Port Lincoln
Kadina
Clare
Renmark
Mildura
Balranald
Hay
West Wyalong
Griffith
Young
Katoomba
Cowra
SYDNEY
ADELAIDE
Gawler
Murray Bridge
Ouyen
Narrandera
Goulburn
Bowral
WOLLONGONG
Kingscote
Kangaroo I
Victor Harbor
Swan Hill
Wagga Wagga
Deniliquin
CANBERRA
Tumut
Queanbeyan
Nowra
Ulladulla
Batemans Bay
LIA
Bordertown
Kingston SE
Naracoorte
Horsham
Echuca
Shepparton
Bendigo
Albury-Wodonga
Wangaratta
Benalla
Cooma
Narooma
Bega
SOUTH PACI
Millicent
Mount Gambier
Hamilton
Ararat
Ballarat
Sunbury
Melton
MELBOURNE
GEELONG
Bairnsdale
Sale
Moe
Traralgon
Portland
Warrnambool
Wonthaggi
TASMAN SEA
500 kilometres
els 18°S and 36°S
YMETRIC TINTS
200
metres
King I
BASS STRAIT
Flinders I
Cape Barren I
Smithton
Burnie
George Town
Ulverstone
Devonport
Launceston
St Marys
Queenstown
TASMANIA
L Pedder
Bridgewater
Kingston
HOBART
Bruny I
Spot elevation
River, perennial
River, non-perennial
Lake, perennial
Lake, non-perennial
Reef
State boundary

## CHAPTER TWELVE

# OCTOBER 2022

Whilst I was growing up my mother often used to call me a little Walter Mitty, a descriptor I didn't warm to at the time. Only as an adult with access to reference authorities like the American Heritage Dictionary can I appreciate her warmth of feeling and astute character analysis of the emerging Des Molloy. *'An ordinary, often ineffectual person who indulges in fantastic daydreams of personal triumphs'* describes me pretty well. I love daydreaming and pretty much always these dreams are indeed filled with spectacular successes. Disappointingly life does not always replicate these cerebral fantasies, but in my world I cling to these imaginary wins until they are proven faulty.

A well-received 'author's talk' at a regional library (and good book sales) planted the embryo of a plan to validate the reasons for an extended springtime jaunt to reclaim Penelope and get over to Tasmania. I quickly identified some key dates. The annual Panther rally for 2022 was to be held somewhere out near Bendigo on the 14th and 15th of October. Arthur's eighth birthday is on October 22nd, so we've got something to work around. Quickly I also ascertain the date of the big public classic motorcycle extravaganza in Tasmania at Oaklands as being on November 20th. Being as Penelope needed fettling of at least a week ... and we'd better put in some contingency time, I tentatively set a potential NZ departure date of September 26th. Learning that there was a rally for old bikes that followed Tasmania's Motorcycle Day, I reckoned heading home from Melbourne at the end of November. Phew ... two months to fill with promotions and fun.

It was easy identifying 135 libraries – less easy sorting out which ones did author's talks … and getting any of them to respond to my enquiries. I had three books to promote, and possibly I would have Penelope as a display prop. I could do libraries in the day and special-interest clubs in the evenings. I could even do a few movie screenings! Of course, I also wanted to roam the Victorian hinterland checking out museums and hamlets of interest. Although it was early winter when I started hitting up suitable libraries, I was amazed to find that those that specialised in what I was proposing, mostly already had their spring bookings locked and loaded. Lacking a publicist or a promoter, and seemingly starting my campaign too late, I finally managed to put together an itinerary that included only two library talks, but five club presentations, three movie screenings, one book shop appearance, a public promo 'stall' and two rallies where I could promote my wares. This was ok and would also give me plenty of time to randomly wander. I also had to admit that I didn't have much pulling power. Although the Ballarat Library considered me and did respond, there wouldn't have been much of a cachet in my appearance when they had just had Anne Cleeves telling all about the Vera and Shetland books and numerable TV series.

And so it was that after a three year gap, once again I crossed the Tasman with a large bag of goodies for Penelope. The wonderful Ferg had co-opted a mate and uplifted Penelope from her storage so when I arrived she was up on the gurney ready for action. Son Joe supplied me with some wheels and an enjoyable time was spent crossing town each day and working with Ferg while Penelope was upgraded once more. All went well in his clean uncluttered space and once again I admire John's slick, unhurried competence. Conveniently John is the Moto Guzzi committee member able to sign me up as a member and get us through the process of getting 'back on the system' with Club plates. This involved getting the ownership reversed from Dan in Darwin to Joe in Melbourne, taking the bike through the obligatory Road Safe check, then a couple of visits to VicRoads. Ultimately and in plenty of time Penelope is resplendent in a new maroon plate and I have the requisite log book. Fully legal is not a term that is always able to be applied to a Molloy vehicle, and when it is, it is usually only a temporary state. I'll try hard this time.

I lack the resolve to head off into cosmopolitan Melbourne on Penelope sans GPS looking for addresses 50 minutes across town, knowing also that I would be returning in the dark. So my first two club nights are done in Joe's VW with Google Maps guiding me. The BSA and Norton Owners' Clubs use the same bowling club for their meetings. Both groups are welcoming and the well-attended nights (a week apart) go well with quite good book sales. An interesting anecdote unfolded from these two gatherings. When I'd reached Joe and Arthur's place in Kensington, I was hardly in the door when I was presented with a box of 35 DVDs of my movie *The Last Hurrah*. "Don't forget these!" I am told … "You're not keeping them here anymore." My reaction was "Bugger! No one has DVD players anymore, I'll never get rid of them." Well, I may not be able to play DVDs, but old duffers who have old motorbikes can and they are all snapped up at $5 a pop. I am also blown away by one guy at the Norton club night. He drives 200 km to get there each month, then drives home after the meeting. A very resolute man especially knowing the dangers of nocturnal animal movements. I was interested that no bikes were evident on either of these nights although lots of weekend runs were scheduled.

The couple of weeks leading up to the Panther Rally were a great combination of family time with Joe and Arthur, time for me (Yes, once again I got to experience Motoclassica) and work. My book promo stuff is work, it involves general admin, countless emails and formulating more detailed plans to lock in the logistics of how I get books around to each venue, especially once I leave the mother-ship. I reactivate a bank account I had back when I had six weeks working in Newcastle before NOT going to

Port Hedland. That involves two mornings in the battle that is a modern bank. Australia is more advanced than NZ by way of being cashless, so when the remaining banks are open, which isn't all that often, they are filled with old folk, all looking bewildered and anxious. Long queues form way before opening time. First World problems!

Anticipatory delight is something I revel in, I positively wallow in the joy of thinking how great the upcoming event, adventure ... or whatever, will be. This year's Panther gathering is to be at big, bearded John deGroot's place. John who I had enjoyed fanging along the byways with in both McLaren Flat and in Bundanoon. I sensed from the email contacts I had managed that the core crew who I liked a lot, would all be there out at Casuarina Hill, near Shelbourne ... not that far from Bendigo, so only about 160 km from Kensington. The weather for the first two weeks of October has been appalling with heavy rainfall most days which has led to flooding over much of the state but the forecast for my Friday ride out to John's place is for a dry day but on a diminished network of highways. I am pretty organised by now and have a plastic tub with six click fasteners holding a weather-tight lid on. This big tub holds 30 books and all my cloth banners and sales paraphernalia. Luckily this fits well on the rear carrier and I am able to fit my tent and sleeping pad on top of it.

When loaded, I think Penelope looks wonderful. I always like seeing bikes loaded with travelling luggage because you can clearly see that an adventure is in the air. My leather saddlebags are slung over the rear half of the seat and give a manly look of having 'been there and done that!' I also have canvas throw-over panniers fitted across the petrol tank up front. These are the same ones that I used on the Beijing to Arnhem ride, so they are also suitably weathered and appropriate. A tank bag completes the package. Penelope may be an old classic but obviously she is still a working girl, no glamour ... a bit battered and worn around the edges ... but what a ride!

Late on Friday night I wrote to my followers –

'When I was an opinion writer for the Building Research Association of NZ (BRANZ) I once wrote a piece relating how learned behaviour can lead you to a cropper. Oh yes, I think you know what is coming. Today's adventure was to navigate across a flood-ravaged Victoria, to the Australian Panther Register's gathering near Bendigo. With the familiarity of having done this sort of thing many times in many places, I packed Penelope, kicked her in the guts and rode off ... three metres!

Now Penelope and I do come from another era and another place. She is from a trusting time when bikes had no locks or even keys for the ignition ... you just gave a lusty kick and away you went. We've done that together across five continents. I live a life at home of unlocked doors and keys left in the cars' ignitions. The requirement for security is low in my consciousness but this is Melbourne and Penelope had to be outside in the street.

This perceived need for security meant I put a sturdy wire cable lock through her front wheel muttering as I did so "No one is going to cart you away my darling!"

So today ... loaded and ready to go ... did I do an inspection walk around? Hell no ... feed out the clutch, "Yippee-ki-yay, we're off on an adventure!". Yes, very short-lived and a little painful. We fell to earth (asphalt) so quickly that I didn't even get my foot off the footrest. Shocked and bewildered I lay trapped beneath Penelope for a while. A car ultimately appeared on the quiet back-street, but the driver wouldn't get out to help despite me waving that I needed help. Finally I wriggled free but felt that my foot had faced the wrong way for a while and it was a struggle to get upright and hop off the roadway. I beckoned to the car-driver that I really did need help. He or she then backed up the street and made off to safety?????

Joe was away but his Rumble coffee roastery is only in the next street and

**THE BIG SIT**

*soon one of his crew had been summoned and had run around and righted Penelope. It was only when attempting to back her into the kerb was the cable lock spotted. I am now trying to do the RICE thing with some frozen mixed berries.*

*This is not the end. I've since had the smart advice that you always put the lock through the back wheel and stretch it over the seat so you will see it when you go to ride ... or feel it when you sit.*

*Kia kaha everyone'*

So that was quite a blow to the ego as well as the body. My right ankle soon assumed a blue colour and swelled up impressively. Through my nearly six decades of riding I have been remarkably safe, falling very infrequently and not often hurting myself. Now, in a space of less than a year I have gone 'tits up' twice. In the spring of 2021 I had cartwheeled a little 'Postie Bike' Honda. My carers won't be letting me out soon.

After 24 hours I was hobbling about the place miserable, pining for the fjords so to speak when Joe restored my dignity with the suggestion that subject to me passing a competence drive around the block, I could take the small Rumble van out to the rally. Whilst there was no possibility of getting my 'Texan' riding boot on, with gentle manipulation I could get my foot into my Allbirds merino sneaker with the laced front all opened up. Of course, the painkillers helped and by late morning on the Saturday I was droning up the M79 in the VW Caddy. I knew where the crew were stopping for their big break on the day's run. I'd been in touch with Ferg as I knew he was doing a quick blat out to the gathering on one of his Moto Guzzis, so by the time I arrived at Cairn Curren Reservoir, I was almost old news. It was great to see all the familiar faces and meet a few new ones. As always there were examples of Phelan & Moore's products from the 1920s through to the 1960s. Penelope would have loved it. I chuckle as I see one Panther up the back-up trailer, and laugh out loud when a few km down the road a control cable on Jane Clarke's cute little late 1940s 350 gives up the ghost and it joins the other in a 'ride of shame'.

It is great to get to spend time with Jane and Mick again ... and Tony of course, and Jordan and Carol, and the Watts family from Queensland. This is my fourth Panther rally in Australia and the core of attendees are now old friends as they have shared my journey so far. John and his partner live on a 50 acre conservation-covenanted property 25 km out of Bendigo and just like the previous three rally venues it is ideal for this sort of gathering with several fire pits and sheds and facilities for groups to enjoy . The heavy rains leading up to the weekend has meant that the land is very soggy and five vehicles had got bogged on the Friday in different spots. Not being four-wheel-drive, I make sure I park accordingly. I am a bit away from the main lot of campers. The Caddy is small, but big enough for me to sleep in the back on my pad.

As always with these gatherings the bonhomie is warming for the spirit. There is good food, tales are told, plans made, laughs had, and beers shared. It is all as good as it gets and I am so glad to be there, even if only as a glorified spectator. Finally, it is time for bed and I hobble my way off to the little white van and crawl in the back. I'd already laid out my sleeping bag on my thin Thermarest and looked forward to a snug night irrespective of the weather.

Shortly after getting in and settled, I decided that I should have one last pee being as I had been imbibing enthusiastically and know that no longer can I go all night without relief, even after a 'dry' evening. Confusion sweeps over me as I find that I can't seem to open the back doors that I had not long ago come through. The Mechanism moves a little and the doors bow a little to pressure but something is keeping them shut. I withdraw for a moment to think, then try again, and again and again. There is a cage in the van stopping access to the front. Seemingly I am locked in. No one else is camped in this area of the property and I am outside of shouting distance for assistance.

**THE BIG SIT**

With dread sweeping over me I lie down and think dry thoughts. I know that there is no way I am going to make it through the night intact. I do have a man-bag which I carry over my shoulder when riding, that I figure is waterproof. My thoughts turn to the option of at some time having to empty out my stuff and then pee into the bag. The thought appals me, but I can think of no other option. Where did this ineptitude come from I wonder? I used to be competent, now seemingly I am morphing into a buffoon, a figure to be ridiculed. However, beating myself up isn't going to solve the problem. I sense a long night ahead. I lie still and try breathing slowly. I wonder about meditation and wish I knew more. An hour or more goes by and I can feel the pressure on my bladder getting worse. I check again that the door mechanism isn't just sticking a bit. I don't want to break my way out … well I do want to break my way out, but don't think it would be good for the van or my relationship with Joe if I did manage it.

Then in the inky darkness I catch sight of a flicker of light. It is a torch … someone is out there! I bash the sides of the van repeatedly and shout out until finally I see the light pause, then tentatively make its way towards me. Halleluiah, it is John, a neighbour who is belatedly making his way home on foot. Soon I am free and relieving the pressure freely. I am so glad that I haven't had to turn my bag nor the van into an urinal. I briefly wonder if my believing cousins have been collaborating with their omnipotent invisible friend to play yet another joke on me. This is not an anecdote for Facebook.

On Sunday up at the house I lay out and display my wares. I now have a satin-like fabric world map with all my big rides shown with links to each book. This compliments the photographic banners and it all looks pretty impressive. People like the big photos and book sales go quite well. It is a leisurely day with a ride out to a couple of points of interest for the riders and I tag along in the van, feeling a bit left out. I'm a bit reflective as I know that this will almost certainly be my last Aussie Panther gathering. These folk who have become like family to me may never be met again. At Motoclassica I had established contact with a specialty vehicle shipping company and tentatively talked about Penelope's repatriation. Sobering stuff, especially as there have been new mates met this year to add to the old, but c'est la vie.

The two weeks that follow are mainly spent lying on Joe's sofa making a grandpa-shaped furrow, convalescing, reading and hoping for better things. Outside it rained and rained. A doctor was consulted and various pills and potions obtained. It seems that soft-tissue damage on older folk is a slow heal. There will be no aimless meandering around Victoria's hinterland taking in the sights. With the availability of Joe's car I am still able to fulfil my promo events and take any number of books with me. The Classic Motorcycle Club turn out in good numbers with lots of nice bikes in evidence. Sales are again strong. I feel valued. The last week of October is a struggle of logistics with an entertaining session in a bookshop out in Ballarat on Thursday early evening. This is not my usual Powerpoint presentation, it is just a stand and chat. Surprisingly, it goes extremely well and friends are made. I then had to dash back to base and get myself out to The Vintage Drivers Club on Friday night. This was probably my biggest audience by numbers but disappointingly the sales are not quite in proportion. It had been a worrying time because as the month unfolded we inexorably moved towards what I saw as D Day, or more accurately B (boot) Day. Finally on Saturday 29th Oct I manage to get a sockless foot into my boot and Penelope collaborates by firing into life on the first kick. We are a duo again, with adventures to be had. It is a pretty dull ride the 110 km to Ballarat, but my AirBnB is suited to my needs and I am happy. Ballarat is Victoria's third largest city with about 120,000 people. It has an old centre and the Regent Cinema is a renovated 1930s theatre which compliments the old classic I park on the footpath outside. Joe and Arthur come up for the weekend and provide logistical support with helping and

making me feel I am not Nigel-no-mates … I've got a crew. A good audience roll in and the afternoon is a big success. I always enjoy these face-to-face interactions, meeting people like 88-year-old Keith who had ridden there. Many are my peers, but many are not, and both give me cheer. Book sales are good, sore foot aside, life is splendid. Joe, Arthur and I dine in a suitable pub. This family stuff will soon pause, so I enjoy it while I can.

My book designer Jess, also lives in Ballarat but right at the crucial time both her and partner Matt go down with Covid. That cuts out a possible visit to Matt's new factory where he makes Structurally Insulated Panels (SIPs) for prefabricated buildings etc. I'd been to his old one and had been looking forward to seeing the new one. This now leaves me plenty of time on Monday, so for my return to Melbourne I avoid the freeways by going North-East to the slightly twee town of Daylesford. I admire as we ride through, but I felt that it was too early in the ride for a stop and explore. I am still trying to minimise 'starts'. After Daylesford, we rode along gentle, undulating, mostly empty roads, to the Kiwi-sounding settlements of Trentham and Woodend and Gisborne. For a period I was followed by an ambulance and I wondered wryly if it was 'just waiting … let's see what is in store for this old duffer? … we've heard that he is an accident waiting to happen!'

I gather from the countryside that there is a move afoot for the energy provider AusNet to run a power supply through this region as part of expanding/improving the network. Clearly, this is not popular with all and there were many roadside signs of varying vitriol along the way. Overall it was a lovely ride through lush, green countryside, quite a contrast to the red-dirt further west and north. All in all, this weekend has set my mind at rest because now we are about to embark on the main reason for being here. I've proven I can start Penelope and we're pretty much ready to go. I have sent ahead a big stash of books to a bookshop in Hobart.

*Melbourne Cup day – the race that stops a nation, is always the first Tuesday* of November and whilst most of the state is Flemington-focussed, for me it is a time of preparation (laundry) and decisions. Already I have decided that the weather is not yet warm enough to camp in Tasmania and the tent, sleeping pad and sleeping bag are being set aside. Rufty-tufty Des has given way to the soft man with a core of marshmallow. Tomorrow, I will ride to Lara, do a library talk, then go to the new terminal at North Geelong and catch the evening ferry to Tasmania. This is an all-night journey and we'll see how the recliners go.

I'll see you on the other side ... as they say. I'm hoping the November will unfold differently from the 'wettest October on record.'

The Lara Library gig is a good one. They shower me with gifts (including chocolate) and a diverse audience turn up to listen to the old geezer from New Zealand give a talk and show 'slides', well a modern version of them. Some people might say that an afternoon like this can be 'Death by Powerpoint', but my folk on the day seem to like it and I head off to the ferry departure point in nearby Geelong quite a few books lighter. I'll restock in Hobart. Geelong has only been the departure point for less than two weeks so everything is new and protocols are still settling in. The timing of the Lara talk and the proximity of the ferry wharf has worked out perfectly and after a short interaction with the Customs officer, we go through into a large hanger-like structure.

There was a big line-up of motorcyclists queueing to board and new fleeting friendships were made, both in the line and later on board. This is yet another simple pleasure that the tin-top drivers never get to experience. Interestingly, in complete contrast to our Inter-Island ferry services, you don't tie down your bikes. The crew does this, and they seem to have it down pat. Whilst leaving Penelope I had one of those moments that people of significance must encounter all the time. "Are you Des Molloy?" an older gent asked. On receipt of my nod, Neil and Muriel told me how they'd read and enjoyed my books. Talk about having your ego stroked, this doesn't happen to me often. I'm sure that public recognition would be a double-edged sword though. They're an interesting couple. Neil was from Te Kuiti originally and Muriel from Tasmania. They had had honeymooned around New Zealand on a Triumph Bonneville in 1974 and now were riding a 1985 BMW R65 very similar to the one we have 'resting' in France with son Steve. A lovely couple still riding and revisiting Tasmania on two-wheels for the memories of gone-by times. I suspect I would find many parallels in their lives to Steph and mine's, although we'd honeymooned on a BSA in 1978. Disappointingly I don't see them on board. Maybe they took a cabin.

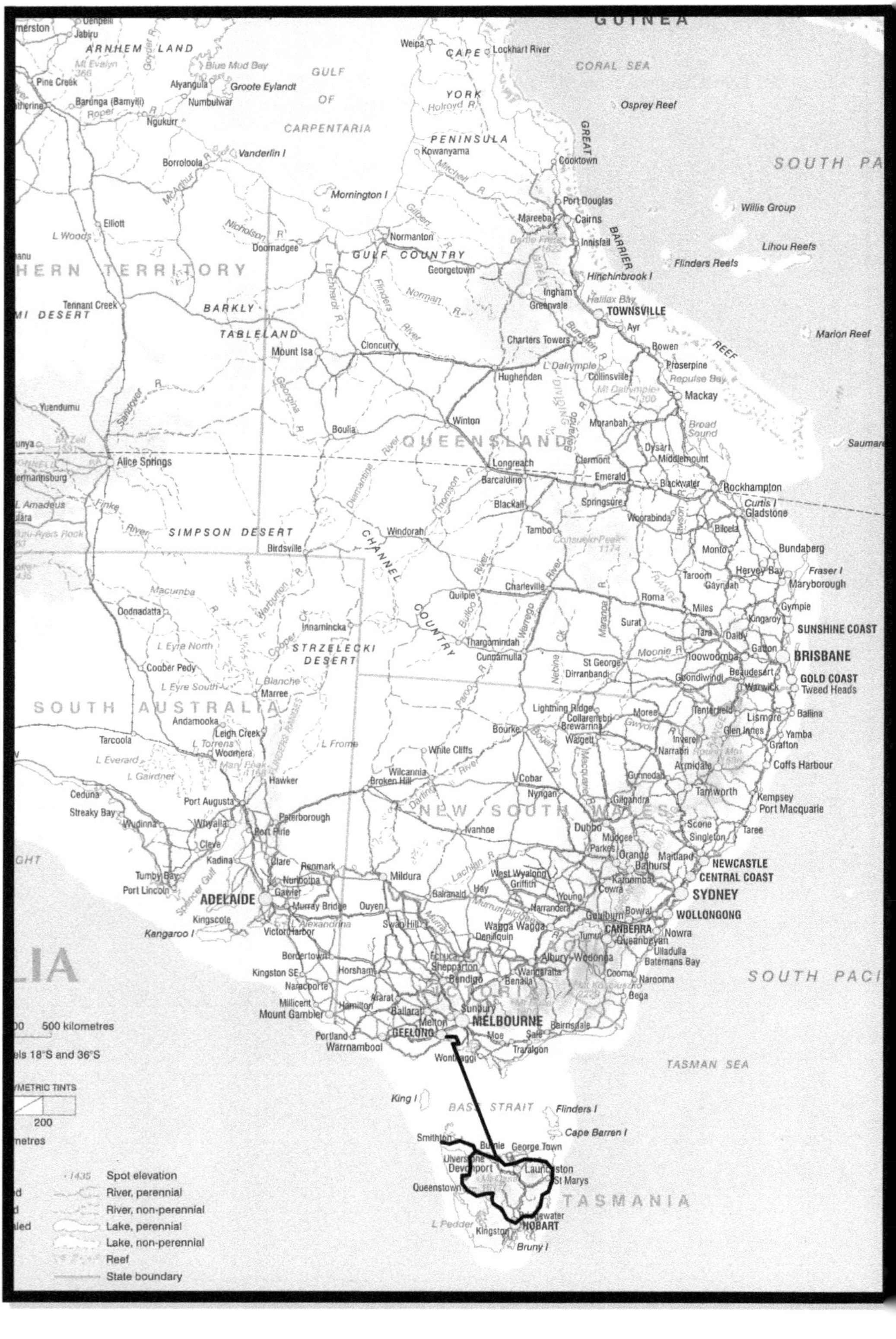

GUINEA
ARNHEM LAND
GULF OF CARPENTARIA
CAPE YORK PENINSULA
CORAL SEA
Osprey Reef
Weipa
Lockhart River
Pine Creek
Jabiru
Oenpelli
Blue Mud Bay
Groote Eylandt
Alyangula
Numbulwar
Barunga (Bamyili)
Ngukurr
Borroloola
Vanderlin I
Kowanyama
Cooktown
SOUTH PA
Mornington I
Port Douglas
Cairns
Mareeba
Willis Group
Elliott
L Woods
Doomadgee
Normanton
Innisfail
Lihou Reefs
GREAT BARRIER REEF
Flinders Reefs
NORTHERN TERRITORY
GULF COUNTRY
Georgetown
Hinchinbrook I
Tennant Creek
Ingham
Greenvale
Halifax Bay
BARKLY TABLELAND
TOWNSVILLE
Ayr
Marion Reef
Mount Isa
Cloncurry
Charters Towers
Bowen
Proserpine
Hughenden
Collinsville
Repulse Bay
Mackay
Yuendumu
Winton
Broad Sound
Boulia
QUEENSLAND
Moranbah
Dysart
Middlemount
Saumare
Alice Springs
Hermannsburg
Longreach
Clermont
Barcaldine
Emerald
Blackwater
Rockhampton
L Amadeus
Curtis I
Gladstone
Blackall
Springsure
Woorabinda
SIMPSON DESERT
Windorah
Tambo
Biloela
Birdsville
Monto
Bundaberg
CHANNEL COUNTRY
Charleville
Hervey Bay
Fraser I
Taroom
Gayndah
Maryborough
Macumba
Oodnadatta
Quilpie
Roma
Miles
Gympie
Innamincka
Surat
Kingaroy
SUNSHINE COAST
STRZELECKI DESERT
Thargomindah
Tara
Dalby
Gatton
BRISBANE
L Eyre North
Cunnamulla
Moonie R
Toowoomba
Coober Pedy
St George
Dirranbandi
Goondiwindi
Beaudesert
GOLD COAST
Tweed Heads
L Eyre South
L Blanche
Marree
Warwick
SOUTH AUSTRALIA
Lightning Ridge
Collarenebri
Moree
Tenterfield
Andamooka
Brewarrina
Lismore
Ballina
Leigh Creek
Bourke
Walgett
Inverell
Glen Innes
Yamba
Tarcoola
L Torrens
Woomera
White Cliffs
L Frome
Narrabri
Grafton
L Everard
Armidale
Coffs Harbour
L Gairdner
Wilcannia
Broken Hill
Cobar
Gunnedah
Hawker
Ceduna
Nyngan
Tamworth
Kempsey
Streaky Bay
Port Augusta
Port Macquarie
NEW SOUTH WALES
Wudinna
Whyalla
Peterborough
Ivanhoe
Dubbo
Scone
Port Pirie
Singleton
Taree
Cleve
Mudgee
Kadina
Clare
Renmark
Parkes
Orange
Maitland
NEWCASTLE
Tumby Bay
Bathurst
CENTRAL COAST
Port Lincoln
Mildura
West Wyalong
Katoomba
ADELAIDE
Gawler
Balranald
Hay
Griffith
Young
Cowra
SYDNEY
Murray Bridge
Ouyen
Narrandera
Goulburn
Bowral
WOLLONGONG
Kingscote
Swan Hill
Wagga Wagga
Tumut
CANBERRA
Queanbeyan
Nowra
Kangaroo I
Victor Harbor
Deniliquin
Ulladulla
Batemans Bay
Bordertown
Echuca
Shepparton
Albury-Wodonga
Kingston SE
Horsham
Bendigo
Benalla
Wangaratta
Cooma
Narooma
SOUTH PACI
Naracoorte
Bega
Ararat
Millicent
Hamilton
Ballarat
Sunbury
Mount Gambier
Melton
MELBOURNE
Bairnsdale
500 kilometres
Portland
GEELONG
Moe
Sale
Warrnambool
Traralgon
Wonthaggi
TASMAN SEA
King I
BASS STRAIT
Flinders I
Cape Barren I
Smithton
Burnie
George Town
Ulverstone
Devonport
Launceston
St Marys
Queenstown
TASMANIA
L Pedder
Kingston
HOBART
Bruny I
Spot elevation
River, perennial
River, non-perennial
Lake, perennial
Lake, non-perennial
Reef
State boundary

## CHAPTER FOURTEEN

# TASSIE, TASSIE, TASSIE!

The crossing to Tasmania was a 12-hour, overnight one. For some reason I allowed more than one insistent 'younger' motorcyclist buy me a beer and I think that helped make the night in the 'Recliner Lounge' pass without too much discomfort. It could also have contributed to just another 'silly old duffer moment' the next morning though. We off-loaded at 6.30 am and as we left the docks I spotted a café so parked up and went in to get the coffee with bacon and egg muffin that was on offer for $10. It was way too early for any of the Devonport points of interest to be open, so I settled back to read a little while the caffeine infusion straightened out my furry head. Reaching into my man-bag brought the realisation that I had left my Kindle on the next seat on the ferry.

Muttering "Bugger, bugger, bugger!" I scuttled back to the terminal building which was close by. Forlornly I told the sweet young thing on the counter my tale of woe, adding that I had been in recliner seat B30. To my surprise, she reached for a radio and instructed someone to go and look. A few minutes later a positive response came back and within ten minutes I was walking back to Penelope with my blushes of ineptness fading away.

Not far from Devonport I found the Don River Railway and lots of old trains and carriages and general railway ephemera. This visit filled in a couple of hours and the 30 minute ride on a Melbourne-built pre-World War 11 railcar showed me just how similar our landscapes are. The track was bordered by ferns and what we would have called Manuka or Kanuka trees. We could have been in Kiwiland.

My goal for the day was to try and make contact with Plastic Pete – a figure from our youthful South American ride ... so named because he was one of a duo we called *The Plastic Expedition*. Derisively but with good humour they had christened our ragtag trio of old British bikes *The Cast Iron Expedition*. In way that travellers do, we had bonded with these two Brits from Tasmania and shared many adventures ... and their oil. Our two Panthers Penelope and Samantha drank oil, partly because we didn't know we were constantly over-filling them to the top mark on the dipstick. Panthers are probably unique in that the oil level should be somewhere on the dipstick between the end and the lower of the two inscribed marks. Knowledge of this peculiarity did not come to us for another 10 or more years. The Plastics were meticulous in servicing their XL 350s and would change the oil every 1,000 miles as per the instruction from Sochiro Honda. In an effort of frugality we would rendezvous where and whenever they were to do an oil change and we would take their waste oil for cycling through our old girls.

**THE BIG SIT**

After many weeks of intermittent travelling together, we had finally parted company on the shores of Lake Titicaca in mid-1977 and we'd lost touch as our lives as grownups took over.

The Visitor Centre staff of the town of Scottsdale knew Peter Willoughby and phoned to let his partner Katrina know that an old acquaintance was going to call in. At their small holding I hadn't got my helmet off before a smiling Pete opened with "Mr Molloy, I recognised that riding style and the sound of Penelope." It had been over 45 years. Of course, the night that followed was just as you would expect as we told old shared tales and the ones that happened 'after'. The only blight was learning that his offsider Mark had passed away a few months earlier. There was one lovely moment before I left next morning. After topping up Katrina's lawn mower with oil Pete slurped a bit into Penelope. So once again we rode off using some of the Plastics' liquid gold. Such a wonderful catch-up.

*Friday was spent riding out to the east coast at St Helens, then meandering down to the evocative-sounding Chain of Lagoons and back inland to the small settlement of St Marys where we are holed up in that old Aussie favourite of mine ... the country town old two-storey pub. Probably I should have left time/room to describe the wonderful riding. Think dappled avenues of trees for a lot on the inland riding ... with twisting narrow roads and a gentle coastal section that is quite like the Kaikoura Coast of NZ. Everything is very verdant, but they've also experienced a wet time and some roads are still closed.*

*I'll get back to you in a couple of days ... maybe*

*Nov 8*

*Good morning all from the coastal town of Triabunna. Yesterday was a delightful ride, firstly through the hills from St Marys back to the coast once again at the Chain of Lagoons, then down the Great Eastern Drive. All was well in my world and Penelope was gently humming along. It was a day for being mellow and smug in the knowledge that big miles weren't needed to*

THE BIG SIT

be covered. Tasmania is not like that. Rides don't get much better than this. Penelope had thrown me a small challenge to resolve back at St Marys. Her exhaust front pipe was showing signs of breaking away from its end flange. This has happened before ... firstly in Mongolia in 2005 and again in Northwest Australia in 2019. I'd had the flange welded on in Broome nearly 10,000 km back. My options were to remove the exhaust completely and block the port with a metal disc or try wiring it back tight into the head. I have tried the latter and it is working so far. Challenge met.

However! Penelope can be a contrary cow sometimes. I am wondering if it is menopause ... because she seems to have hot flushes. This has been happening around Australia and it has had the brains' trust baffled. In previous years, further north when hot she would develop a misfire. Convinced it was temperature related but not totally sure I have bought an infrared heat-sensing gun. This has shown me that the normal temperature between the exhaust ports is consistently 212°C. Yesterday, about 60 km after filling up, I sensed a slight slowing of the engine, whipped in the clutch and glided to a halt at the side of the road. The temperature between the ports was 364°. In her past, Penelope has endured high ambient temperature up to 50°C in Iran and Pakistan and similar in Central America ... and never complained. What is different? Before coming to Aus, due to the poor condition of the fins I treated her to a new cylinder head produced by the Panther Owners Club. Surely a new head couldn't be the problem? Have any other owners experienced issues with the club heads? I'd love some feedback.

So I have lifted the carb needle again, to richen Penelope up a little and we'll continue on gently. It is an easy ride to Hobart and I will monitor her temperature like all good carers would.

The East Coast of Tasmania in early November is proving to be a wonderful time and place to meander along. The roads are largely deserted, the sights pleasing and the temperature quite benign. There are a couple of times when I could have done with my tent. It seems that post-Covid, there are lots of people out and about, and more than once I am turned away from likely accommodation places because they are fully booked. It is interesting that the roads are not reflecting this, but maybe they are and I just don't know how deserted they really are normally. I was lucky to get the last cabin available in Triabunna at a rate that made me wince, but the location was good and an evening's walk saw me down on the water-front eating fish and chips, determinedly keeping the gulls away and thinking how good life was.

One of the wonderful things I am enjoying about Tassie, is how small it is. This means you can be unhurried. I could have rushed from top to bottom in a single day, as many do. My original plan for Hobart had been to stay with Bob Findlay, a fellow Kiwi and Panther owner. He's been helping oil some of the wheels for me with regards to my upcoming presentations. His situation has recently changed and his house is prepped for selling and not really conducive to having a grubby visitor so I forgo staying with Bob and his wife (Yes, I have done it again and forgotten a spouse's name!) and head downtown. I have to say that the entry to Hobart from the East on a moto is impressive and a little daunting, as you have to cross over the Tasman Bridge. This arches up and over the Derwent River. It is nearly one and a half kilometres long and there is a wind blowing as I cross. The 60 m height above the water feels like double that and I don't enjoy the experience. This, of course is the bridge that had a middle span wiped out by a bulk ore carrier in 1975 resulting in 12 deaths (seven crewmen and five motorists). This disaster isolated a large part of Eastern Hobart's population and with only small barges to get vehicles across the Derwent or a 50 km detour, crosstown movements were paralysed for some time. It was two years before the bridge opened again and it operates to this day under tightened safety regulations. These days all traffic is kept off the bridge when large ships are transiting below. The river depth at the collision point is 35 m and the wreck of *Lake Illawarra* lies on the bottom, still with a concrete slab on top of it, without presenting a navigation hazard to smaller vessels.

Nov 13

*OK, well I have done Hobart and I have to say I was most impressed. For a variety of reasons I was in the downtown YHA and this meant I was able to do lots of stuff on foot. On my first morning, I had done three museums by lunchtime.. The Maritime Museum, the Mawson Replica Hut Museum, and the Tasmanian Museum and Art Gallery are all in a cluster near the harbourside, and near my digs. All three museums were brilliant and I left each uplifted by the thought that I knew more than when I went in ... except that I may have reached a point where my knowledge and memory hard drive is pretty much full ... and it is possibly now 'one in, one out!' I can't share all my learnings with you, but here are a couple.*

*I know how big Australia is because I have ridden around it. Seeing a map of Antarctica with Australia overlaid on top, I was surprised to see that Australia is the smaller. As Kiwis, we hear a lot about our Scott Base and also the US's McMurdo Sound, because they are supplied out of Christchurch. The Australian Antarctic Territory, unknown to most Kiwis, is massive. It is over 40% of the total area and the biggest of all the claims. And Mawson ... look him up, he was a legend.*

*Another of the 'I never knew that' snippets involved the Japanese in WW11. They had a submarine which carried a float plane that they launched off with a big rubber band ... or some such. This plane flew over Sydney, Melbourne and Hobart without ever being shot at. The sub and plane then came to NZ and flew over both Auckland and Wellington. They were checking out shipping numbers and locations etc. They went to Fiji and Samoa doing the same sort of thing but also torpedoed at least one vessel. Their next mission took them across to the US and the pilot bombed forests in Oregon near the town of Brookings hoping to get a wildfire, going. He tried again after three weeks but neither attempt was very successful. Decades later President Kennedy helped facilitate a controversial visit of reconciliation.*

*Of course, no visit to Hobart would be complete without going to MONA. For those who may have been living under a rock, or have had no need to know these things, this is the famous underground Museum of Old and New Art. It is a privately funded initiative of David Walsh and is the largest in the Southern Hemisphere. It is set in a vineyard and overlooks the harbour which allows access up 99 steps. The complex is massive and supports two fast catamaran ferries from downtown. About 1.5 million people visit each year. The art collection is eclectic and a sign when you enter alerts you to the 'adult content'. Oh yes, there was some stuff in there that you probably wouldn't want your mum to see. A whole wall of plaster casts of female genitalia was confronting. I was scared to look at wall too closely in case I was thought* to be a pervert. I did hear a bloke say "I think I recognise that one!" No one nearby dared to smile at the witty crassness of this utterance. The architecture was amazing and the complex would have been very challenging to build. I presumed that it was built from the top down.

And Penelope? Well, I blocked off her left exhaust port as she was getting quite a bit of blow-by past my wired fix. Interestingly the temperature at the port seems to have dropped from about 212 – 220 to around 185. She feels a bit restricted, but we're not in any hurry. The Vintage and British motorcycle clubs hosted me for a night in an old pub on the waterfront. This was a good night and I sold a pleasing number of books. The next night I was treated to an evening meal with my Panther-man Bob and his wife. They made me very welcome and there is nothing better than a home visit when you are out on the road.

My last appearance in Hobart was an Author's Talk at the Hobart Library and whilst it was not a big gathering it was enjoyable and again I sold enough books to have made it worthwhile. One downside was a lady backing into Penelope in the downstairs carpark and knocking her over. She has been 'tits up' before, it was just a shame to see the broken mirror. My talk was attended *by Jo and Gareth Morgan, the notable Kiwi motorcycling adventurers and it was good to have them there as they added to the enjoyment with their participation in parts.*

*So I am now not in Hobart … but I will tell you more about that later.*

I'd enjoyed Hobart and being based in a hostel right down near all the action meant that I was able to roam on foot, which whilst my right one was not yet great, I was increasingly able to get further and further each day. I don't like cities much but do quite enjoy people-watching and looking for differences to what I am used to at home. I know that sometimes comparisons are not valid when you are not comparing like for like. I was blown away by the number of pedestrians wearing ear pods. It seemed that most did. Now in my home town, they don't, but that is not really a fair comparison as Takaka is so small it doesn't have commuters walking from buses and trains to places of work. However I didn't recall the same numbers of white dangly things hanging out of ears in Melbourne. Another observation of regional differences arose when talking to a young woman at the YHA who had just arrived on a motorbike and she was appalled that she couldn't just park it on the footpath. "We can in Melbourne!" she moaned. For me Hobart is normal as all our bigger cosmopolitan centres in NZ don't allow parking on the footpath and actively work to keep riders away. I am always amused to see bikes parked on the footpaths in downtown Melbourne (and in French cities). Luckily we could both squeeze down the side alley to get behind the hostel.

My relationship with the bookshop storing my supply of books is a little odd. Initially, they had reached out to me because I was doing an author's talk at the library and they more-or-less partner with the library on these occasions. Of course I had to restock with books before my talk to the bike clubs so had gone to the store and I was a little surprised to find none of my books on display … but at least they were out the back. Then after the club talk I had to restock again for the library … and yes, still no books on display. Then on the library day nobody from the shop turned up ... which the library said was unusual. Of course, I had to again restock for heading off to Queenstown, and I arranged for a couple of boxes to be uplifted for the big Oatlands Motorcycle Day and the Girder Fork Rally which followed. Still no books on display. The staff were always nice but my original contact who I think was an owner was never met and I gather he was away on paternity leave.

Nov 15

Kia ora all!

For those that care ... I am now holed up in a backpackers in Queenstown on Tasmania's West side, not quite out at the coast. It is raining heavily, forecast to not hit 10° and there will be snow down to 600 m, which is a bit of a worry as the next place I am aiming for is at 1,000 m. People are being advised not to do outdoor activities in this area. My $40 room is very much like I imagine a prison cell to be. In contrast my previous two nights were in sumptuous luxury, in a refurbed turn-of-the-20th- Century dwelling that in NZ we would call a villa. I was being hosted by the Paragon Cinema folk so they provided this without charge. It would have still been good value at the $160 a night normally charged.

The ride across to Queenstown was everything you expect Tasmania to provide. The roads were semi-deserted. They undulated, twisted, turned and regularly gave you beautiful lakes to look at. An echidna scampered across the road in front of me at one point, the first I have spotted in the wild in 25,000 km. The countryside was of course green and lush. Passing a large cherry farm made me think, once more marvelling at how little I know. The only place in NZ where we grow cherries is in Central Otago where the landscape is barren and a tawny hue. It is dry, arid and bitterly cold in the winter. Supposedly frosts are needed to 'set' the fruit and they always hit the market around this time of year. The landscape here was nothing like that – it was verdant. There were snow warning signs so obviously, it gets cold enough. Of course, the evidence of hundreds and hundreds of trees showed that it could be done. My only criticism of the ride was the lack of spots to pull over and get a photo, hence the paucity of scenic images.

Queenstown is an old mining town with a current population of about 1,800, way down on the numbers here in the mining boom times, or even the hydro construction times of the 1980s. To the casual visitor, like me, it looks like time has passed it by. This in many ways results in some good things. Because there has been very little development there is no reason to pull down the old buildings. There is no real hinterland to support so the main industry seems to be tourism. There is adventure tourism in the nearby rivers and neighbouring Mt Owen has 35 km of mountain bike trails. Probably the biggest attraction though is the historic railway which heads through to the coast at Strahan. A steam 'rack and pinion' Abt train goes halfway, down to the imaginatively named Dubbil Barril, where it meets another historic train which has come up to meet it from Strahan. This one is a diesel. Each of the train trips is about four hours return, and whilst I was tempted, the cheap seats were all full and $180 might be reasonable but I felt the voices from home uttering "You're going to spend how much on a little train trip?"

My movie screening in the Paragon Theatre was not a sell-out but I always judge the event by how enjoyable it was for all of us, me included. It is a wonderful venue and I even managed to get a 'walk in' by chatting to the driver of the Hobart University promo rig that had parked in the car park next door ready to begin a roadshow the next morning. Rob had nowhere to go, so came into the movies and had a beer etc. A lovely connection. I also chuckled at the news that I did better than Keith Potger of The Seekers who played the Paragon a few weeks back. His mid-week morning matinee only attracted five people. We did better than that ... and I sold 12 books.

I've just been hit with the news that even though it is only Tuesday, the organisers have decided to cancel the big outdoor classic motorcycle show on Sunday at Oaklands that was to be my big, all-day, static display in the *public eye. Bugger! You can't manage nature though.*

What a difference a day ... or two makes. By Wednesday the weather Gods had done their thing and it was time to put my 'Big Boy's pants' on and hit the road. I had decided to ride out to the coast at Strahan to look out over The Southern Ocean and loop around before heading to the North Coast and Bass Strait. The middle of the island was still too snowy and cold. So after a final brekkie at my preferred Tracks Café at the Railway Station, I layered up with all my cold weather clothes and reminded myself that seven degrees is OK.

Although rain threatened it never eventuated and my ride to Strahan was an hour or so of muffled joy. Only one car passed me and whilst there were a couple of viewing spots where I could have taken a record of the ride, when your phone is five layers in ... the effort seemed all too hard. Again I enjoyed the closeness of what we call bush. Not all eucalypts, there are quite a few cross-over trees from NZ. Lots of ferns abound and in some areas Manuka and possibly Kanuka are prominent. Myrtles were previously common but are seen less and less. On this West side of the island, Wet Eucalypt forests are overall the most prevalent and interestingly they need forest fires to regenerate, unlike the Dry Eucalypts from the East Coast which don't.

I've often repeated the refrain of how wonderful it is that 'they've never found the cure for motorcycling.' So it was with a smile on my dial that I cruised into the small coastal settlement of Strahan and eased to a halt in front of the BP gas station. As I walked in to pay, a sudden realisation swept over me. Yes, it was another 'silly old duffer' moment. Why can't they work on a cure for age-related enfeeblement and dufferdomness? Chalk up another one for me! I had left my man-bag back at the Queenstown backpackers outside where I had loaded up. This contained my wallet, pills, passport, kindle, phone charger, log book etc ... in other words, more or less all of my life on the road. Cursing the lack of a 'minder', I assured the petrol guy I would pay via the internet when I was reunited with a card and turned the old girl around and back we went.

Yet again good fortune shone on me … or it was again one of the cousins' interactions with their omnipotent deity. I know they really do include a "Look after Des" in their prayers when I am 'afoot'. It was a huge relief to find the bag sitting on the trailer side, just as I had left it. The 'What ifs' had been intruding for all of the 45 km or so back. Just as they had been when three storeys underground at MONA, I realised that I didn't have my bike jacket with me anymore. I was so mortified by my dufferdomness, that I hadn't owned up to that one at the time.

Reunited with my life, I rode back out of Queenstown and was soon on the scenic A10 Murchison Highway which took me all the way across to the northern coastal settlement of Somerset. With the snow supposedly now down to 900 m it was always above us as the highest point of the A10 is just on 700 m. Near the small settlement of Rosebery I passed two of Tasmania's controversial industries. Suddenly on this forest-lined highway, there was a break in the trees and I could see hundreds of utes and cars

**THE BIG SIT**

parked off to the side and there were buildings and heavy machinery in evidence. This was the Bluestone tin mining operation, the only tin production mine of any size in Australia. Down the road a bit, there was clear-felling forestry. Both of these operations seemed at odds with the seemingly untouched, craggy environment I was riding through. Some of the snow-clad peaks were just like our Queenstown's Remarkables. I smiled when passing near Waratah that I saw the forest-harvesting attachment on a digger that at home is called 'a Waratah'. I think it is a generic term like some places call all vacuum cleaners 'the Hoover'. I wonder if they call it a Waratah here in Waratah … I hope so.

About 30 km from the coast suddenly we burst out onto pasture land, with all the normal animals, houses, barns, fences and individual trees. The Bass Strait was immediately ahead and as blue as could be. I'd been warned by a backpacker in Queenstown that Somerset is a 'shit hole' … and she was a redhead – and we intuitively know things us redheads. Well, the holiday park was full, the first pub was full, and just when I was thinking dark thoughts about Somerset, it was found that the 'other' pub had one room available. Phew! I was told that the only spot for Penelope would be straight in front of the pub as they had CCTV. For some reason, I was a tired old man and after carrying most of my luggage upstairs in three trips, I decided that the box of books could stay on the back overnight, it was just too heavy to lug up to my room. There were no meals available but there was a Chinese Restaurant a short walk away, and food for two meals was bought.

I'd been contacted by a 'follower' who was keen to meet for coffee and a chat. "When and where?" I'd responded. He then told me there was a bakery just down from the pub and that he was an early riser. "What time do they open?", thinking that some cafes don't open till nine or even ten. "Five am, but we could do a bit later." We agreed on 7.30 and so Colin came into our lives. Interesting and gregarious, he liked to chat, I liked to listen … I liked to chat, he liked to listen, and the time flew by, then I asked him if there was anyone in town he'd recommend for stainless steel welding. "Hell yes!" So now Penelope has a welded mirror stem and a fixed-up exhaust. Such a good job done by Dennis Welding & Engineering. Thanks Andrew … or was it Dave or Peter, I am still not always very good at remembering names.

Being as it was only lunchtime and I had already learned that there were no beds available in the pubs, I decided that we should head out to the historic town of Stanley (pop 590) which is more or less at the top, left corner of Tasmania and a fishing port. It is overlooked by a flat-topped, old extinct volcano commonly named The Nut. It had been sighted by Bass and Flinders when they sailed around Tasmania in 1798. They called it Circular Head which is now the name of the area. So I rode along the coastal highway through a reasonably warm afternoon. At one point I thought Penelope was getting hot (she wasn't!) so paused by the side of the road and had a rest. A van stopped and out hopped a motorcyclist who had shared several beers with me on the sailing over. He is converting a shed into habitable construction nearby. A small and enjoyable interaction.

I stay in an ocean-side luxury spa cabin for the night at Stanley as it was the only one left. The $180 tariff made me wince. Spas seem to be a huge waste of water to me, but I decided that I should get my money's worth while I was there, and with the thought that it might soak out some of the oil-infused colouring of my grubby paws.

19 Nov 2022

*As I sit here alone in my $40-a-night caravan in Mole Creek, toasting my 73rd birthday, looking out the window to some pretty steady precipitation, I am quite buoyant and satisfied with the ways things have gone over the last couple of days. Yes, I was going to ride into town and splash out on a nice meal at the pub … but looking out at Penelope in the wet, it didn't seem worth it. A tub of two-minute noodles is not my usual celebratory fare, but* *it did the trick.*

*Yesterday, (Friday) was a funny old day with a few issues, mostly down to my ineptness. After my luxurious night on the Stanley foreshore, nice and early I walked up to the main street to see if there was a café open. The old part of town perches up high at the base of The Nut and is only one street wide and seemingly made up entirely of late nineteenth-century houses and commercial buildings. I felt the street was an amalgam of images from books I have read and movies I have seen. For some reason, I thought of 'The Shipping News' as I strolled along the deserted thoroughfare. Then I saw the hoardings recalling the movie filmed there a few years back. 'The Light Between Oceans' was set in West Australia but filmed in Stanley as well as in NZ's Oamaru and the Taieri Gorge Railway also featured. It is an interesting town with a lot of history and I could picture myself in a little room overlooking the view, writing away at a wooden Victorian desk.*

*I hadn't ridden 20 km when I sensed Penelope's distress and once again we paused at the side of the road in an inappropriate place. In an attempt to make her less incontinent, I had repeated the mistake of legions of amateur*

**TASSIE, TASSIE, TASSIE**

mechanics before me. I would have sworn that I sparingly used silicon sealant to try and make the oil feed to the cylinder head not weep oil as it has been doing. In my eyes, there was no way that the silicon could migrate into the slender oil feed pipe and block anything. We have adverts in NZ with a sloganised good intention married to a response of "Yeah, right!" Once she had cooled down, I indeed removed the silicon blockages. A Police vehicle turned up just as I was getting ready to move on. He'd had several reports of a motorcyclist sitting at the side of the highway reading a book.

Now nervous about my fiddling and Penelope's well-being, I pulled off the road after another short spell into a reserve and to my absolute horror, the magic heat gun showed 425° between the ports. Once again expletives were expleted and bewilderment washed over me. Were we going to have to do the rest of the ride in 15 km chunks? I messaged Colin, my mate from yesterday that I was only limping along so didn't know when I would be able to drop in as intended. Just to add to the confusion, there was no cell phone coverage so my message didn't go till later and his offer to come and pick me up also wasn't received.

But that Omnipotent One above ... if he/she (non-binary?) exists, sent me some cheer, firstly by way of a TasNetworks engineer Doug, who gave me water and offered to rescue me if I needed it. He would have gone back to Devonport and got a trailer. Then two characters of a similar vintage to me pulled over and one said "Well bugger me ... an old Panther!" They got out of the car and the other said "I've just read a book where an old guy rides one of these from Beijing to Holland."

Of course, I inform him that this is indeed us and next minute he is on the phone talking to a mate he has lent the book to. That mate then wants to talk, to make sure the story is not all make-believe. It is a small world and these surprising links cheered us all up. I did one more small chunk before stopping at a gas station food place where the young woman didn't know if they had wifi ... and the food was dire. However, it was here that probably the Omnipotent One decided that he/she had had enough fun for the day and sent down the thought "Check the photo you took of the temperature gauge reading 425° and see if it is Centigrade!" Yes, the silly old duffer had somehow got the reading of 422.6°F ... which is only 217°C ... and that seems to be normal for her!

Well, the day got a lot better then, once we knew it was me not Penelope. Meanwhile, Colin had decided to come and look for me because my message came through while I was riding along. Ultimately I dropped up to his place where we used a bit of Teflon tape on the pipe threads and I admired his eclectic collection of bikes, cars, mowers, rotary hoes, clag etc. Some would say he is a hoarder. Colin does admit that his collecting has got a bit out of control over the years and he should start sorting and parting out. I love the thought that his wife is a librarian and together we chuckle at the image of

**TASSIE, TASSIE, TASSIE**

her applying the Dewey Decimal Classification system to his vast cornucopia of 'stuff'.

Somehow the day had fled and Penelope and I had to put some real miles in before the curfew that is dusk in these parts. The coast road from Somerset back towards Devonport was ok because whilst busy it was four-lane and with the sun out and the changing seaside vistas to look at, I was not unhappy. Leaving the coast and heading inland was the real joy though. Suddenly we were on roads that didn't always even have a centre line. We climbed up, over and through the Gog Range Regional Reserve, passing through Paradise and we chuckled at the sign to Nowhere Else before getting to the rustic charm of the Mole Creek Holiday Park and a proffered beer around a fire pit. They tell me there are platypuses in the adjoining river. Happy as … tomorrow is another day and I only have a short ride to where the Girder Fork Rally is to begin on Monday morning. Tomorrow is a 'meet and greet' BBQ, if the rain stops!

The ride to Hadspen was predictably pleasant and not in the least bit arduous. We make a stop at a traction engine museum which impresses and eat in a small spot which doesn't. The food is forgettable and the two-storey iconic pub on the corner of town is closed except for a gambling room. I've noticed and not admired the Australian tolerance of gambling. TV advertising for betting on sports results and the horses is very common and back in Ballarat I has gazed in amazement at a sign outside an inner-city hotel promoting their casino bar as being open 23 hrs a day.

For three days, we are based in Hadspen, sharing a cabin with Jim and Louise from Penguin. I wonder what people from Penguin are called? Penguiners? I should have asked them. I also wonder what people from Nowhere Else are called … or Melbourne's suburb of Batman … Batmen?

We roam far and wide on the Tasmanian VMC Girder Forks Rally. Yes, I know Penelope doesn't have girder forks but the group welcomed us anyway. The attendance was down on what they would have hoped but with a smaller group, it was much more manageable and intimate. We were able to spend good quality time with all the others at the rally. The evenings are particularly enjoyable as, apart from the first night at a hotel restaurant, we commune on site with simple BBQ-type meals and a sufficiency of drinking and good cheer. There was the ability to display my wares and books were sold.

Now as many of you will know by now, Penelope is a Yorkshire-born, working-class girl ... sort of a below-stairs parlour-maid with attitude. At the other end of the social scale is the aristocracy and in two-wheel terms, this would mean something like a Brough Superior. Now George Brough must have been a cocky and arrogant sort. His dad made Brough motorcycles and when young George went out on his own making bikes, he called them Brough Superiors which must have been a bit of a slap in the face for his father. Although George's bikes were constructed of bought-in parts, they were always of the highest quality and specification. A master of promotion he sold to the rich-and-famous and was legitimately allowed to brand his bikes 'The Rolls Royce of motorcycles'. Lawrence of Arabia was a big fan, sadly losing his life on his seventh one (his eighth was on order), when he swerved to miss two young lads on bicycles, in heavy rain.

The doctor who tried to save his life became a campaigner for crash helmets. But getting back to our rally. Now Penelope has never even been near a Brough of either standard fare or a Superior type. To our surprise, there were two Brough Superiors in attendance, an SS80 (80 MPH) and the SS100 … the crème de la crème of the ilk, guaranteed to do the old Imperial ton. It was on an SS100 that Lawrence lost his life. So 'nellops' now has friends in high places. It has to be said that their throaty syncopated sound is so good it should be bottled and sold.

After the final day's fun on Wednesday, I packed up and made my way in a leisurely fashion along an alternate route to the small town of Latrobe (Pop 4,200) where the holiday park provided a good little cabin for $75. Next to me were John and Mick, two mature BMW riders from NSW. Learning that one of my rides and books was a Robert Pirsig re-enactment, John scurried inside and brought out his copy of Zen and the Art of Motorcycle Maintenance. He's halfway through and whilst he won't admit to 'enjoying' it, he acknowledges its importance and has earmarked it for Mick to read next. And as a big bonus for me, they bought copies of all three of my books. A very convivial night involving red wine followed.

The next day I wrote to my followers –

*Well, it is a fairly fatigued and tired old man penning this last Tasmanian missive from the library in Devonport. I should have more oomph, but it is what it is, we'll look at iron levels when I get back. Tonight is the ferry ride back to the mainland and tomorrow I hope to source a crate for 'her out there' and the process of getting everything home begins.*

*Kia kaha*

*Des*

The ferry departure times can vary as much as three hours depending on their passenger numbers making one extra sailing … or not. So my departure could have been six pm or nine pm. I go to the port early and settle in to a quiet beer and reflection at the dockside bar. There are a couple of riders already there having a meal and we while away the time probing each other's rides etc. They are on Ducati Multistradas with 164 brake horsepower, so more than six times as powerful as Penelope. They are from the wine-growing area of Margaret River over in the West. They blasted their way across the width of the big continent in almost no time at all, then looped around Tassie in two-and-a-half days! They intend getting new tyres when back on the mainland, then doing a 'track day' at The Bend raceway in South Australia, before once more fanging it across the long straight Nullabor Plain. They are a good guys to hang out with. They are a bit concerned when they see a large Police contingent with dogs turn up and settle in to the neighbouring carpark. It seems one of them has a small private stash of weed. Word from the barman is that a big number of an outlaw bike gang are probably going to travel with us. To the relief of my new mates, the Police stand down and leave. Only one gang member and one 'prospect' travel with us. When all the riders travelling are assembled in the concourse, we have plenty of time to mingle and chat. Penelope always brings in admirers and the box of books are another talking point. Wonderfully, I sell five books while waiting to board. Bonus!

The sailing across to Geelong and subsequent ride back to Melbourne are uneventful and I reflect that Tasmania has been everything I hoped it would be and more. The back roads are sealed and deserted. Wherever you look, there will be a 'mountain', you may even be going to go around it, or even partially over it. Some areas are heavily 'wooded' or bush-clad, others pastureland, or even crops. Of course, I have sampled their famous product, the apple, a Royal Gala. There are places I never went to, things I didn't do, but I enjoyed everywhere I went, and everything I did.

*Well, the Aussie adventure is over. I will be in the big silver bird in the morning back to Wellington ... a couple of days on the Kapiti Coast and home to The Bay on Friday. Penelope is on a Harley Davidson pallet and will be transported*

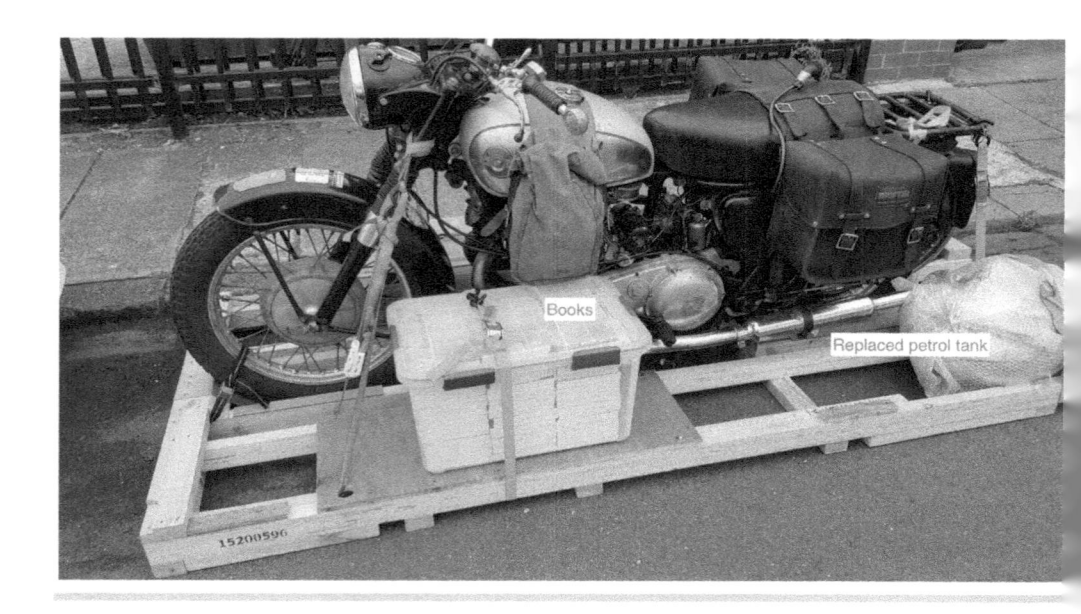

*to Nelson via a Roll-on/roll-off ferry. Being as this is the final 'home time' I am bringing back the petrol tank I swapped in Darwin, and the wobbly wheel, and a couple of boxes of books. Fingers' crossed it all works well.*

*So no more posts from me for a while. Thanks for coming along for the ride and for the many positive comments.*

*Des … going home for a rest.*

A book is nothing without readers and I appreciate all of you, especially those who have managed all three Penelope books. I'd like to think that maybe we have inspired others to go off on an adventure. Often the media portray adventurers who trek across the Sahara, kayak around Greenland or row the Atlantic as 'Inspirational'. I think not, as those extreme epics are way beyond any normally functioning person. However, anyone can get on their moto and point it down the road … it just takes a decision.

And a final postscript: Penelope arrived home at the end of January 2023 and after a minimal amount of tweaking she is cantering around The Bay like a bought one. We've not done any long rides … maybe we never will.

**NO ONE SAID IT WOULD BE EASY**

A YOUTHFUL FOLLY ACROSS THE AMERICAS ON OLD BIKES

A PRECURSOR TO THE LAST HURRAH BY

**DES MOLLOY**

An outrageous sortie on a pre-war BSA and two obscure, obsolete Yorkshire-made, single-cylinder Panther motorbikes. Poorly funded, with little planning, the ride depends on good luck, blind loyalty and terminal optimism. The struggle is managed with a youthful naivety. This is a recollection of a youth well-spent. Love and adventure are in the air with every chapter a precarious adventure.

*A fantastic insight to an intrepid sojourn. Makes you feel as though you're experiencing the ups and downs of their adventures along the way. They must have been mad!* – Amazon UK review

*Loved every minute of it, got totally caught up in the adventure, the fun, trials etc. Well written, full of humour, didn't want it to finish.* – Donna, NZ

*Brilliant Book! If Des Molloy had written this book shortly after completing his travels, I have no doubt that it would already be in every motorcyclist's library and Des would be living in luxury, supported by a constant stream of royalties. I hope he soon is. This is an epic book about truly epic travels.*
– Nick Adams (author), Canada

*Brilliant! A first class read from start to finish. Congratulations.*
– Peter Fleming (author), NZ

*'No One Said it Would be Easy' grabbed me within the first pages. Set in the 1970s, this is the inspirational and wonderfully described story of the slightly mad, seat-of-the-pants, ride from the USA through Central America and down through South America.* – Sam Manicom (author), Britain

**Available Online at www.kahukupublishing.com**

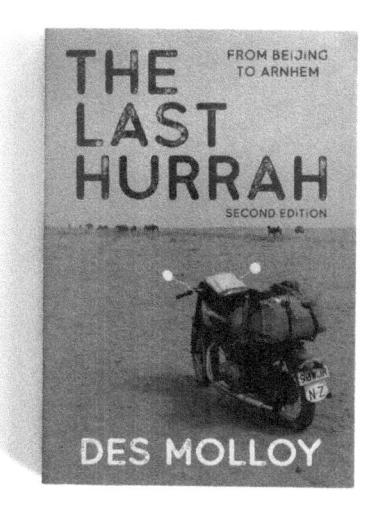

Des Molloy and Dick Huurdeman look like the sort of guys who should be sedately steering a sleigh in a Santa parade, not riding old single-banger British bikes half way across the world through some of the most difficult and remote terrain imaginable. Des's son Steve joined this intrepid pair as a cameraman and general factotum for the highs and lows of an incident-packed three-month trek from Beijing to Arnhem on 'Penelope', a 1965 Yorkshire-made 650cc Panther, and 'Dutch Courage', a 1954 Norton 600.

*The Last Hurrah is a truly inspirational tale and just goes to prove that although the chassis may show the patina of age, the spirit of the finely tuned engine underneath never dies!'* – Nadine Mills, Oxford

*It will warm your heart and your spirit and leave you wanting more. Next thing you know, you will be out back packing your own motorbike for a journey.* – 'D D'

*'Des: not sure if you'll get this or not, but I just wanted to say that your book is ABSOLUTELY FANTASTIC '!*
Lynda Blair, Ducati rider New Zealand

*'Hi Des, I've just ordered yet another 'Last Hurrah' I'll be keeping this copy on a piece of elastic! Your book is that good - I lend it out never to see it again- it's that good!'* – Ann Renouf

*Des is one of those story tellers you want to meet and just kick back and listen to his yarns. Genuinely a 'triffic book from a 'triffic author. Do yourself a favour... and buy this book!!* – Jay (UK)

## Available Online at www.kahukupublishing.com

In July 1968 a mentally insecure philosophy teacher began a motorcycle ride across the US with his not-yet 12-year-old son. Robert Pirsig's journey was immortalized in his best-selling book *Zen and the Art of Motorcycle Maintenance*.

Des Molloy and team, on the correct-period 1965 bikes follow the wheel-tracks of their antecedents, recording their thoughts and comparing with the best-selling philosopher.

*Other motorcyclists have re-enacted Pirsig's ride over the years, but none get close to Molloy's meticulous odyssey. The thing I particularly love about Des's books is the fact that there is no back-up vehicle, media frenzy, sponsorship or signed book contract. Des represents us all, a normal Joe enjoying an adventure and making the most of his time on Earth. Long may it continue.*
– George Lockyer, Bike Rider Magazine

*What a ride. There is so much that I really enjoyed about this book. The anecdotes and adventures of travelling across America in the wake of Robert Pirsig's epic journey roll off Molloy's pen as easily and enjoyably as he puts his motorcycle into his favourite twisted, curving roads.* – Brian Wilson

## Available Online at www.kahukupublishing.com

# WANT MORE ADVENTURES?

If you enjoying my musings, I write regular short stories that I share via my website for small digital donation.
Des to add text.

## www.kahukupublishing.com/short-stories

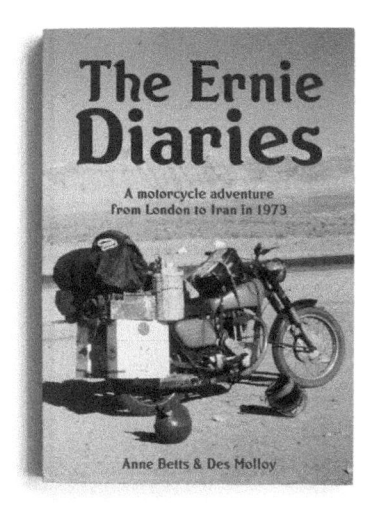

**The Ernie Diaries**

*A motorcycle adventure from London to Iran in 1973*

Anne Betts & Des Molloy

I think that at some stage in every young person's life, they dream of riding off into the sunset on a noisy, anti-social motorbike. Sometimes it is simply a thirst for adventure, other times it is to throw off a yoke of convention that is threatening to define ... and constrict. – Des Molloy

*As a travelogue, The Ernie Diaries is a wonderful journey. As a record of those days and those times, it is invaluable. It was a rare treat to read and find myself so thoroughly immersed in their journey. I heartily recommend it to anyone who rides, who has been in love, and who has been changed by the world thy observed.* – Peter Elliot, Kiwi Rider magazine

*The Ernie Diaries is proof that the innocence of youth and a determined spirit will have you seeing the world with very different eyes ... it is a must read.*
– Traverse magazine Australia

*It achieves what a good travel book should: It inspires the reader to just take off into the wild blue yonder and see what happens. I enjoyed it.*
– George Lockyer, Bike Rider Magazine

*It reads more fun than a travel book and more interesting than young people having fun book.* – Brian Wilson

### Available Online at www.kahukupublishing.com

# Everyday People.
# Amazing Adventures.

*Kahuku*
Publishing Collective